Essays and Studies 2010

Series Editor: Peter Kitson

The English Association

The objects of the English Association are to promote the knowledge and appreciation of the English language and its literature, and to foster good practice in its teaching and learning at all levels.

The Association pursues these aims by creating opportunities of co-operation among all those interested in English; by furthering the recognition of English as essential in education; by discussing methods of English teaching; by holding lectures, conferences, and other meetings; by publishing journals, books, and leaflets; and by forming local branches.

Publications

The Year's Work in English Studies. An annual bibliography. Published by Blackwell.

The Year's Work in Critical and Cultural Theory. An annual bibliography. Published by Blackwell.

Essays and Studies. An annual volume of essays by various scholars assembled by the collector covering usually a wide range of subjects and authors from the medieval to the modern. Published by D.S. Brewer.

English. A journal of the Association, *English* is published three times a year by the Association.

The Use of English. A journal of the Association, *The Use of English* is published three times a year by the Association.

Newsletter. A *Newsletter* is published three times a year giving information about forthcoming publications, conferences, and other matters of interest.

Benefits of Membership

Institutional Membership

Full members receive copies of *The Year's Work in English Studies*, *Essays and Studies*, *English* (3 issues) and three *Newsletters*.

Ordinary Membership covers *English* (3 issues) and three *Newsletters*.

Schools Membership includes copies of each issue of *English* and *The Use of English*, one copy of *Essays and Studies*, three *Newsletters*, and preferential booking and rates for various conferences held by the Association.

Individual Membership

Individuals take out Basic Membership, which entitles them to buy all regular publications of the English Association at a discounted price, and attend Association gatherings.

For further details write to The Secretary, The English Association, The University of Leicester, University Road, Leicester, LE1 7RH.

Essays and Studies 2010

Textual Cultures: Cultural Texts

Edited by
Orietta Da Rold and Elaine Treharne

for the English Association

D. S. BREWER

ESSAYS AND STUDIES 2010
IS VOLUME SIXTY-THREE IN THE NEW SERIES
OF ESSAYS AND STUDIES COLLECTED ON BEHALF OF
THE ENGLISH ASSOCIATION
ISSN 0071–1357

First published 2010
D. S. Brewer, Cambridge

D. S. Brewer is an imprint of Boydell & Brewer Ltd
PO Box 9, Woodbridge, Suffolk IP12 3DF, UK
and of Boydell & Brewer Inc.
668 Mt Hope Avenue, Rochester, NY 14620, USA
website: www.boydellandbrewer.com

ISBN 978–1–84384–239–2

A CIP catalogue record for this title is available
from the British Library

This publication is printed on acid-free paper

Printed in Great Britain by
CPI Antony Rowe, Chippenham and Eastbourne

Contents

Illustrations

Abbreviations

BMC	*Catalogue of Books Printed in the XVth Century Now in the British Museum, Part I* (London: British Museum, 1908)
CCCC	Cambridge, Corpus Christi College
CPG	*Clavis Patrum Graecorum*, 5 vols. & supplement, ed. M. Geerard, F. Glorie, *et al.* (Turnhout: Brepols, 1974–98)
EETS	Early English Text Society
ISTC	*Incunabula Short-Title Catalogue*, online at http://www.bl.uk/catalogues/istc
LALME	Angus McIntosh, M. L. Samuels, and Michael Benskin, *A Linguistic Atlas of Late Mediaeval English*, 4 vols. (Aberdeen: Aberdeen University Press, 1986)
NIMEV	Julia Boffey and A. S. G. Edwards, *A New Index of Middle English Verse* (London: British Library, 2005)
PG	*Patrologia Graeca*, ed. J. P. Migne, 161 vols. (Paris: Migne, 1857–1866)
PL	*Patrologia Latina*, ed. J. P. Migne, 221 vols. (Paris: Migne, 1844–1903)
STC	*Short-Title Catalogue of Books Printed in England, Scotland and Ireland, 1475–1640*, ed. A. W. Pollard and G. R. Redgrave (London: Bibliographical Society, 1976–1991)

Notes on Contributors

Erika Corradini holds a Ph.D. in late Anglo-Saxon and early medieval culture and manuscript studies (from the University of Leicester). Her research focuses on the collection of books housed at Exeter Cathedral in the late eleventh and twelfth centuries, its formation, development and readers. She has recently been involved in a detailed examination of manuscripts containing homilies written in the English vernacular for the use of a bishop and has been analysing their relevance in the administration of pastoral care.

Julia Crick is Associate Professor in History at the University of Exeter. She has published on various aspects of the history and culture of early medieval Britain, including a number of studies of manuscripts, palaeography and textual transmission. Her books include *The Historia Regum Britannie of Geoffrey of Monmouth, III: A Summary Catalogue of the Manuscripts* (1989), *The Historia Regum Britannie of Geoffrey of Monmouth, IV: Dissemination and Reception in the Later Middle Ages* (1991), and, with Alexandra Walsham, ed., *The Uses of Script and Print, 1300–1700* (2004). Her most recent book, *Charters of St Albans*, was published in 2007 in the British Academy series, Anglo-Saxon Charters.

Orietta Da Rold is a lecturer in medieval literature at the University of Leicester and is interested in how literature is influenced by questions of materiality, reading-habits and book production. She has published widely on medieval manuscript culture and scribes, focusing chiefly on the period 1100–1500. She is the co-founder (with Elaine Treharne) of the English Association Special Interest Group in the History of Books and Texts.

A. S. G. Edwards is Professor of Textual Studies, De Montfort University. He writes mainly on manuscripts and texts between the fourteenth and sixteenth centuries, and is currently engaged on an edition of *The History of Griseld the Second*, a poem about Katherine of Aragon by the sixteenth-century poet William Forrest, and (with Julia Boffey) *A Companion to Fifteenth-Century Poetry*.

Martin K. Foys is an Associate Professor of English and Communication Arts at Hood College, and currently a visiting professor of English at Drew University. He is the author of *The Digital Edition of the Bayeux Tapestry* (2003), and *Virtually Anglo-Saxon: Old Media, New Media, and Early Medieval Studies in the Late Age of Print* (2007). Most recently, he has co-edited and contributed to the volume *The Bayeux Tapestry: New Interpretations* (2009); he is also a director of the *Digital Mappaemundi* project.

David Gants is Associate Professor in English at Florida State University, and the digital humanities specialist in the History of Text Technologies programme. He publishes on bibliographical, textual, and technological matters, and is the electronic editor of the *Cambridge Edition of the Works of Ben Jonson*. He is also director of the Early English Booktrade Database project, which seeks to describe, quantify and classify every book published in the *STC* period. He serves on the council of the Bibliographical Society of America as well as chairing its fellowship committee and is a member of the advisory board for the Oxford Works of Edmund Spenser.

Ralph Hanna is Professor of Palaeography at the University of Oxford. He has written widely on later medieval manuscripts and their contexts. His most recent book-length study is *London Literature 1300–1380* (2005).

Robert Romanchuk is Associate Professor of Slavic at the Department of Modern Languages and Linguistics, Florida State University. He studies the history of education in the Orthodox Christian Middle Ages. He has published a number of articles in this area, as well as a book, *Byzantine Hermeneutics and Pedagogy in the Russian North: Monks and Masters at the Kirillo-Belozerskii Monastery, 1397–1501* (2007). He is currently working on a new book, *Byzantine Letters and Spiritual Direction at Balkan Courts: Hesychasts and the Language Arts, 1330–1443*.

Margaret M. Smith retired recently as Reader in Book Design History from the University of Reading. She is associate editor for printing and reproduction technologies of *The Oxford Companion to the Book* (2010). She is now a free-lance researcher in book design history, and in the history of west Suffolk.

Liberty Stanavage is currently finishing her dissertation, 'Domesticating Vengeance: The Female Revenger in Early Modern Drama, 1566–1700', at the University of California, Santa Barbara, where she is a Ph.D. candidate. She specialises in early modern drama, but also works on medieval and Restoration literature. Her current research interests include female revenge in early modern literature, publics and anti-publics in the broadside ballad and material textuality in manuscript culture.

Elaine Treharne is Professor of English at Florida State University and Visiting Professor of Medieval Literature at the University of Leicester. She is the author or editor of some twenty volumes, and has written over thirty articles on Old and Middle English manuscripts and their contents. She is currently completing *The Ideology of English* and working on *The Sensual Book*. She is general editor of *Essays and Studies* (from 2011 onwards) and, with Greg Walker, of the new series, *Oxford Textual Perspectives*.

Whitney Anne Trettien has a masters degree in comparative media studies from Massachusetts Institute of Technology, where she produced a born-digital thesis on seventeenth-century experimental poetry. She is currently a researcher at MIT's HyperStudio Digital Humanities Lab and a doctoral student in English at Duke University.

Introduction

ELAINE TREHARNE

IN THE RECENT 2008 Research Assessment Exercise in the United Kingdom – a qualitative audit and analysis of all academics' publications and research – the English Subject Panel made its report on the state of the discipline and potential future directions.[1] In the detailed description, the panel noted the major strengths in scholarship in a number of fields, including manuscript-based studies and 'history of the book and the sociology of texts'. The buoyancy of this area of research is evinced, too, by the creation of new groups, centres, degree programmes and book series all focused on the history of the book in the broadest sense[2] – an area of investigation that properly understood should extend from the emergence of sustained literacy in early cultures to contemporary digital technologies. While this volume cannot claim to have attended to every major facet of textual history along this extensive chronology, the range of material covered here does cover a good deal of ground from the Byzantine period to the Anglo-Saxon and Anglo-Norman periods into the high Middle Ages; and then hurtling through the early modern period, via Pepys, to the publication of electronic forms of bibliographic study.

The aim of this volume was never to be comprehensive in coverage, but rather to publish the work of scholars whose approaches to books, words and texts are engaging, innovative and always rigorous. Readers

---

[1]   This is available as a pdf file from http://www.rae.ac.uk/pubs/2009/ov/ under Panel M, 'English Language and Literature'. This document in itself, of course, as a product of its specific historical moment, ably illustrates the overarching concept of this book – to demonstrate a range of interpretative approaches centring on the text (manuscript, metaphor, writing, code) in its cultural context.

[2]   For example, the English Association Special Interest Group in the History of Books and Texts founded in 2007 (http://www.le.ac.uk/engassoc/fellows/book.html); the Centre for Manuscript and Print Studies, founded at the Institute for Advanced Studies in London in 2001 (http://ies.sas.ac.uk/cmps/index.htm); the newly founded History of Text Technologies Program at Florida State University (http://hott.fsu.edu/); and the Princeton University Center for the History of the Book and Media, established in 2002 (http://web.princeton.edu/sites/english/csbm).

will find the contributors' investigations into the materiality of the book within its varied physical, metaphorical, historical, intellectual and social ambients to be diverse but inspiring, manifesting a concern to exploit the multiple interpretative possibilities yielded by the text in context. This concern is apparent whether the writer is treating one author (like Whitney Trettien's focus on Samuel Pepys); one manuscript (like the Ellesmere Chaucer, scrutinised by A. S. G. Edwards; or Bodley 647, the subject of Ralph Hanna's essay; or Erika Corradini's thorough treatment of Cambridge, Corpus Christi College 421; or Exeter Cathedral Library 3514, the focus of Julia Crick's discussion; or Liberty Stanavage's excellent analysis of the *York Register*); a whole group of manuscripts (such as those examined by Orietta Da Rold and Robert Romanchuk); printed incunabula (as in Margaret Smith's nuanced account of red); or virtual materials (considered by David L. Gants and Martin K. Foys). The way that manuscripts are used and interpreted by their multiple readerships forms the focus for some of the essays here, while regarding the textuality of texts and their physical remediation attracts the attention of others.

All the writers here demonstrate convincingly the importance of scholarship on the material text in its context, and how the book is materialised synchronically and diachronically through such sustained attention. All eleven scholars also indicate and exemplify new directions for research, illustrating how the meticulous evaluation of one case study or set of related studies can provide significant evidence to help re-present the larger picture of textual and bibliographic studies in a new light. And this volume shows convincingly that textual culture is not simply about manuscript or print or digital text; it must ultimately include all technologies from the earliest period to the present day. Moreover, each case study here not only focuses on the cultural text to reflect on its moment of production, but also simultaneously provides an insight into the meaning inscribed upon the cultural text by twenty-first century scholarship.

Both editors would like to thank the contributors for their exemplary scholarship and professionalism in working with them to get this volume in and out on time. Orietta Da Rold wishes to thank her co-editor for *bonam viam ostendere*, and Inan and Elif for their patience. All participants in this project owe a large debt of gratitude to the many libraries and librarians involved for their assistance in providing access to manuscripts, incunabula and images. Final thanks go to the English Association for supporting the work of scholars in English across the globe, and special thanks go to Helen Lucas and Peter Kitson. The editors dedicate this volume to Professor Gordon Campbell: as he approaches his retirement, we wish him many congratulations on his years of work, his complete commitment to the profession at large and his collegiality and good humour in the face of it all.

The Composite Nature of Eleventh-Century Homiliaries: Cambridge, Corpus Christi College 421

ERIKA CORRADINI

THE PRODUCTION OF English vernacular homilies in the eleventh century has often been studied with regard to textual transmission and adaptation. Much focus has been placed on the eleventh-century practices of adapting earlier sources to the needs of new users, and to studying the different purposes underlying the original production of, for instance, Ælfric and Wulfstan.[1] These studies provide invaluable evidence regarding the interests and concerns of those preachers who were interested in using Ælfric and Wulfstan's homiletic texts in the eleventh and early twelfth centuries. However, the form in which such adaptations of earlier homilies were collected physically and conceptually has not been easy to comprehend or to describe, because codicological analyses are only just beginning to illuminate eleventh-century homiletic production from a scriptorial perspective. Treharne's studies in the palaeography and codicology of eleventh- and twelfth-century English vernacular manuscripts have uncovered the multilayered structure of homiletic codices as far as the organisation of both the codicology and content are concerned.[2] Many eleventh-century vernacular homiliaries seem indeed to have lacked the liturgical coherence that

---

[1] Most recently on the subject see H. Magennis and M. Swan, eds., *A Companion to Ælfric* (Leiden: Brill, 2009); M. Swan and E. Treharne, eds., *Rewriting Old English in the Twelfth Century* (Cambridge: Cambridge University Press, 2000); A. Conti, 'Revising Wulfstan's Antichrist in the Twelfth Century: A Study in Medieval Textual Re-appropriation', *Literature Compass* 4/3 (2007), 638–63; J. Wilcox, 'Ælfric in Dorset and the Landscape of Pastoral Care', in F. Tinti, ed., *Pastoral Care in Late Anglo-Saxon England* (Woodbridge: The Boydell Press, 2005), 52–75.

[2] E. Treharne, 'Producing a Library in Late Anglo-Saxon England: Exeter, 1050–1072', *The Review of English Studies* 54 (2003), 155–71; E. Treharne, 'The Bishop's Book: Leofric's Homiliary and Eleventh-Century Exeter', in S. Baxter, C. Karkov, J. Nelson and D. Pelteret, eds., *Early Medieval Studies in Memory of Patrick Wormald* (Farnham: Ashgate, 2009), pp. 521–37. I am indebted to Professor Treharne for giving me the opportunity to read an earlier version

characterised the initial arrangement of Ælfric's two series of *Catholic Homilies* as conceived by the author himself, for example.[3] Seemingly, many eleventh-century collections of homilies show hardly any liturgical rationale in the form in which they currently stand. This liturgical inconsistency may well be due to the fact that the volumes in which they appear have undergone substantial codicological and palaeographical alterations, often carried out in different stages throughout very long periods of time; however, in most cases it is difficult to discern liturgical, and at times thematic, coherence, even after a reliable codicological reconstruction of the volumes in question has been attempted and completed.[4] The complexities of what may be termed an inconsistent nature make the explicit cogency of eleventh-century codices almost unintelligible when one seeks to make sense of their function and cultural value. This is even more the case because these volumes contain homilies whose contents and rigid preaching diction, when studied outside a liturgical context, do not facilitate the modern scholar's comprehension of their cultural significance, or the meanings that they had for eleventh-century audiences – whenever it is possible to identify those audiences, that is. One may observe that the principle underpinning many eleventh-century composite homiliaries seems to rest on the provision of a varied selection of texts, which can often occur independently from any specific religious occasion. Thus, their compilation does not provide readings for a complete liturgical cycle, as one might expect in contemporary English as well as Latin homiliaries, for example.[5] What these codices offer, perhaps, is not readings for the

of her work on manuscripts, which was of enormous benefit to the research underpinning the compilation of this paper.

[3]   Examples of manuscripts arranged according to a liturgical rationale beyond Cambridge, University Library, Gg 3.28, the manuscript which is believed to be a remarkably close copy of Ælfric's original production, are Cambridge, Corpus Christi College, 198, s. xi[1], from Worcester; Oxford, Bodleian Library, Bodley 340 and 342, s. xi[2], from Rochester, described in N. R. Ker, *Catalogue of Manuscripts Containing Anglo-Saxon* (Oxford: Clarendon Press, 1957). Some examples of eleventh-century composite codices in which Ælfric's homilies are not arranged according to the liturgical year and are interspersed with religious materials other than homilies are Oxford, Bodleian Library, Hatton 115, s. xi[ex], at Worcester in the thirteenth century; Hatton 113 and 114, s. xi[3/4], from Worcester; London, British Library, Cotton Vitellius D.xvii (or rather what remains of it), s. xi[med], of unknown origin.
[4]   Treharne, 'The Bishop's Book', pp. 523–6.
[5]   H. Gneuss, 'Liturgical Books in Anglo-Saxon England and their Old English Terminology', in H. Gneuss and M. Lapidge, eds., *Learning and Literature in*

liturgical cycle, but rather a flexibility of choice which is reflected in an unprecedented intellectual dynamism, as their composite, versatile nature would suggest.

Thus, I shall seek to demonstrate that the loose structure of some of these codices, those that seem not to have been deliberately planned, was less haphazard than one might expect, and that the ostensibly disorganised make-up of such books is not as incoherent as it looks at first glance. The unsystematic construction of many eleventh-century homiletic codices would actually enhance the potential adaptability of these homiliaries for new uses and audiences.[6] Only volumes with rather fluid formal boundaries could have easily been (re-)adjusted to provide materials to fulfil new preaching necessities and re-purposed – if such a term can be allowed – without losing their religious and cultural significance. A detailed analysis of CCCC 421 will demonstrate that homiliaries in early medieval times had a rather long life. Their longevity is due to a continuous updating of both their physical form and content, which was facilitated by the fluid structural boundaries characterising such manuscripts. The codicological history of CCCC 421 is particularly interesting because it reflects the gradual completion of a process through which the volume was disaggregated and expanded with new materials in subsequent phases; the theoretical and methodological implications of this progression are of critical importance to a fuller understanding of the production of homiliaries in the eleventh and early twelfth centuries and of their use.

Cambridge, Corpus Christi College 421

The volume was produced at the beginning of the eleventh century, considerably revamped in about the 1050s, and was still in use many years later at the end of the century. The history of the codex from the end of the eleventh century until its acquisition by the sixteenth-

---

Anglo-Saxon England (Cambridge: Cambridge University Press,1985), pp. 91–142, p. 123. Gneuss implies that eleventh-century religious institutions were likely to have Latin homiliaries to cover the liturgical cycle.

[6]   One relevant example of such collections, beside the one here under scrutiny, is Paris, Bibliothèque Nationale de France, lat. 943 (Ker, *Catalogue*, no. 364) containing two homilies for the same feast, that is the dedication of a church, now edited in R. Brotanek, *Texte und Untersuchungen zur altenglischen Literatur und Kirchengeschichte* (Halle: Niemeyer, 1913), pp. 3–27.

century antiquarian archbishop Matthew Parker is, unfortunately, unknown.[7] Once in the archbishop's possession, however, the codex became part of his collection of medieval books, which was eventually donated to Corpus Christi College, Cambridge, upon the death of the archbishop in 1575, where they remain to this day.[8]

The older nucleus of CCCC 421 – including pages 99–208 and 227–345 – was produced at the beginning of the eleventh century in a centre supposedly affiliated with Canterbury, if not Canterbury itself.[9] Originally, the codex was a companion volume to CCCC 419, with which it shares structure, script, and *mise-en-page*. Together, the two companions provided a fairly extensive collection of homilies, mostly by Ælfric and Wulfstan. Over time, the two volumes received a significant number of spelling updates, some of which are likely to have been executed at subsequent stages. Changes in the orthography of words would suggest that the two manuscripts were in use for a long period of time, long enough for the necessity to revise the spelling to arise. Such alterations do not appear consistently throughout the two volumes, but tend to concentrate within the limits of individual texts. This unsystematic approach to revision was plausibly adopted for homilies being prepared for delivery, thereby suggesting that only some of the texts in these two volumes were used at times after their original production.[10] Although it is difficult to know exactly *when* each of the phases of the spelling revision was carried out in the two companions, let alone

[7]   Ker, *Catalogue*, no. 69, pp. 117–18; although Ker's *Catalogue* remains the principal term of reference for CCCC 421, the manuscript has more recently been palaeographically and codicologically described in J. Wilcox, *Anglo-Saxon Manuscripts in Microfiche Facsimile*, vol. VIII (Tempe: Arizona Center for Medieval and Renaissance Studies, 2000), pp. 7–13. The Parker Library on the Web project has the most updated and complete description of the relevant codex at   http://parkerweb.stanford.edu/parker/actions/page.do?forward=home   (last accessed 1.08.2009)
[8]   The Latin heading 'Liber Sextus' followed by a summary of the manuscript's contents inclusive of page numbers now on fol. iir was added to the volume in the archbishop's time, as also suggested by the sixteenth-century script. Wilcox, *Anglo-Saxon Manuscripts*, p. 8.
[9]   Wilcox, *Anglo-Saxon Manuscripts*, p. 7, indicates that the origin of CCCC 421 is unknown. However, its linguistic and textual features point to Canterbury as far as the physical production of the codex is concerned, contrary to what the contents of the manuscript would indicate.
[10] Ibid., p. 8.

by whom,[11] it is plausible to think that part of the changes affecting words would have depended on the scriptorium where the books were modernised and prepared for use, and the conventions adopted by the scribes working for that scriptorium. Interestingly, one recurrent change in CCCC 421 and 419 is the alteration of **i** to **y**. The technique of attaching the longer limb of **y** to the existing **i** and squeezing it between it and the following letter is very much in evidence and particularly frequent in vernacular manuscripts entirely produced at Exeter in the third quarter of the eleventh century. Corrections in Exeter-produced vernacular manuscripts are indeed very few, and even at a glance it may be noted that they mostly consist of **i**-to-**y** changes.[12] Such consistency in revising spelling conventions beyond the limits of one single manuscript would indicate that at a certain point it was decided that the entire corpus of vernacular codices was to be updated and **i** altered to **y** when occurring in certain positions.

It is in itself unsurprising that CCCC 421 and 419 should host corrections added in a style shown in Exeter-produced and corrected manuscripts, since it is accepted by scholars that by the mid-eleventh century the two volumes had been added to the collection of books that belonged to Leofric, who was bishop of Exeter in the years 1050–72. However, the implication of these alterations has a much deeper significance for our knowledge of the history of these codices than one might expect, because they reveal that not only were the manuscripts being repeatedly used before they came to Exeter, but also that, once in Leofric's hands, they were still orthographically updated and harmonised according to the spelling habits used by the bishop's scribes and to which the users of these volumes were accustomed. The language appraisal of the two companions supports the idea that the homiletic texts contained in the two codices needed a linguistic revision when being prepared for delivery. In this regard, spelling alterations, without really changing the meaning of words, would have ensured maximum clarity of the texts, for their delivery to be as smooth and hesitation-free as possible. Bearing this in mind, not only do such corrections offer a snapshot of spelling habits in mid-to-late eleventh-century Exeter, but concurrently underline the utilitarian function of the works that

---

[11] In most cases it is impossible to distinguish critical differences between the hands that made the alteration. This is because corrections are minimal, though frequent.

[12] CCCC 190, pp. 315–19 and London, British Library, Cleopatra B.xiii are but two examples.

CCCC 421 and its companion contain. The style and nature of the corrections showing in these two codices illustrate that they were intended for reading the texts out in front of an audience.[13] This is indicated by changes being often carried out in a mimetic fashion, in an attempt perhaps to camouflage the alterations and harmonise them with what is written on the page in a non-intrusive manner so that the deliverer could read them easily and without interruption.[14]

Homiletic comparanda

The presence in CCCC 421 and 419 of corrections which are written in typical Exeter hands and of a kind recurring in manuscripts written and used at Exeter in the third quarter of the eleventh century is, however, not the only piece of evidence supporting the idea that the two companion volumes were in use at Exeter and underwent revision there – and radical revision at that.[15] Two sets of eight quires in

[13] See Treharne, 'The Bishop's Book', passim, and A. Conti, 'The Taunton Fragment and the Homiliary of Angers: Context for New Old English', The Review of English Studies 60 (2009), 1–33, p. 32. Conti suggests that the homiliary of Angers, unlike CCCC 421, was used as a guide for preachers in writing sermons. Clearly, manuscripts for compiling homilies such as those admirably described and analysed by Conti were not unusual, though copies have hardly survived, probably owing to the deterioration inherently caused by their utilitarian nature. Although it is evident that practical functions are generally and justly associated with vernacular homiliaries, the uses for which they were employed varied, as reflected in their diverse physical characteristics. On the latter point see also Wilcox, 'Ælfric in Dorset', p. 61.

[14] Examples of these minutiae are CCCC 421, p. 180, the word 'wyrðe', line 1, was written in the margin; p. 190, line 3, 'godspelle' obtained correcting 'ge<erasure>spelle'; p. 196, line 5, i was changed to y in the word 'dysiga'; p. 244 a rather lengthy portion of text was orderly written in the footer of the page; p. 334, line 12 i was altered to y in the word 'cwyde' and line 18 the word 'dufte' was overwritten on erasure (rather than in the interlinear space); to name only a few examples. Similarly, CCCC 419, p. 11, line 4 the word 'þe' was squeezed between two words slightly above the line; p. 13 i was changed to y in the words 'togehyran', line 12 and 'wyle', line 15. At points when lack of space does not allow for squeezing a letter cluster in the right position, the correction is written above the word and the place where it should be read signalled with a visible comma-like stroke of the pen, see CCCC 419, p. 29, line 5 and again line 13 the words 'mancynne' and 'olehtan' (this is also visible in CCCC 191, fol. 114 another Exeter codex). These are only a few of the many examples of corrections unobtrusively carried out in these volumes.

[15] CCCC 419, p. 55 above lines 4 and 8. The script of this set of corrections

total, produced at Exeter in the third quarter of the eleventh century, were inserted into CCCC 421 at some point during Leofric's episcopacy. The Exeter portions of CCCC 421, now covering pp. 3–98 and 209–24, were originally part of another collection of homilies entirely compiled by Exeter scribes, perhaps before the arrival of CCCC 421 and its companion at Exeter. This collection of homilies is now extant as London, British Library, Cotton Cleopatra B. xiii and London, Lambeth Palace, 489.[16] The Exeter sections of CCCC 421 share script and page layout with these two codices and it is such palaeographical grounds that suggest they were originally intended to be part of the same collection of homilies, including texts now appearing in three different volumes. Although it is possible that the texts contained in Lambeth 489 and Cleopatra B.xiii were bound in the two volumes in which they now appear in the sixteenth century, the acquisition of CCCC 421 and CCCC 419 by Leofric may have reasonably instigated re-organisation and revision of the entire homiletic collection already in place at Exeter. This explains the similar spelling updates found throughout the four volumes, and the insertion into CCCC 421 of units belonging to the collection originally copied and assembled at Exeter, now represented by Lambeth 489 and Cleopatra B.xiii.

If this was the case, as seems plausible, the texts now contained in the four volumes together would have formed the homiletic collection which Bishop Leofric used to fulfil his preaching duties.[17] Although there is no apparent episcopal flavour to CCCC 421 and CCCC 419, contrary to what has been noted with regard to Cleopatra B.xiii and Lambeth 489,[18] the simple fact that CCCC 421 shows codicological connections with them is sufficient grounds to place it in a context which is likely to be different from that at the beginning of the century, when the manuscript was made. In these circumstances it would appear that CCCC 421, and by implication its companion volume, were reshaped as a collection and placed in a context where they would

---

is clearly of the Exeter type as reflected in the distinctive features of insular **g**, **a** and **d** and in the angular shape of minims.

[16] The connections between these four volumes have been evidenced in T. A. M. Bishop, 'Notes on Cambridge Manuscripts. Part II', *Transactions of the Cambridge Bibliographical Society* 2 (1954–8), 185–99, p. 198, and more forcefully supported in Treharne, 'The Bishop's Book', pp. 524–8, where a detailed codicological analysis of the three volumes is presented.

[17] Treharne, 'The Bishop's Book', pp. 524–8.

[18] P. Clemoes, *Ælfric's Catholic Homilies. First Series*, EETS, ss 17 (Oxford: Oxford University Press, 1997), p. 22.

fulfil new and different functions, namely serving specifically episcopal preaching.

The Exeter-compiled portions that now appear in CCCC 421 were probably produced alongside the texts now contained in Lambeth 489 and Cleopatra B.xiii, as suggested by a strikingly similar script and identical page make-up.[19] Compilation of these materials in all probability dates to an early phase of the scribal activities at Exeter, possibly dating to the early 1050s, which predates the acquisition of CCCC 421.[20] It is not impossible that Leofric may have built his homiliary gradually, rather than all at one time. Such an endeavour as assembling a homiliary from scratch would have indeed necessitated accessibility to a range of resources that for financial reasons and the poverty of Exeter prior to his time Leofric could not have had at his disposal when he commissioned the production of the texts in Lambeth 489 and Cleopatra B.xiii.[21] Limited accessibility to resources and lack of funds may have been the reasons behind the acquisition of a further set of homilies at a later stage, when presumably the bishop could afford their purchase or just when these were made available to him for whatever reason. Another reason may have been more simply that the bishop wanted authoritative homiletic materials to add to the preaching resources that he already possessed and thereby to build a respectable collection. Later acquisition of CCCC 421 and its companion would thus explain the radical reorganisation of the whole collection and linguistic updating.

Although little is known about the activities involved in procuring books from other institutions, there are reasons to believe that at a

[19] Treharne, 'The Bishop's Book', pp. 4–5; the features here described by Treharne are in evidence in the Exeter-copied sections of CCCC 421. There is, however, general disagreement on the number of hands at work in these manuscripts owing to their remarkable similarity.

[20] E. Drage, 'Bishop Leofric and the Exeter Cathedral Chapter, 1050–1072: A Reassessment of the Manuscript Evidence' (Ph.D. dissertation, University of Oxford, 1978), ch. 4. Judging from Drage's excellent assessment of the Latin palaeography of Leofric's manuscripts, it would seem that a rush of scriptorial activities took place for Exeter concurrently with Leofric's establishing his see there and consequent consecration in 1050.

[21] Drage, 'Bishop Leofric', especially pp. 206–28, and more recently P. W. Conner, *Anglo-Saxon Exeter: A Tenth-Century Cultural History* (Woodbridge: Boydell, 1993), pp. 21 and 226–35, for an edition of Leofric's inventory of goods. On marginalisation of the diocesan see representing Devon and Cornwall see J. Hill, 'Leofric of Exeter and the Practical Politics of Book Collecting', in S. Kelly and J. J. Thompson, eds., *Imagining the Book* (Turnhout: Brepols, 2005), 77–98, p. 82.

certain point in his career Leofric may have needed a collection of homilies that offered a wider selection of texts, and themes perhaps, and that in consequence of this necessity he asked assistance from other centres, which, like Canterbury, housed larger book repositories.[22] In the later years of his episcopacy, Leofric was undoubtedly in a more favourable financial position than he was when in 1050 he established his episcopal see at Exeter.[23] Now, his importance and renown within the English episcopate would have made him closer to bishops of other rich dioceses, through whose friendship and collaboration he could have brought to Exeter more books than the institution owned when he took charge.

There is, however, one other reason why Leofric may have felt that there was a necessity to expand his episcopal collection of homilies: the intensification and perhaps diversification of his diocesan duties. The later part of the eleventh century saw radical changes in the English church, partly due to the multiplication of parish churches and the consequent fragmentation of the ecclesiastical unity once represented by the cathedral, whose pastoral rights the bishop administered as an unchallenged authority in his own diocese.[24] New churches were consecrated in unprecedented numbers, almost everywhere in England, at about the time when Leofric was in charge. Judging from the number of homilies for the dedication of a church apparent in the bishop's homiliary – four out of approximately forty homilies in total – Leofric was actively engaged in consecrating new churches in his diocese.[25] The multiplication of ecclesiastical institutions with rights to administer pastoral care to the parishioners in place of the episcopal authority entailed a major effort on behalf of the bishop to safeguard his spiritual power and his administrative control over smaller churches.[26] It was mainly through preaching, I believe, that the bishop would have been able to assert a firm administrative and spiritual hold on the institutions of his diocese and communicate his spiritual power effectively to his community of souls. It is in this context that the acquisition of

---

[22] Conner, *Anglo-Saxon Exeter*, p. 2.
[23] Hill, 'Leofric of Exeter', pp. 83–4. Relocation of his diocesan see to a city certainly impacted on the status of the bishop.
[24] J. Blair, *The Anglo-Saxon Church* (Oxford: Oxford University Press, 2005), p. 8, and more specifically with regard to Exeter, p. 403.
[25] Treharne, 'The Bishop's Book', *passim*.
[26] F. Barlow, *The English Church, 1000–1066* (London: Longman, 1963), pp. 199–200.

texts, which like those in CCCC 421 were not bound to any specific liturgical day and therefore could be used on general occasions, should be evaluated and their utility assessed.

Preaching opportunities

Together the two companion volumes travelling from Canterbury to Exeter provided a wider selection of general homilies at a time when preaching duties intensified at Exeter as a consequence of episcopal figure and its leading power being threatened by the disintegration of the cathedral's unity with regard to pastoral rights.[27] This helps explain the need for a homiliary with a clear episcopal focus, now bound into Lambeth 489 and Cleopatra B.xiii, which supplied texts useful for the bishop to accomplish his public duties and administer the care of the souls. Another two codices, now CCCC 421 and 419, in addition, furnished texts for rather more general occasions that might be used during masses for celebrating the anniversary of a church's dedication, or in synods, for example, before the congregation.

Preaching in these two types of situation would have probably intensified in the ecclesiastical panorama outlined above, as synods and the celebration of a church's anniversary would have provided the exact kind of context in which the bishop might stress that smaller churches were subject to his spiritual and temporal power and depended on episcopal sovereignty.[28] If the transfer of the quires from the text group consisting of Lambeth 489 and Cleopatra B.xiii to CCCC 421 is examined in this light, it does not seem to be at all a matter of chance that they should contain homilies that were well worth reading on such occasions and whose general nature may have been the reason for inclusion in a miscellaneous manuscript like CCCC 421. Four of the five Ælfrician homilies copied at Exeter and bound into CCCC 421 at the beginning of the codex are dedicated to the celebration of an unnamed apostle, of many martyrs, of an unnamed confessor and of the holy virgins and occur in the codex rubricated as follows:

pp. 3–25 In die sancto pentecosten
pp. 25–36 In natale unius apostoli

[27] Blair, *The Anglo-Saxon Church*, pp. 489–90.
[28] On the different kinds of churches in Devon in 1050 see N. Orme, *English Church Dedications with a Survey of Cornwall and Devon* (Exeter: University of Exeter Press, 1996), p. 22.

pp. 36–54 In natale plurimorum sanctorum martyrum
pp. 54–76 In natale unius confessoris
pp. 76–96 In natale sanctarum virginum[29]

Given their general nature, it is plausible to think that such homilies would have been suitable for preaching on the anniversary of any church in the diocese which was dedicated to one or more of the saints, as was usually the case.[30] In this way it would have been possible to adapt these homilies for delivery in virtually every church of the diocese every year on the day when the anniversary occurred for as long a period of time as desired. That these texts were suitably adapted to such occasions can also be inferred by the presence in Leofric's personal missal – a tenth-century volume from Arras, now Oxford, Bodleian Library, Bodley 579 – of as many masses corresponding to the celebration of an apostle, many martyrs, a confessor and the holy virgins.[31] Crucially in addition to these, a mass for the virgins and one for St Mary ad Martyres were copied and incorporated into the missal in Leofric's time by scribes working for him.[32] Beside their adaptability, these homilies when read aloud in church in the emphatic style of Ælfric's prose would have made an impression on an audience of laymen and on the clergy, who resided in or staffed local churches, and reminded them of the tenets of basic doctrinal instruction worth repeating by the bishop, or the canons assisting him in his duties, on any occasion, as a way to underline the presence of the episcopal authority in religious matters.[33]

From an episcopal perspective, diocesan synods would have been equally suitable arenas for the bishop to preach. A number of eleventh-century manuscripts bear evidence that it was not inappropriate for the bishop to deliver homilies in this kind of situation. In fact, a miscel-

---

[29] Editions of these texts are available in Clemoes, *Ælfric's Catholic Homilies. First Series*, no. 22, pp. 354–64; M. Godden *Ælfric's Catholic Homilies. The Second Series*, EETS, ss 5 (Oxford: Oxford University Press, 1979), nos. 35 (pp. 299–303), 37 (pp. 310–17), 38 (pp. 327–34) and 39 (pp. 327–34), respectively.
[30] Orme, *English Church*, pp. 35–6 and Blair, *The Anglo-Saxon Church*, p. 399.
[31] F. E. Warren, ed., *The Leofric Missal as Used in the Cathedral of Exeter* (Oxford: Clarendon Press, 1883, repr. 1968), pp. 170–3 in Part A representing the original core of the codex.
[32] N. Orchard, *The Leofric Missal*, vol. I (London: The Henry Bradshaw Society, 2002), p. 224.
[33] Leofric adopted the enlarged version of the continental Rule of Chrodegang to govern a community of canons at Exeter; an edition of this rule is A. Napier, *The Old English Version of the Enlarged Rule of Chrodegang with the Latin Original* (London, 1916), p. 91, lines 28–32.

lany of materials such as that contained in CCCC 190 – a volume
with an Exeter provenance and housing Exeter additions, which brings
together under one cover canonical and ecclesiastical laws, pastoral
letters, ecclesiastical grades and excerpts on the liturgy – suggests that
such collections might be assembled to be used in synodal contexts.[34]
Another manuscript bearing some resemblance to CCCC 190, especially part B, shows some evidence that materials like penitentials,
benedictionals, confraternity regulations and, ecclesiastical laws were
stitched together in the form of a book to be used in synods, mostly
for guiding priests and other clergy. CCCC 190, part B, shares these
types of text with Paris, Bibliothèque Nationale, lat. 943.[35] In addition
to these texts, the latter codex contains a paragraph in English for the
bishop to read in conclusion of synodal assemblies.[36] When studied in
its immediate manuscript context, this passage indicates clearly that
manuscripts with such mixed structures and diverse selections of texts
were evidently used in diocesan assemblies and, perhaps more importantly, give us a fairly good idea of the people who participated in a
synod (mostly priests, abbots and abbesses[37]), thereby providing us with
an impression of the potential audiences for the homilies that these
books contain.

Bibliothèque Nationale de France, lat. 943 has a clear episcopal focus
and has been associated with the bishop of Sherborne, a neighbouring
diocese to Exeter. It may well be then that such texts circulated quite
easily and that habits were shared among dioceses in the south-west
and west of England. Homiliaries such as CCCC 421 contained pieces
that suited synodal preaching. The homilies contained in CCCC 421,
pp. 209–24, are one such example, as is Ælfric's homily for Pentecost
at pp. 3–25, since synods usually took place at Pentecost – and what
great opportunities these were for a bishop to remind the congregation
of the respect that was to be commended to his power.[38]

The Exeter-copied quires constituted excellent material for incorporating into a codex like CCCC 421. The latter book, in distinc-

[34] M. F. Giandrea, *Episcopal Culture in Late Anglo-Saxon England*, Anglo-Saxon
Studies (Woodbridge: The Boydell Press, 2007), pp. 116–17.
[35] Ker, *Catalogue* no. 364.
[36] Brotanek, *Texte und Untersuchungen*, pp. 27–8.
[37] Consistent with D. Whitelock, D. Brett, *et al.*, eds. *Councils and Synods,
with Other Documents Relating to the English Church I A. D. 871–1066* (Oxford:
Clarendon Press, 1981), no. 40
[38] J. L. Kupper, *Liège et l'église impériale XIᵉ–XIIᵉ siècles* (Paris: Societé d'edition
Les Belles Lettres, 1981), pp. 259–61.

tion to Lambeth 489 and Cleopatra B.xiii, already contained homilies for minor liturgical feasts prior to its enlargement. It would then seem reasonable to think that because of their general contents Leofric felt that the Exeter quires needed to be relocated in a context that was more congenial to the uses that he had in mind. It is plausible that the removal of the Exeter-copied portions from the Lambeth 489 and Cleopatra B.xiii collection to CCCC 421 influenced the function of the latter codex, which seems rather different in the third quarter of the eleventh century from the use imagined for it at its origin at the beginning of the century. Homiliaries such as CCCC 421 and 419 in their early-eleventh-century context were books purposefully produced for the circulation of the homilies of Ælfric and Wulfstan in a priestly environment, as they provided texts for priests to deliver in their churches. Their possible Canterbury origin and provenance emphasise this function even further, provided that Canterbury or the scriptoria associated with this centre, if one such consortium ever existed,[39] had a leading role in disseminating homilies, especially Ælfric's *Catholic Homilies*, through predication by priests.[40] The acquisition of CCCC 421 for Leofric's homiletic collection and its subsequent modification also entailed re-contextualisation and re-purposing of the texts in an episcopal frame. The contextual framework of CCCC 421 indicates that the dissemination of late-tenth-century ideas for a programmatic ecclesiastical reformation, as anticipated by Ælfric and Wulfstan, happened at episcopal level on a wider scale than in previous times, and reflected the expectations of the two authors for eleventh-century bishops. Rather differently from the situation in the first decades of the eleventh century, a reform of the Church relied very much on episcopal initiative, regardless of bishops' secular or monastic background.[41] Episcopal use of monastic-reform preaching materials in the later eleventh century in a sense bespeaks respect and consideration for the ideals that had inspired authors like Ælfric and Wulfstan to encourage an institutional reform of the Church. However, at the same time dedi-

---

[39] Wilcox, 'Ælfric in Dorset', p. 59; E. Treharne, 'Scribal Connections in Late Anglo-Saxon England', in Cate Gunn and Catherine Innes-Parker, eds., *Texts and Traditions of Medieval Pastoral Care: Essays in Honour of Bella Millett* (York: York Medieval Press, 2009), pp. 29–46.

[40] Wilcox, 'Ælfric in Dorset', p. 61.

[41] Barlow, *The English Church*, pp. 5–6. In the third quarter of the eleventh century the number of secular and monastic bishops was even, though seculars held the most important sees, including Canterbury, Winchester and London.

cated bishops like Leofric, Wulfstan II of Worcester (1062–95) and Hereman of Sherborne (1058–78) felt the need to re-configure and adapt those texts physically as well as conceptually. Homiletic texts were therefore extracted or excerpted according to interest or even popularity and repositioned for new uses.[42] Disembodiment from their original textual context facilitated the dissemination of those texts in many respects. It was an accepted practice in the eleventh and twelfth centuries that homilies could be produced as independent textual units – if contrary to Ælfric's original intentions – regardless of contextual coherence. Moreover, memorised passages and excerpts repeatedly copied in composite compilations formed units of texts transferred from manuscript to manuscript, as the case of CCCC 421 has clearly shown. Breaking of formal boundaries, whether textual or codicological created a modern way of sharing contents and knowledge, which, indifferent to the original rigidity of texts and collections, allowed for more thematic and structural flexibility than can be accounted for in earlier codices.

Conclusion

The 'de-construction' of CCCC 421 and a closer study of the phases of its re-construction have revealed that the manuscript's cultural and intellectual value was preserved by disrupting its original codicological integrity. This process of adding and subtracting textual units or even sections in vernacular homiletic codices seems to have been quite a common procedure in the late eleventh century. Although such composite homiliaries hardly ever reflect the intentions of the people authoring the texts that they contain, one might observe that the simple fact of juxtaposing texts by different authors, when not of a different type, is an expression of their users' interests and of the books' cultural function. CCCC 421 shows that earlier manuscripts contained exciting materials in a form that their subsequent users, such as Leofric, may have found limiting for their purposes, hence the changes.

Much as vernacular composite homiliaries were in vogue in the latter part of the eleventh century and well into the twelfth, there is very little palaeographical or codicological evidence that such codices as CCCC 421, Lambeth 489 and Cleopatra B.xiii were much in use

[42]   M. Swan, 'Old English Made New: One Catholic Homily and its Reuses', *Leeds Studies in English*, n.s. 28 (1997), 1–18, see esp. pp. 1–2 and 15.

at Exeter after Leofric's death in 1072, however. This may well be due to a Norman bishop, Osbern FitzOsbern, taking over at Exeter upon Leofric's death. Whether or not he ever made use of the rather generous collection of vernacular books that Leofric had used before him is still unknown. While under Osbern's episcopacy the cathedral book collection kept growing through the bishop's action, the production of vernacular books came to a halt.[43] All scriptorial activities, in fact, seem to have continued on a minimal scale, mostly for creating legal documents. The lack of vernacular manuscripts in Bishop Osbern's acquisitions and the abundance of mostly patristic books, perfectly in line with most of his colleagues and contemporaries,[44] however, confirms the different nature of his intellectual interests when compared with Leofric's. It would seem then that CCCC 421 and other codices of the same kind were simply neglected, other books being preferred to them for whatever cultural or political reasons. After Leofric's death the manuscript does not seem to have been much in use, as lack of any palaeographical evidence prior to the changes carried out by Matthew Parker and his son in the sixteenth century suggests. Whatever the life of CCCC 421 was in the centuries following the death of Leofric, it is the early history of the manuscript that is crucial to understanding how books were produced in late Anglo-Saxon and early medieval England. Through studies like this we can realise how much the idea of books and the ways in which they disseminate knowledge have changed through time.

---

[43] Treharne, 'Producing a Library', p. 169.

[44] T. Webber, 'Script and Manuscript Production at Christ Church, Canterbury, after the Norman Conquest', in R. Eales and R. Sharpe, eds., *Canterbury and the Norman Conquest: Churches, Saints and Scholars, 1066–1109* (London: Hambledon Press, 1995), 145–58; R. Thomson, 'The Library of Bury St Edmunds Abbey in the Eleventh and Twelfth Centuries', in R. Thomson, ed., *England and the Twelfth-Century Renaissance* (Aldershot: Ashgate, 1998), 617–45, pp. 630–6; R. Gameson, 'Manuscrits normands à Exeter aux XIᵉ et XIIᵉ siècles', in P. Bouet and M. Dosdat, eds., *Manuscrits et enluminures dans le monde normand (Xᵉ–XVᵉ siècles)* (Caen: Presses Universitaires de Caen, 2005), 107–27, p. 108.

The Power and the Glory: Conquest and Cosmology in Edwardian Wales (Exeter, Cathedral Library, 3514)

JULIA CRICK

HISTORIANS OF THE MODERN and pre-modern worlds have often sought to make connections between the boundaries of states and the shape of their respective historiographies; in recent years they have scrutinised archival processes and the preservation of artefacts of the past, and they and their literary peers have examined the historical narratives which imposed order on the past and gave meaning to its remains.[1] National historiographies are thus commonly ascribed active properties, as means by which elites might recognise and realise a collective future for their nation, stifle opposing views and assert a common will. If we accept the general principle that fields of historiographical interest will often coincide with political boundaries, actual or imagined, something impressed on historians by empirical observation, whether according to the model outline above or in ignorance or defiance of it, it follows that when competing historical trajectories meet they may be expected to generate turbulence at the very least.[2] This paper concerns a book

[1] Two collections of essays illustrate these trends very interestingly: Len Scales and Oliver Zimmer, ed., *Power and the Nation in European History* (Cambridge: Cambridge University Press, 2005) and Francis X. Blouin and William G. Rosenberg, ed., *Archives, Documentation, and Institutions of Social Memory: Essays from the Sawyer Seminar* (Ann Arbor, MI: University of Michigan Press, 2006). For illustration of the range of applications and discussion of their Foucauldian resonances see Anupama Rao, 'Affect, Memory, and Materiality: A Review Essay on Archival Mediation', *Comparative Studies in Society and History* 50.2 (2008), 559–67, kindly drawn to my attention by Maria Fusaro. I wish to record my thanks to David Dumville, Elizabeth Duncan, Daniel Huws, Oliver Padel, Paul Russell, David Thornton, Peter Thomas, librarian of Exeter Cathedral, and the staff of the Special Collections room at the University Library, Exeter, all of whom have assisted in the preparation of this paper by answering enquiries or by going to unusual trouble to make material available.
[2] See n. 3. For a less concrete example, note the appetite for universal history in the imperial realm of Germany: Valerie Flint, 'World History in the Early Twelfth Century: The "imago mundi" of Honorius Augustodunensis', in R. H. C. Davis and J. M. Wallace-Hadrill, eds., *The Writing of History in the Middle*

copied at a time of war before and during Edward I's conquest of Wales, a volume in which Welsh and English versions of history met and intersected.

The origins of Exeter 3514

By and large medievalists have embraced the broad historiographical trends just outlined, pursuing the connections between narrative and nation, construing the construction of narratives of national pasts as a form of nation-building, although they have produced fewer studies which analyse in the same vein the collection and deposition of information.[3] Here they have at their disposal, of course, an additional form of record not available to their modern colleagues. In a manuscript culture the act of authorship stands in a very active relationship with other processes of book production, more active, we could argue, than in a culture dominated by print. The copying of each book represents a small-scale act of origination, comparable with authorship in some respects: a lesser investment of skills, time and resources, certainly, but an activity involving a measure of selection from received tradition, whether received tradition is accepted wholesale, as a body of texts, or only in part.[4] Jacqueline Stodnick has recently attempted to construct a link between the two distinct forms of scholarly enquiry – codicology and discourse analysis – looking at the nation in truly skeletal form, as collections of king lists reproduced in manuscript.[5] I will make no attempt to replicate her method here, but we can learn much from her attention to the significance of copying as a process, potentially as

Ages: Essays Presented to Richard William Southern (Oxford: Oxford University Press, 1981), p. 214.

[3] Among numerous examples of the former see Patrick J. Geary, The Myth of Nations: The Medieval Origins of Europe (Princeton: Princeton University Press, 2002), pp. 15–40; for a move towards the latter see David Pratt, The Political Thought of King Alfred the Great (Cambridge: Cambridge University Press, 2007), esp. pp. 338–50.

[4] For discussion see Mary Swan, 'Authorship and Anonymity', in Phillip Pulsiano and Elaine Treharne, eds., A Companion to Anglo-Saxon Literature (Oxford: Blackwell, 2001, 2nd edn 2008), pp. 71–83; Patrick Geary, 'Medieval Archivists as Authors: Social Memory and Archival Memory', in Blouin and Rosenberg, eds., Archives, pp. 106–13.

[5] Jacqueline Stodnick, '"Old Names of Kings or Shadows": Reading Documentary Lists', in Catherine E. Karkov and Nicholas Howe, eds., Conversion and Colonization in Anglo-Saxon England (Tempe, AZ: MRTS, 2006), pp. 109–31.

a political one, and from her willingness to shift attention to an area which some might consider poetically and historically arid: the difficult featureless territory of the medieval list. As Stodnick and others have shown, such texts serve to order historical and geographical knowledge in ideologically significant ways.[6] In some circumstances, such as those which surround the creation of the volume to be discussed here, acts of transcription carry particular significance: old texts gain new meaning. That the combined content resists reduction to the status of manifesto or nationalist tract, that the story it tells is not quite a consistent (or, indeed, a national) one, reinforces another point about the culture from which it comes. Both sides of this particular political divide belonged to a common culture and shared a literary language and a particular cosmological vision. This shared inheritance only served to intensify the resulting competition for territory.

In late-thirteenth-century Wales not just the production, but the writing down of texts became a process heavy with political significance. After more than two centuries of sustained English military pressure and colonisation, the conquest of Edward I ended the last Welsh ruling dynasty with the death of Llywelyn ap Gruffudd in December 1282; Edward subsequently acted to appropriate Llywelyn's assets and ensure that any potential claimants died heirless.[7] The finality of these actions provoked an immediate cultural reflex. Rees Davies has described the 'ideology of disinheritance', which lent renewed vigour to a movement to copy Welsh historical and poetic texts and to translate Latin history into Welsh.[8] The conquerors likewise acquired texts,

[6]   The classic contribution is David Dumville, 'Kingship, Genealogies and Regnal Lists', in P. H. Sawyer and I. N. Wood, eds., *Early Medieval Kingship* (Leeds: The School of History, University of Leeds, 1977), pp. 72–104, reprinted in David N. Dumville, *Histories and Pseudo-histories of the Insular Middle Ages* (Aldershot: Ashgate, 1990), XV.
[7]   R. R. Davies, *Conquest, Coexistence and Change: Wales 1063–1415* (Oxford: University Press, 1987), pp. 333–88, esp. 351–4, 360–3.
[8]   Davies, *Conquest*, pp. 435–6; Rees Davies, 'Race Relations in Post-conquest Wales: Confrontation and Compromise', *The Transactions of the Honourable Society of Cymmrodorion* s.n. (1974 [1975]), 45–7. For a different view of the process see Helen Fulton, 'Class and Nation: Defining the English in Late-Medieval Welsh Poetry', in Ruth Kennedy and Simon Meecham-Jones, eds., *Authority and Subjugation in Writing of Medieval Wales* (Basingstoke: Palgrave, 2008), pp. 191–212. For a list of Welsh manuscripts copied at this time see Daniel Huws, 'Llyfrau Cymraeg 1250–1400', *National Library of Wales Journal* 28.1 (1993), 19–20, translated in Daniel Huws, *Medieval Welsh Manuscripts* (Cardiff: University of Wales Press, 2000).

apparently through a process of active collection. Edward II had in his possession an anthology of Welsh bardic poetry, recently copied but in archaic diction, so it has been argued.[9] Archbishop John Pecham of Canterbury (1279–92) cited in his negotiations with the Welsh the Laws ascribed to the tenth-century king Hywel Dda. Pecham perhaps knew the thirteenth-century manuscript of that text kept at Canterbury in the later Middle Ages, and possibly instigated its arrival there.[10]

The present study concerns a manuscript long associated with Edwardian Wales by the *Cronica de Wallia*, its most famous text, which contains material probably derived from the southern Welsh Cistercian monasteries of Whitland and Strata Florida (and prior to that, from the English Benedictine house at Bury St Edmunds), and which concludes in 1285, three years after Llywelyn's death.[11] More than half a dozen scribes worked on the manuscript (see Appendix 1; Figs. 1–3), some of them contemporaneously, a number achieving high calligraphic standards, including one working in or after 1266 (Hand 2) and another in or after 1285 (Hand 4). Exeter 3514 was thus copied in the decades either side of the Edwardian conquest, probably in a milieu very close to the political centre. Abbots of the Cistercian order were used as intermediaries between the Welsh and the English; after Llywelyn's defeat members of Cistercian communities were required to swear allegiance to the English king, even if their sympathies remained questionable afterwards, as before.[12]

[9] Andrew Breeze, 'A Manuscript of Welsh Poetry in Edward II's Library', *National Library of Wales Journal* 30.3 (1997), 129–31.
[10] Daniel Huws, 'Leges Howelda at Canterbury', *National Library of Wales Journal* 19.4 (1976), 341, and plates XIX, 5–6, reprinted in Huws, *Medieval Welsh Manuscripts*; Aberystwyth, National Library of Wales, Peniarth 28 (http://digidol.llgc.org.uk/METS/lhw00003/physical?div=2&subdiv=0&locale=en&mode=reference). On Pecham see Huw Pryce, *Native Law and the Church in Medieval Wales* (Oxford: University Press, 1993), pp. 70–3.
[11] *The Historia Regum Britannie of Geoffrey of Monmouth, II. The First Variant Version: A Critical Edition*, ed. Neil Wright (Cambridge: D. S. Brewer, 1988), pp. lxxxiii–lxxxiv. On the place of origin, see Thomas Jones, '"Cronica de Wallia" and Other Documents form Exeter Cathedral Library MS. 3514', *Bulletin of the Board of Celtic Studies* 12 (1946–8), 29; Kathleen Hughes, 'The Welsh Latin Chronicles: Annales Cambriae and Related Texts', *Proceedings of the British Academy* 59 (1973 [1975]), 246–50.
[12] Whitland having been attacked by English agents in 1258 and Cwmhir, Strata Florida's neighbour, ultimately receiving Llywelyn's body for burial:

It will be argued here that Exeter 3514 is a Welsh book, one read and at least partially copied in conquered Wales. Some have doubted that it was a wholly Welsh production, whether their view was determined by the texts contained in the manuscript, some of them certainly of Welsh origin but most not, or by its physical appearance, which conforms to European norms in many respects. The evidence to be discussed below suggests that the manuscript must be regarded as a totality and that Welsh elements pervade its composition, possibly from its earliest point. Certainly the texts that it contains combine to present a version of history which can scarcely be regarded as a neutral one, as we shall see.

Inside the book

Exeter 3514 provides a composite account of universal history whose cumulative effect is to locate the British present in human history and ultimately to place that history within the cosmos. The effect is achieved by the aggregation of clusters of texts, many familiar, some relatively rare or unique, which span vast tracts of space and time. This is done in a controlled and minutely detailed fashion. A series of genealogical texts documents the passage of time from Creation to the present through unbroken chains of named individuals (see Table 1), likewise a world map fitted neatly inside a text of Isidore's account of the winds (Fig. 1) terminates the vast geographical compass of the first book of Honorius of Autun's *De imagine mundi*, and a series of diagrams of the spheres.[13] The volume thus contains lists of the sort which attracted Stodnick's attention, accommodated beside bulky and universally available constituents, texts which one might expect to find in almost any late-thirteenth-century library in western Europe: pseudo-Methodius, Honorius of Autun, Dares Phrygius, Geoffrey of Monmouth, Henry of Huntingdon.

David H. Williams, *The Welsh Cistercians*, 2 vols. (Tenby: Cyhoeddiadau Sister-siadd [Caldey Island, Tenby], 1983–4), II, 36–9, 41–2, 49–50. See also Rhŷs W. Hays, 'The Welsh Monasteries and the Edwardian Conquest', *Studies in Medieval Cistercian History Presented to Jeremiah F. O'Sullivan* (Spencer, MA: Cistercian Publications, 1971), pp. 110–37.
[13] PL 172.119–33 (Book I.I–XXXVI). See Appendix 1, item [6].

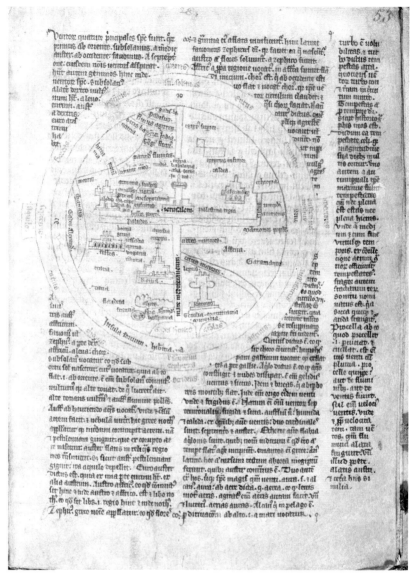

Figure 1. Exeter, Cathedral Library, MS. 3514, p. 53: the OT map located within Isidore, *Etymologiae*, XIII.XI. Published by permission of the Dean and Chapter of Exeter Cathedral

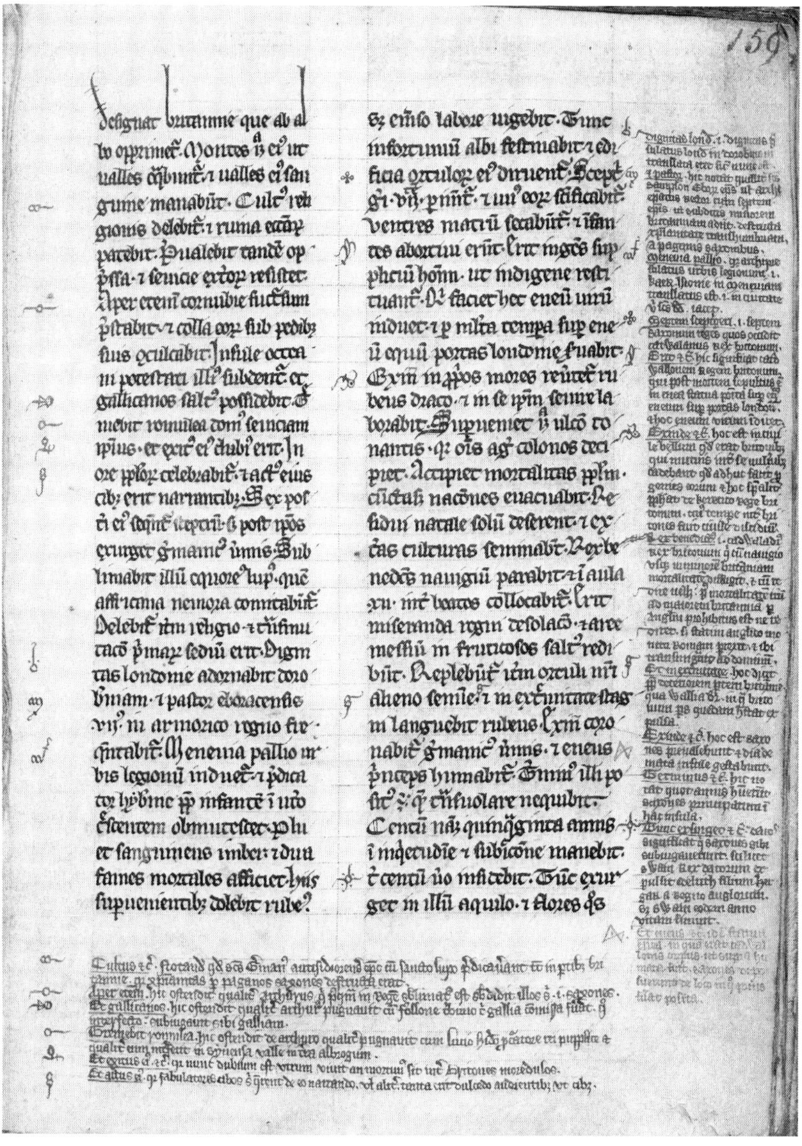

Figure 2. Exeter, Cathedral Library, MS. 3514, p. 159: glosses on the Prophecies of Merlin. Published by permission of the Dean and Chapter of Exeter Cathedral

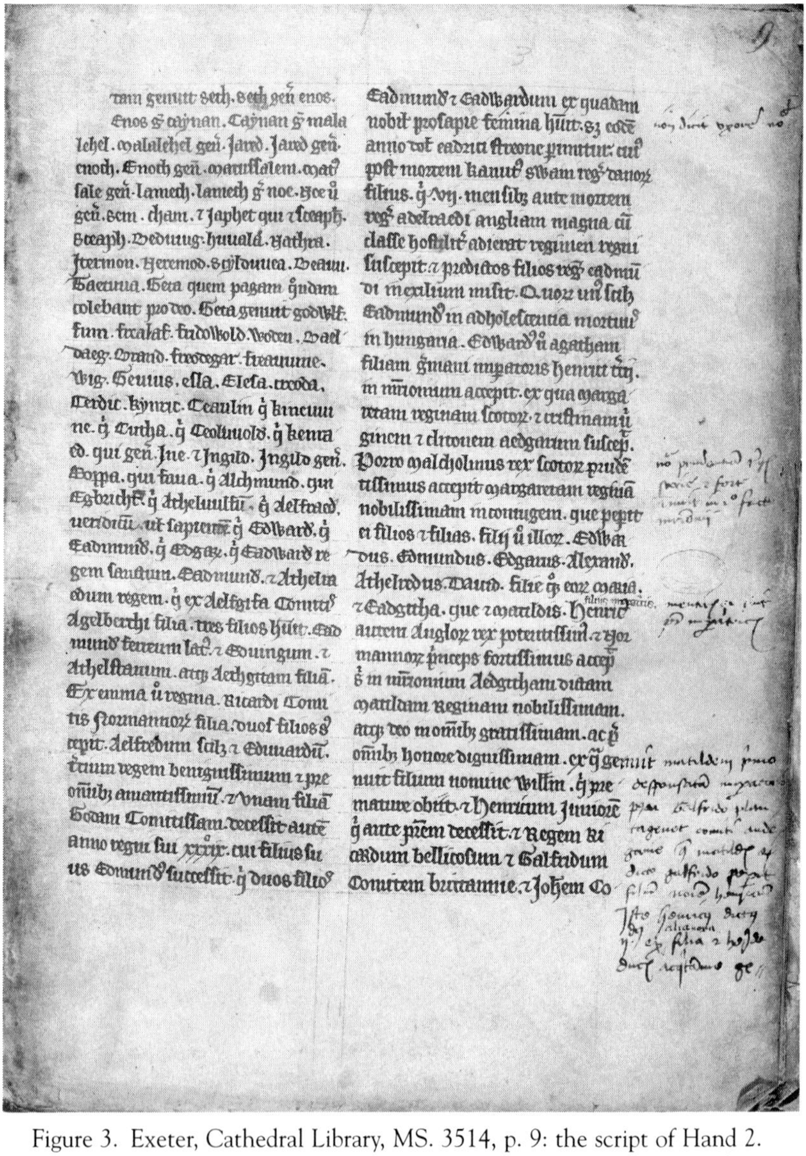

Figure 3. Exeter, Cathedral Library, MS. 3514, p. 9: the script of Hand 2.
Published by permission of the Dean and Chapter of Exeter Cathedral

Table 1. Cosmological time as spanned in genealogical and historical
texts in Exeter Cathedral 3514, quires I–XI

The texts are listed according to numbering assigned in Ker's description
(above, n. 27) and described in Appendix 1.

Creation	Old Testament	Trojan war	post-Roman era	Present

Ker 2a (pp. 9–10 Appendix 1 [2]). English kings from Adam to Henry III
(1216–72)

——————————————————————————>

Ker 2b (pp. 10b–18 Appendix 1 [3]). *De aduentu Anglorum* (448–734)

                                        ——————————>

Ker 2d (pp. 21b–30 Appendix 1 [5]). French kings from Pharamundus to Philip
IV (1285–1314)

————————————————————>

Ker 4(a) (pp. 54–6 Appendix 1 [7]). British kings from Adam to Cadwallader

                    ——————>

Ker4(b) (p. 56b Appendix 1 [8]). Kings of Gwynedd from Llywelyn ap Gruffudd
(1256–82) to Adam

————————————————<———————————

Ker 4(c) (pp. 56b–57b Appendix 1 [9]). Trojan genealogy from Noah to Brutus

————>

Ker 4(d) (pp. 57b–58a Appendix 1 [10]). Kings of Wessex (from 'Æthelwold' [son
of Ecgberht, and so presumably Æthelwulf of Wessex, 839–58] to Noah)

————————————<————————

Ker 4(e) (pp. 58a/b Appendix 1 [11]). Norman kings (806–Henry III)

                              ——————>

Ker 5 (p. 60 Appendix 1 [12]). English kings from Cynegils (611–?642) to Henry
III

                              ——————>

Ker 6 (pp. 61–66b Appendix 1 [15]). French kings from Gratian and Valentinian
(379–83) to 1230s

                        ——————>

Ker 7 (pp. 67–93 Appendix 1 [16]). Dares

            ——————>

Ker 8 (pp. 94–218 (Brutus to Cadwallader), Appendix 1 [17]). Geoffrey of
Monmouth

                    ——————————>

One modern commentator, describing the manuscript for a Welsh audience, noted that it contained the basic materials of Welsh history.[14] The implications of this description merit exploration, but even leaving aside the Welsh associations of texts and classes of texts read widely elsewhere,[15] the implications of the configuration of texts presented here are clear enough. In Llywelyn's lifetime (ruler of Gwynedd 1256–82) Welsh claims to dignity, sovereignty and legal independence were being staked on the genealogical routes being advertised in this manuscript, tracks traced back through Trojan ancestry to the Old Testament and thus quite distinct from those traced for English kings in most historical texts, not least in the genealogies in the same manuscript. Indeed, the work of the latest-looking scribe of Exeter 3514 left no room for doubt. He copied not only a recent history of the Welsh, to 1285, but a genealogy of the French kings, up to and including the ruling monarch Philip IV, demonstrating that they, like the Welsh, were descendants of the Trojan ruling house, and thus, by implication, cousins.[16]

The book had reached its present state at latest by the early fourteenth century when a scribe recorded on the first flyleaf in an anglicana hand twenty-one items which it contained, two of which are now lost, suggesting that the contents then ran to more than 530 pages.[17] This demonstrates that even at the start of its life the new materials in the book occupied only a small fraction of its volume. Indeed, alongside the pan-European works already listed, Exeter 3514 contains a significant volume of material apparently imported directly from England, some very recently. David Dumville established beyond question that

[14] Brynley Roberts, 'Pen Penwaedd a Phentir Gafran', *Llên Cymru*, 13 (1974–81), pt iii–iv (1981), pp. 278–9. I am indebted to Dr Oliver Padel for my knowledge of this article and for sending me a partial translation.
[15] This is a point which could be developed. On universal history in Edwardian Wales see Caroline Brett, 'The Prefaces of Two Late-Thirteenth-Century Welsh Latin Chronicles', *Bulletin of the Board of Celtic Studies* 35 (1988), 63–73. On cosmology and geography see Alison Peden, 'Science and Philosophy in Wales at the Time of the Norman Conquest: A Macrobius Manuscript from Llanbadarn', *Cambridge Medieval Celtic Studies* 2 (1981), esp. 28, 40–1, 44–5. Also Alfred Hiatt, 'The Map of Macrobius before 1100', *Imago Mundi* 59.2 (2007), p. 171, no. 20.
[16] Hand 4. See Appendix 2 and discussion, pp. 33–5.
[17] The list is printed as the first column of the table in Appendix 1. Ker noted that two items were missing, my numbers [14] and [15], and his total reached 22: N. R. Ker, *Medieval Manuscripts in British Libraries* (Oxford: Clarendon Press, 1969–2002), II, 822.

the manuscript was built on an existing textual core of twelfth-century origins, a compendium of Anglo-Norman episcopal and abbatial lists prefacing a text of Henry of Huntingdon's epic account of English history, the *Historia Anglorum*.[18] This cluster circulated in twelfth-century Normandy and the precise configuration represented here has been traced to the Norman monastery of Saint-Wandrille, although the version here was copied from an exemplar whose medieval associations place it in eastern England.[19] Neil Wright recognised that this core can be isolated from the remainder of Exeter 3514 not just as a cluster of texts, but as a distinct codicological and palaeographical unit: it occupies ten quires separable from the rest (XII–XXI) and is written in two hands, which Ker identified as 'earlier than the rest', and which are not found elsewhere in the volume.[20]

We should be scrupulous to avoid conflating textual and physical origins, however, and to assume that these quires were themselves copied outside Wales. Instances of textual indebtedness pervade the volume from start to finish. The second quire contains two texts of probable East Anglian origins, a heptarchic history, and the account of the death of Bede (Ker items 2(b) and (c)), while both the Welsh Latin chronicles which end the manuscript draw on recent material from Bury St Edmunds, for the 1250s and early 1260s, so Hughes has suggested.[21] None of these items can be separated from the compilation as a whole; the scribes of the texts in question appear elsewhere in the volume (see Appendices 1–2).

Such debts do nothing to dent the Welshness of the manuscript, as manifested in a variety of texts: the Welsh chronicle material already mentioned, annotations relating to Welsh history and geography catalogued by Ker, and symptoms of Welsh interest contained in a variety of other Latin texts.[22] First, the compilation contains another textual

---

[18] David N. Dumville, 'An Early Text of Geoffrey of Monmouth's *Historia Regum Britanniae* and the Circulation of Some Latin Histories in Twelfth-Century Normandy', *Arthurian Literature* 4 (1985), 1–36, reprinted in Dumville, *Histories*, XIV, pp. 6–16. These are represented as shaded blocks in the table below (Appendix 1).

[19] Dumville, 'An Early Text', pp. 14–15. The exemplar was London, Lambeth Palace 327: Wright, *The Historia*, p. lxxxii; *Henry, Archdeacon of Huntingdon. Historia Anglorum. The History of the English People*, ed. and transl. Diana Greenway (Oxford: University Press, 1996), pp. cxxxv–cxxxvi.

[20] Ker, *Medieval Libraries*, II, 822.

[21] Hughes, 'The Welsh Latin Chronicles', pp. 246–7.

[22] Ker, *Medieval Libraries*, II, 823–4.

cluster that appears in manuscripts of Welsh origin or provenance. In
Exeter 3514 this occupies much of quires IV–XI and it consists of the
genealogies of the last prince of Gwynedd, Llywelyn ap Gruffudd, then
a genealogy of the Trojans to Brutus, and a distinctive version of Dares'
Trojan History and the First Variant version of Geoffrey of Monmouth's
History of the Kings of Britain.[23] While the First Variant and Vulgate
version of Geoffrey's text suggest that the crown of Britain has been
lost forever, in manuscripts of this group allowance of this harsh judgement is mitigated ('nisi post longum tempus') and the possibility of
Welsh recovery anticipated.[24] Another indicator of Welsh origin, the
extensive marginal commentary on the *Prophecies of Merlin*, written
perhaps in the same hand as that of p. 53 (see Figs. 1 and 2), contains
unique information of interest to a Welsh readership but meaning-
less in an English or French context: the styling of Henry II 'Bricht
cadarn' (strong arm) at §114.4, the record of the killing of the sons of
Owain ap Edwin by Owain Gwynedd, founder of the Gwynedd ruling
dynasty, an event traceable to 1125 (§113.17).[25] More telling still is the
mangling of important English names: Edgar is 'Hetgar' and the king
whom William the Bastard defeated in 1066 is recorded as 'Geraldum
filium Ethwini': Harold Godwinesson.[26] Such errors bespeak a distance
from English history and it is this, together with the familiarity with
Welsh language and history, which makes the commentary unique in
the tradition of exegesis of the *Prophecies of Merlin*.[27]

---

[23] Wright, *The Historia*, pp. xciii–xcvi, cv. MSS. cDES. See Julia C. Crick,
*The Historia Regum Britannie of Geoffrey of Monmouth, III: A Summary Cata-
logue of the Manuscripts* (Cambridge: D. S. Brewer. 1989), nos. 55, 67, 68, 70.
See below, Appendix 1, items [7]–[9], [16]–[17].

[24] Wright, *The Historia*, pp. ci–cii, civ, §186/7.

[25] Printed by J. Hammer, 'Bref commentaire de la *Prophetia Merlini* du ms
3514 de la Bibliothèque de la Cathédrale d'Exeter (Geoffrey de Monmouth,
Historia regum Britanniae, l. VII)', in *Hommages à Joseph Bidez et à Franz Cumont*
(Brussels: [Collection Latomus, 2], 1949), p. 116. Hammer gave the reading
'Brihtcadain'. I am grateful to David Thornton for discussion of these points.
On the killing of Owain ap Edwin's sons see David E. Thornton, 'Owain ab
Edwin (d. 1105)', in *Oxford Dictionary of National Biography*, 60 vols. (Oxford:
University Press, 2004).

[26] Hammer, 'Bref commentaire', pp. 114–15. Both readings have been checked
against the manuscript and the first corrects Hammer's reading 'Hergar'.

[27] But note, however, that the author of the First Variant version conjures a
seventh-century king of England named Æthelstan, an error which is surely
symptomatic of a similar distance. Wright noted the error but took it as indica-
tive of the redactor's incompetence, *The Historia*, p. lxxiii.

Neil Ker, who described the volume for his series *Medieval Libraries of Great Britain*, noted that it was 'written in England or Wales'.[28] Neil Wright regarded the book as a hybrid, with a core 'written in the mid-thirteenth century in an unidentified British scriptorium' expanded 'when the book had reached Wales', probably at Whitland.[29] Nonetheless, close palaeographical examination makes it difficult to escape the conclusion that much of the volume is Welsh: the distribution of the scribal stints connects material of obviously Welsh origin with the rest. Indeed, if we suppose the core section to be the work of a monastic scriptorium in eastern England in the mid-thirteenth century, we encounter marked anomalies, particularly in the scale of the book and the proportions of the script. Exeter 3514 answers neither of the descriptions that fit many English books of the thirteenth century: it is neither a large handsome two-column production written in Gothic bookhand and decorated with elegant filigreed initials, nor a tiny, compact, closely written workaday volume in simplified and less formal script. We see a volume which does not conform to these norms: a mid-sized volume (252 x 187 mm), neither very large nor pocket sized, whose script, layout and decoration cannot be described as truly Gothic (see Appendix 2). In addition we find a scattering of insular abbreviations popular in much earlier centuries. The Welsh provenance of some of the contents of the manuscript, together with the fact that certain palaeographical features link the work of scribes across the entire volume, constitute reason to suppose that the entire volume was copied in Wales (see Appendix 2). The combined evidence of contents and the distribution of scribal stints suggests that this took place in the second-half of the thirteenth century, in two, possibly three campaigns: the replication of the Anglo-Norman core, the major work of expansion in or after 1266 (Hand 2 and related work), and the copying of the final texts after Llywelyn's death (Hand 4). This conclusion poses important questions, not least the quality and extent of the scribal resources available in a Welsh house at a time of political and military crisis. The decoration in the newer part of the volume was unfinished, and the

---

[28] Ker, *Medieval Manuscripts in British Libraries*, II, 824. See also Dumville, 'An Early Text', p. 10: 'a Welsh book of the mid-thirteenth century'. The manuscript is tentatively assigned to Whitland in N. R. Ker, *Medieval Libraries of Great Britain: A List of Surviving Books, Supplement to the second edition*, ed. Andrew G. Watson (London: Royal Historical Society, 1987), p. 68.
[29] Wright, *The Historia*, pp. lxxxii, lxxxiii.

red and blue filigreed initials in the core were crude and perhaps a little
old-fashioned, but the work was completed to generally consistent and
calligraphic standards.[30]

Genealogical time

Whether or not this hypothetical reconstruction is accepted in its
entirety, the alternative is to suppose that the whole, Cambro-Latin
and all, was copied in an English centre, subsequently to receive
glosses by scribes interested in Welsh affairs. This second reconstruction, already the less economic of the two, looks the least tenable
because the compilation carried an ineluctable political message. It
established the divinity of the lineage of Brutus, first king of Britain; it
laid out the unbroken descent of the dynasty of Gwynedd from Adam
to the present incumbent, Llywelyn ap Gruffudd, 'cognatus Dei'; it
rehearsed the utterly different historical trajectory of the English kings,
descending via Sceaf, son of Noah, an obsolete route claimed for the
West Saxon kings three hundred years before but rejected before the
Norman conquest.[31] This genealogical information encoded a birth-
right – a lineage documented as far as the Creation, via the heroes
of classical antiquity, moreover one free at every stage from the taint
of association with the English and their Germanic forebears – and
commentary was provided in the accompanying histories of Troy and
Britain.[32] Whether the scribes worked during or immediately after the
lifetime of Llywelyn ap Gruffudd, these were important messages. Archbishop Pecham's negotiations with the Welsh princes conducted after

---

[30] On archaism in Peniarth 28 (a mid-thirteenth-century manuscript of Welsh
origin written in European script and localised to Wales by its contents) and
in Welsh manuscripts in general see Huws, 'Leges Howelda', p. 343. For discussion of broadly analogous problems in identifying Hiberno-English manuscripts
see John J. Thompson, 'Mapping Points West of West Midlands Manuscripts
and Texts: Irishness(es) and Middle English Literary Culture', in Wendy Scase,
ed., *Essays in Manuscript Geography: Vernacular Manuscripts of the English West
Midlands from the Conquest to the Sixteenth Century* (Turnhout: Brepols, 2007),
pp. 113–28.
[31] On the route and its obsolescence see Daniel Anlezark, 'Sceaf, Japheth and
the Origins of the Anglo-Saxons', *Anglo-Saxon England* 31 (2001), 13–46.
[32] Indeed, a contemporary annotator treated the histories of Dares and Geoffrey as a unit, providing a running commentary in marginal rubrics written on
carefully ruled lines throughout the entirety of the two texts.

Llywelyn was declared a rebel in 1264 and before his death in 1282 returned to the question of ancient right; laws enjoyed by the Welsh princes and their forebears from the time of Camber, son of Brutus; the princes' inheritance (*hereditas*) from the time of Brutus, their possession of Snowdon as an appendage of the principality of Wales, 'as their forebears had held it from the time of Brutus', all the time linking this to 'language, traditions, laws and customs' ('linguam, mores, leges et consuetudines').[33] The antiquity and separateness of Welsh law, whose origins Geoffrey had conveniently documented when he not only asserted the antiquity of the dynasty of Britain but associated its laws with the founding moment, became a matter of urgent political concern in this and subsequent generations and were spelled out in the genealogical texts in this manuscript.[34]

Exeter 3514 contained matter of ideological importance to the Welsh but its contents resist reduction to the requirements of any one party. Rather, we see the tug between claimants to the same ground. The volume presents Welsh history within a much larger cosmology drawn from the common intellectual and religious tradition in which both sides participated. The copying here in Latin of materials from the European tradition, most in circulation for a century, and some for half a millennium, many imported, some within living memory, represents an assertion of intellectual and aesthetic standards and the continuity of much older traditions. The place of Welsh history was staked out here in time and space using the universal language, in texts copied in contemporary European script which a leading modern expert was unable to localise to England or Wales. As is well known, Edward and subsequent English monarchs usurped the Galfridian tradition, merging the English royal genealogy with the Trojan, and portraying themselves as the descendants of Brutus and Arthur and the heirs to their dominions.[35] It is perhaps no surprise that the latest annotating hands in

---

[33] Charles Trice Martin, ed., *Registrum epistolarum fratris Johannis Peckham archiepiscopi Cantuariensis*, 3 vols. (London: Longman, 1882–5), II, no. CCCLVIII, pp. 469–71. Discussed by Davies, *Conquest*, pp. 351–2, 373–4; Davies, 'Race Relations', 35–42.

[34] J. Beverley Smith, 'The Legal Position of Wales in the Middle Ages', in Alan Harding, ed., *Law-Making and Law-Makers in British History: Papers Presented to the Edinburgh Legal History Conference, 1977* (London: Royal Historical Society, 1980), pp. 21–53.

[35] Discussed most accessibly by R. R. Davies, *The First English Empire: Power and Identities in the British Isles 1093–1343* (Oxford: University Press 2000), pp. 40–3.

Exeter 3514 that betray signs of Welsh interest date from the fourteenth century. The cultural defences erected in this handsome volume were overridden; it was in the hands of the bishop of Lincoln by Tudor times and appears never to have returned to Wales.[36]

Appendix 1. Fourteenth-century contents-list (fol. ii)
with identifications

In isto uolumine continentur libri subscripti	Pages in MS	Ker	Textual notes
[1] In primo quidam tractatus qui incipit 'quomodo in principio creauit de celum et terram' et in fine eiusdem tractatus de antichristo	1–6	1	Pseudo-Methodius
[2] Item genealogia ab Adam usque ad Edwardum filium Henrici regis	9–10	2(a)	Unprinted genealogy of English kings to Edward I (1272–1307)
[3] Item de aduentu Anglorum in Britanniam cum geneal<og>ia regum scilicet Iutarum Cantuariorum, Saxonum Australium, Occidentalium, Orientalium, Meditaraneorum (sic), Deirorum, Berniciorum, et de sancto Oswaldo.	10–18	2(b)	Unprinted history of the Anglo-Saxon Heptarchy, derived from the Annals of St Neots[37]
[4] Item de transitu Bede uenerabilis	19–21	2(c)	Death of Bede[38]
[5] Item genealogia regum Francie	21–30	2(d)	Unprinted genealogy of the French kings from the Trojan, Pharamund, to Philip IV (1285–1314)

---

[36] Ker, *Medieval Libraries*, II, 823–5.
[37] Discussed by Dumville in David N. Dumville and Michael Lapidge, ed., *The Annals of St Neots* (Cambridge: D. S. Brewer 1985), p. xxi.
[38] Dumville and Lapidge, *The Annals*, pp. li–lii.

[6] *Item quidam tractatus [ ] qui dicitur speculum mundi et de quatuor uentis principalibus*	43–53	3(a)–(g)	Honorius of Autun, Book I, followed by world map surrounded by text of Isidore, *Etymologiae*, XIII. XI.2–end 'De uentis'[39]
[7] *Item genealogia ab Adam (sic) usque ad Brutum et de regibus a Bruto usque ad Cadwaladrum ultimum regem Britonum*	54–6	4(a)	Unprinted genealogy of the kings of Britain from Adam to Cadwallader
[8] *Item genealogia a Lewlino filio Griffini ascendendo usque ad Adam*	56	4(b)	Retrograde genealogy of Llywelyn ap Gruffudd[40]
[9] *Item genealogia a Ciprio usque ad Brutum*	56–7	4(c)	Unprinted genealogy of Brutus
[10] *Item genealogia Anglorum*	57–8	4(d)	Retrograde genealogy of the West Saxon kings from Æthelwold, father of Alfred the Great, to Noah, from William of Malmesbury, *Gesta regum Anglorum*, ii.116[41]
[11] *Item genealogia Normannorum*	58	4(e)	Unprinted genealogy of the Normans from AD 806 to Henry III
[12] *Item de longitudine et latitudine et prouinciis Anglie \et de episcopatibus Anglie/ et de quibusdam Regibus quot annis regnauerunt*	58–60	5	Unprinted account of the geography of Britain[42]
[13] *Item de nominibus regum a Bruto ad Kadwaladrum*			Lost
[14] *Item Beda de concordia maris et lune*			Lost
[15] *Item genealogia regum Francie et de Willelmo Bastard. Et ceteris regibus Anglie succedent*	61–6	6	Unprinted

[39] PL 82, col. 479–81. Previously unidentified. Ker 3(g).
[40] Printed and discussed by David E. Thornton, 'A neglected genealogy of Llywelyn ap Gruffudd', *Cambridge Medieval Celtic Studies* 23 (1992), esp. pp. 11–12.
[41] Mynors, Winterbottom and Thomson, *Gesta regum*, pp. 176–7. Not previously identified.
[42] Welsh content discussed by Roberts, 'Pen Penwaedd'.

[16] *Item Dares Frigius de historia Troianorum*	67–93	7	Dares Phrygius
[17] *Item historia Britonum translata a Britannica lingua in latinum*	94–218	8	Geoffrey of Monmouth, *Historia regum Britannie*, First Variant Version[43]
[18] *Item historia Anglorum composita ab Henrico archidiacono Huntendonensi que diuisa est in .x. libros ut patet in principio libri quem ipse composuit*	226–450	10	Henry of Huntingdon, *Historia Anglorum*[44]
[19] *Item historia Ricardi dicti sine timore, ducis Normannie, et ceteris ducibus succedentibus et de Willelmo Bastard et ceteris regibus Anglie usque ad coronacionem Regis Henrici filii Iohannis Regis*	450–504	12	Unprinted
[20] *Item quedam cronic. de Wallia*[45]	507–19; 522–3	13	'Cronica de Wallia', to 1266[46]
[21] *Item cronic. de Anglia*	?523–8	?15	Chronicle to 1285[47]

[43] Wright, ed., *The Historia*.

[44] Greenway, *Henry*, pp. cxxx–cxxxi (sigla Ex[1] and Ex[2], copied from two different versions).

[45] Jones expands as *Cronica* but *cronicon* would be a valid transcription: Thomas Jones, '"Cronica de Wallia" and Other Documents from Exeter Cathedral Library MS 3514', *Bulletin of the Board of Celtic Studies* 12 (1946–8), 27–44.

[46] Jones, 'Cronica', pp. 29–42.

[47] Jones edited the final pages (pp. 527–8): 'Cronica', pp. 42–4.

Appendix 2. Hands

It is clear that a number of scribes worked on the manuscript and that several worked in collaboration. Ker recorded two important observations which have shaped all subsequent criticism of the manuscript, that his items 9 and 10 (Henry of Huntingdon's *Historia* and the preceding episcopal lists, represented by shading in Appendix 1), were 'earlier than the rest', and that the bulk of the later part of the manuscript, namely pp. 1–66, 507–18 (his articles 1–6, 13) were 'in one hand'.[48] Examination of the manuscript over several months has convinced me that while the first judgement stands, the second should be modified, because although we observe many generic similarities within the folios indicated, perhaps as many as five sets of activity can be identified, possibly the work of five different scribes. This view remains tentative – it may be erroneous to equate these separate stints with separate individuals. Although distinct differences of practice can be observed, some of these might be changes wrought within the hand of an individual writing over a number of years. In particular, there is much to connect Hands 1 and 2; Hand 5 is possibly a higher grade version of Hand 1. There are more positive identifications, however, in particular the linking of the *Cronica de Wallia* with Hand 2 and the second Welsh chronicle with Hand 4.

Two general conclusions emerge. The first is that certain idiosyncrasies characterise the work seen throughout the volume. First, common features link the added texts (Hands 1–6 below), but there are also points of similarity between the core and added sections (see description of Hands 7 and 8 below). While there are a number of stylish and calligraphic performances, none of the scribes writes quite what one might expect for late-thirteenth-century bookhand. Indeed, given that the manuscript is far from the diminutive and most of the script is not small either, the bookhand employed looks unusually relaxed and informal. Scribes are reluctant to display fusion or breaking of minims; when the two-compartment **a** is employed, we find the looped form more characteristic of anglicana than the coffin-shaped letter common in bookhand of this date. There are some idiosyncrasies. Several scribes employ the ancient gate-shaped insular *enim* compendium (Hand 6, 7,

---

[48] Ker, *Medieval Libraries*, II, 822, 824.

8). Two scribes write above the top line, despite the tendency to write below it by the middle of the thirteenth century.

Hand 1
pp. 1–3r20; 43–52, ?53, 54–60; possibly seen elsewhere (see Plate 1)
Regular and stylish Gothic bookhand, moving towards semi-quadrata, with some breaking of minim strokes at the base line (e.g. **r** occasionally written with diagonal foot). Brown ink. Some lateral compression. Familiar kind of hand seen elsewhere in volume. ?Slightly earlier than Hand 2. Broadly similar aspect but different usages (pencil ruled, written below top line, 32–5 lines). Two-compartment **a** with top compartment closed by a looped stroke, but also straight-backed version with split minim stroke serving as the head; round-backed **d** in left margin; pierced **p** and **t**; some flagging of ascenders; fusion **be, bo, do, de, he, pe**; crossed *et*-nota.

Hand 2
pp. 3b–12b, 61–6; ?507–18, 518–19 (see plate 3).[49]
Scribe working in or after 1266–copied *Cronica de Wallia* entry for this year on p. 519. Gothic bookhand, brown ink, very similar to Hand 1 but different usages. Propensity to flourishes and exuberance, some fusion of minim space. 2-compartment **a** but occasional use of the split-backed form seen in Hand 1; round-backed **d** with downward tick extending decoratively into left margin; long **I** with two bosses and forked ascender; double **ll** with hairline top (late feature), occasionally **x** with horizontal hairline stroke, fusion of **bo, de, do, po**. Features which distinguish this from other hands in the volume: 8-shaped **g** with angular bowl closed by diagonal hairline stroke, preference for uncrossed over crossed *et*-nota, although crossed version does appear, descender of **q** turns leftwards; cup-shaped top to descending abbreviation stroke on abbreviation – *or(um)*; *aR(um)* ligature with upper-case R; tendency to extend ascenders at top of page and likewise descenders at foot.

Hand 3
pp. 13a–21b, 522 line 24–523 line 16
Generic similarity to adjacent hands in this section, but written with much thicker nib which lends the script a squat appearance. No

---

[49] Page 507 is illustrated by Jones, 'Cronica', p. 30.

breaking of minim-strokes. Two-compartment **a** but also the straight-backed type, cf. Hand 1; crossed *et*-nota; fusion **do, po**, but not **be, de, he**. Distinctive features: formation of **w** with rightwards hooked stroke descending beneath the interlocked **v**; rounded **g** with disproportionately small lower compartment.

Hand 4
pp. 21b–30a; 36–40, 523–8
Looks like more evolved version of script of Hands 1 and 2. The scribe was writing in or after 1285 (copies Ker item 2(d) which ends in or after 1285 and Ker item 15 which ends at 1285). Blacker ink. Later features include more breaking of minim-strokes, especially visible at tops of minims (semi-quadrata), but also see **a** with a break in the stroke forming the top compartment and broken **r** in *-rum* abbreviation; tagged ascenders eg. **g, b, h**; **x** crossed by horizontal hairline stroke. Also looped two-compartment **a** (as in Hand 1), 8-shaped ground **g**, crossed *et*-nota. Stylish and playful (e.g. 25b l. 22 [C]um itaque – rabbit/mouse drawn inside decoratively extended **u**).

Hand 5
pp. 43a – b, 94a – b
Large bookhand with lozenging at tops of minims, bearing generic similarities, especially to Hand 1. Employs the same form of **r** with the foot on the baseline and the looped two-compartment **a**. Distinctive forms include a large-headed open **a** and an 8-shaped **g** with horizontally elongated sinuous lower compartment. Resembles Hand 1 and could be the same scribe practising a higher grade of script.

Hand 6
pp. 67–218 (see main text, plate 2)
32 lines; relatively large squat four-line script with indented or tagged ascenders, especially the hairline top on double **l**. Some lateral compression but as with other hands in the volume the script does not fit the normal conventions of Gothic bookhand: neither fusion nor breaking of minim strokes. Very black ink in places, e.g. pp. 100–15. Sometimes resembles Hand 1 (e.g. p. 169). Two-compartment **a**, squat straight-backed **d** as well as round version; **g** tends to sit on the baseline rather than descend below it; round **s**; **x** with hairline cross-stroke; crossed *et*-nota generally used but uncrossed occurs. Note the use of the Insular *enim* compendium on the catchword at the foot of p. 142 and on p. 143 line 1.

Hand 7
pp. 223–300
Small Gothic bookhand with little fusion and no breaking of minim
strokes. The most distinctive letter is a pinched s-shaped **g**. **a** with
large open head, often closing to a second compartment, angular **h**
descending below the baseline, crossed *et*-nota and **x**, **t** sometimes
pierced. N.B. Split-headed **a** occurs (cf. Hand 1) as does the looped
two-compartment **a** . *aR(um)* abbreviation is found (as in Hand 2) and
the whole has the same upright and busy aspect. Several insular symptoms: recurrent use of the old insular *enim* compendium and of the
division-sign compendium for *est*, with a comma replacing the lower
point.[50] The top line is written.

Hand 8
pp. 301–450
a has a tiny head. 8-shaped **g**, crossed **et**-nota, pierced **t**, crossed **x**.
Resembles Hand 3 quite closely, except in the formation of **w** (described
above). Very black ink.[51]

Hand 9
pp. 451–604
Squat proportions. Protogothic resembling other hands in the volume.
Small-headed **a**, short-backed **d**, 8-shaped **g**, round **s** in final position,
pierced **t** following **c** and **s**.

[50] I thank Elizabeth Duncan of the University of Aberdeen for discussion of
this matter. Her volume on abbreviations in Gaelic manuscripts is forthcoming
from Aberdeen University Press.
[51] Greenway associated change of hand with change of text from version 5 to
6 on p. 442: *Henry*, pp. cxxx–cxxxi. I note a temporary change of aspect there.

Manuscript Production before Chaucer: Some Preliminary Observations[1]

ORIETTA DA ROLD

THIS PAPER CONCERNS books written in England in the centuries before Chaucer; it considers some of the current trends in our understanding of manuscript production from the twelfth to the fifteenth centuries. It represents ideas and questions which I formed during my work on two projects funded by the Arts and Humanities Research Council, which catalogued manuscripts from very different points on the medieval chronological spectrum. On the one hand, 'The Production and Use of English Manuscripts: 1060 to 1220' project (EM Project) deals with manuscripts containing English texts that were copied between the end of the eleventh and the beginning of the thirteenth century;[2] on the other, the 'Manuscripts of the West Midlands' project (MWM Project) has catalogued manuscripts linguistically localisable to the West Midlands and datable to the fourteenth to fifteenth centuries.[3] Working on these projects brought a realisation that there is scope for more detailed study of the production of medieval manuscripts containing English from the twelfth to the fourteenth centuries. A perusal, for instance, of the electronic catalogue of the MWM Project and the manuscripts available in the EM Project offers an impressive collection of data, which includes the incipits and explicits of texts, palaeographical and codicological information, and art-historical obser-

[1] I should like to thank Elaine Treharne for the numerous conversations and discussions on medieval manuscript production, and for her careful reading of this essay. Any errors remain my own.

[2] This project is still being developed. For further details on the project, see 'Our Project in a Nutshell', in *The Production and Use of English Manuscripts 1060 to 1220* (http://www.le.ac.uk/ee/em1060to1220, 13 October 2009); for an overview on the research questions of the project, see Orietta Da Rold, 'English Manuscripts 1060 to 1220 and the Making of a Re-source', *Literature Compass*, 3 (2006), 750–66 and Mary Swan and Elaine M. Treharne, eds., *Rewriting Old English in the Twelfth Century*, Cambridge Studies in Anglo-Saxon England 30 (Cambridge: Cambridge University Press, 2000).

[3] *A Catalogue of Vernacular Manuscript Books of the English West Midlands, c.1300–c.1475* (http://www.mwm.bham.ac.uk, 13 October 2009).

vations. However, one is left to wonder what these data are telling us about the production and the use of these books and the transmission of medieval texts. What is the picture that these resources paint? It is certainly a complex scenario with several missing components, which, however, we can start to put together by questioning the available evidence. Information about the textual content of the majority of these manuscripts is readily available in numerous indexes of medieval verse and prose, and various editions which have appeared over the years,[4] but more work needs to be done on the manuscripts and their respective physical contexts. These contexts would provide further evidence for an assessment of the circumstances that effected and affected the transmission of English texts, and offer a better understanding of the intricate matrix of medieval book production. There is still much mystery surrounding the origins of many manuscripts, their mode of production, and who wrote them, and for whom.

There are, of course, obvious exceptions to this vacuum of evidence, especially in the later period. Fourteenth-century manuscripts such as the Auchinleck Manuscript (Edinburgh, National Library of Scotland, Adv 19.2.1), the *Gawain*-Manuscript (London, British Library, Cotton Nero A.x) and the Harley Manuscript (London, British Library, Harley 2253) are well known to medievalists. Recently scholars have re-examined some of the assumptions regarding the production of these particular manuscripts. There may have been no scriptorium which produced the Auchinleck manuscript (it may have been a professional workshop), and we certainly know a great deal about the creation and function of Harley 2253 in the literary context of the fourteenth century.[5] The

---

[4]   See the new and updated version of *Index of Middle English Verse*, Julia Boffey and A. S. G. Edwards, *A New Index of Middle English Verse* (London: British Library, 2005); Boydell & Brewer has published some twenty volumes of the *Indexes of Middle English Prose* (for a complete list, see Boydell & Brewer's online catalogue). On texts from the early medieval period, see A. Cameron, 'List of Old English Texts', in R. Frank and A. Cameron, eds., *A Plan for a Dictionary of Old English* (Toronto, University of Toronto Press, 1973), pp. 25–306. The Early English Text Society, since its foundation in 1864, has published 126 volumes in the Extra Series, 334 volumes in the Original Series and another 23 volumes in the Supplementary Series. These books contain Medieval English texts either in editions or in facsimile reproduction; see http://users.ox.ac.uk/~eets/, 13 October 2009.
[5]   On the Auchinleck Manuscript, see David Burnley and Alison Wiggins, 'Importance', in D. Burnley and A. Wiggins, eds., *The Auchinleck Manuscript* (http://www.nls.uk/auchinleck/editorial/importance.html#Chaucer, 13 October 2009); Alison Wiggins, 'Are Auchinleck Manuscript Scribes 1 and 6 the

great multilingual anthologies such as Oxford, Bodleian Library, Digby 86, Cambridge, Trinity College, B.14.39 and Cambridge, University Library, Gg 1.1 have also come under scrutiny recently.[6] Larger collections of Middle English texts, such as Oxford, Bodleian Library, Laud Misc. 108, have also been considered in important recent articles.[7]

Ascriptions of manuscripts

Thomson and Morgan, in *The Cambridge History of the Book in Britain*, offer an outline of manuscript production of the period from 1100 to 1400 and explain that:

> A major shift within the period occurred over the quarter-century either side of c. 1200, during which the dominance of the monastic book gradually, and almost completely, gave way to town-based commercial production for a variety of markets including the monasteries themselves, but also focusing on the universities, the mendicant orders and the secular church. Not only were books now produced in a different way and in different localities, but they differed, both physically, and in their content, from their twelfth-century predecessors.[8]

The contributors' interesting essays support this overview, and the thematic coverage is excellent, with essays considering religious and lay texts, as well as providing contextual information about key production

Same Scribe? Whole-Data Analysis and the Advantages of Electronic Texts', *Medium Ævum* 73 (2004), 10–26 and Ralph Hanna, *London Literature, 1300–1380* (Cambridge: Cambridge University Press, 2005), pp. 104–47; on Harley 2253, see Susanna Greer Fein, ed., *Studies in the Harley Manuscript: The Scribes, Contents, and Social Contexts of British Library MS Harley 2253* (Kalamazoo, MI.: Medieval Institute Publications, 2000).

[6]   See the impressive discussion on vernacular manuscript production offered by Tony Hunt, Julia Boffey, A. S. G. Edwards *et al.*, 'Vernacular Literature and Its Readership', in Nigel J. Morgan and Rodney M. Thomson, eds., *The Cambridge History of the Book in Britain* (Cambridge: Cambridge University Press, 2008), pp. 367–96.

[7]   See also A. S. G. Edwards, 'Epilogue: MS Laud Misc. 108 and Other English Manuscripts', forming part of a collection of essays on Laud 108 edited by Kimberly Bell and Julie Nelson Couch, forthcoming from Brill. My thanks to A. S. G. Edwards for showing me a copy of his work in advance of publication.

[8]   Nigel J. Morgan and Rodney M. Thomson, 'Preface', in *Cambridge History of the Book in Britain*, p. xvii.

milieux such as books for preaching, books of instruction and books containing English literary texts.[9] It is surprising, however, that the editors did not dedicate more room to the discussion of English texts copied between c.1100 and c.1400. It is true, as Boffey and Edwards argue, that:

> Any attempt to give a concise account of the history of early Middle English literature, and of the material aspects of its production and transmission, faces both quantitative and qualitative difficulties. The relative paucity of surviving materials from the earlier part of the period is striking when compared with that from the latter fourteenth century during Richard II's reign.[10]

Their views on the limited availability of evidence are shared by numerous scholars,[11] and they are undeniable. Furthermore, the scope of the chapter itself probably did not allow for an expansive interpretation of all that can be found copied in English in this early period. If we are directed by strict guidelines about what constitutes 'Middle English Literature' and what constitutes an 'original' composition, texts classified as such could be limited; but should we disregard these labels, it may be possible to consider other types of evidence with overwhelming results (that is, evidence of texts that are 'copies' and 'early Middle English'). Moreover, texts written in English in this period should be considered symptomatic of a multilingual production, rather than thought of as marginalised output; as such, English texts might most usefully be studied along with Latin and French.[12] It is perhaps the

---

[9] Alexandra Barratt, 'Spiritual Writings and Religious Instruction', in *Cambridge History of the Book in Britain*, pp. 340–66, Alan J. Fletcher and Anne Hudson, 'Compilations for Preaching and Lollard Literature', ibid., pp. 317–39, and Hunt, Boffey and Edwards, 'Vernacular Literature', *passim*.

[10] Hunt, Boffey and Edwards, 'Vernacular Literature', p. 381.

[11] See, for instance, Seth Lerer, 'Old English and its Afterlife', in David Wallace, ed., *The Cambridge History of Medieval English Literature: Writing in Britain, 1066–1547* (Cambridge: Cambridge University Press, 1999), pp. 7–34, and Christopher Cannon, *The Grounds of English Literature* (Oxford: Oxford University Press, 2004), esp. pp. 10–49.

[12] This is of course a difficult task, because of the sheer number of manuscripts. However, new connections could be found in perusing publications and catalogues, such as Brian Woledge and Ian Short, 'Provisional List of Twelfth-Century Manuscripts Containing French', *Romania* 102 (1981), 1–17; Ruth J. Dean, *Anglo-Norman Literature: A Guide to Texts and Manuscripts* (London: Anglo-Norman Text Society, 1999); R. A. B. Mynors, Rodney M. Thomson

constant search for the beginning and the end of a period and the question of what is 'literature' which often lead scholars to marginalise any type of data-set. The linguistic divide between Old and Middle English compartmentalises our understanding of the Middle Ages without offering any possibility of flexibility, a flexibility which is very much present in the written context of medieval manuscripts.[13] Scholars often direct 'attention towards the fifteenth century – and to the foundations of Modern Literary Culture without realising that by doing so they neglect the past'.[14] The coexistence of Old and Middle English, Latin and French, for instance, in twelfth- and early-thirteenth-century (as well as later) manuscripts deserves further consideration.[15] Discovering the possible places in which these multilingual books were produced might open new avenues of research and contribute to the debate on metropolitan and provincial book production.[16]

and Michael Gullick, *Catalogue of the Manuscripts of Hereford Cathedral Library* (Cambridge: D. S. Brewer 1993); and Rodney Thomson and Michael Gullick, *A Descriptive Catalogue of the Medieval Manuscripts in Worcester Cathedral Library* (Cambridge: D. S. Brewer, 2001).

[13] For a response and discussion on the issue of periodicity, see E. M. Treharne, 'Categorization, Periodization: The Silence of (the) English in the Twelfth Century', in Rita Copeland, Wendy Scase and David Lawton, eds., *New Medieval Literatures* 8 (Turnhout: Brepols, 2006), 248–75

[14] Ralph Hanna, *London Literature, 1300–1380*, p. 2.

[15] See, for instance, Cambridge, University Library Ii.1.33, a manuscript copied towards the end of the twelfth century by two main scribes, one of which had linguistic competencies in Old English, Early Middle English, Latin and French. See Orietta Da Rold, 'Homilies and Lives of Saints: Cambridge, University Library, Ii. 1. 33', on the website of *The Production and Use of English Manuscripts 1060 to 1220* (http://www.le.ac.uk/english/em1060to1220/mss/CULIi.1.33.htm, 20 October 2009). Doyle also advocated this tripartite approach for fourteenth- and fifteenth-century manuscripts; see A. I. Doyle, 'English Books in and out of Court from Edward III to Henry VII', in V. J. Scattergood and J. W. Sherbone, eds., *English Court Culture in the Later Middle Ages* (London: Duckworth, 1983), p. 163, and Tony Hunt, 'Insular Trilingual Compilations', in Ria Jansen-Sieben and Hans van Dijk, eds., *Codices Miscellanearum: Brussels Van Hulthem Colloquium 1999* (Brussels: Archives et Bibliothèques de Belgique, 1999), pp. 51–70.

[16] See, Hanna, *London Literature, 1300–1380*. A. I. Doyle, 'The English Provincial Book Trade before Printing', in Peter Isaac, ed., *Six Centuries of the Provincial Book Trade in Britain* (Winchester: St Paul's Bibliographies, 1990), pp. 13–14; M. A. Michael, 'Urban Production of Manuscript Books and the Role of the University Towns', *Cambridge History of the Book in Britain*, pp. 168–94; Rodney M. Thomson, 'Monastic and Cathedral Book Production', *Cambridge History of the Book in Britain*, pp. 136–67.

Framing new questions

Within the debates on languages, on the absence of evidence and on reconstructed histories, data relating to the manuscript production of vernacular texts before Chaucer ought to be quantified. It may be reasonable to start by asking the obvious question: what is the evidence for English manuscript production between 1100 and 1400? The short answer is: greater than one may anticipate. There is a significant number of manuscripts: at least 32 manuscripts from the twelfth century, 116 from the thirteenth century and 74 from the fourteenth-century.[17] Their number increases as we progress to the late fifteenth century, but the thirteenth century is very well represented, thanks particularly to the work of the Tremulous Hand – the famous annotator and glossator from the Worcester area.[18] These manuscripts contain English texts of various kinds and forms, from secular to religious themes, from prose to poetry. They also include law codes, administrative matters, science and medicine.[19] These texts have different functions and they are mapped onto the page in different ways, but nevertheless they are written in English.[20] This evidence insists on a reconsideration of our under-

[17] These are preliminary numbers drawn from 'Portal to Manuscript Descriptions: List of Manuscripts', *Production and Use of English Manuscripts* (http://www.le.ac.uk/ee/em1060to1220, 13 October 2009); Margaret Laing, *Catalogue of Sources for a Linguistic Atlas of Early Medieval English* (Cambridge: D. S. Brewer, 1993); and *A Catalogue of Vernacular Manuscript Books of the English West Midlands, c. 1300–c. 1475* (http://www.mwm.bham.ac.uk, 13 October 2009).

[18] For an overview, see Christine Franzen, *The Tremulous Hand of Worcester: A Study of Old English in the Thirteenth Century* (Oxford: Clarendon, 1991); on the Tremulous Hand and his manuscript context, see Christine Franzen, 'On the Attribution of Additions in Oxford, Bodleian Ms Bodley 343 to the Tremulous Hand of Worcester', *A Quarterly Journal of Short Articles, Notes, and Reviews* 16.1 (2006), 7–8; Christine Franzen, 'The Tremulous Hand of Worcester and the Nero Scribe of the *Ancrene Wisse*', *Medium Ævum* 72.1 (2003), 13–31. The manuscripts of the Tremulous Hand have been published in facsimile by Christine Franzen, *Worcester Manuscripts*, Anglo-Saxon Manuscripts in Microfiche Facsimile 6 (Tempe, AZ: Medieval and Renaissance Texts and Studies, 1998).

[19] On content see, for instance, Boffey and Edwards, *A New Index of Middle English Verse*; N. R. Ker, *Catalogue of Manuscripts Containing Anglo-Saxon* (Oxford: Clarendon Press, 1957; repr. with supplement, 1991); Laing, *Catalogue of Sources for a Linguistic Atlas of Early Medieval English*; *LALME* I, pp. 59–291. On the indexes of Middle English prose, see n. 4 above.

[20] Orietta Da Rold and Mary Swan, 'Linguistic Contiguities: English Manuscripts 1060–1220', in Elisabeth Tyler, ed., *Conceptualizing Multilingualism in England, 800–1250* (Turnhout: Brepols, forthcoming 2010). See also Elaine

standing of multilingual manuscript production in this period, and, in particular, on a re-evaluation of labels relating to scribal activities and writing environments. Questions might usefully be asked about who these scribes were: were they professionals; were they amateur? Can we really talk about scribes and their dialects at the same time as talking about scribes and their localisation? How, as scholars, can we be sure we mean what we think we mean in relation to scribes and their activities?

Scribes and their activities

Answering questions about scribes and their working environments is a major undertaking, and excellent work has been done on key scribes.[21] Parkes has provided us with the terminology to discuss scripts,[22] and useful overviews as well as case studies can be found in numerous publications.[23] Yet there is room to think about how we could answer the questions I posed above, especially in the light of the increasing availability of electronic resources. The catalogue of MWM, for example 'is a web-based catalogue containing searchable descriptions and reference images of over 150 manuscripts in which one or more texts have been located by dialect to the West Midlands counties of Gloucestershire, Herefordshire, Shropshire, Staffordshire, Warwickshire, and Worcestershire, covering the period c. 1300–c. 1475'.[24] Around fifty-seven of these manuscripts can be dated to the thirteenth and fifteenth centuries.[25] They showcase a variety of productions, which vary in content,

Treharne, 'Post-Conquest Old English', in Phillip Pulsiano and Elaine Treharne, eds., *The Blackwell Companion to Anglo-Saxon Literature* (Blackwell, 2001), pp. 403–14.

[21] See, for example, the work on the scribe of Harley 2253 by Carter Revard in 'Scribe and Provenance', *Studies in the Harley Manuscript*, pp. 21–109. Malcolm Parkes has published a prosopography of medieval scribes in M. B. Parkes, *Their Hands before Our Eyes: A Closer Look at Scribes*, The Lyell Lectures Delivered in the University of Oxford, 1999 (Aldershot: Ashgate, 2008), pp. 156–60.

[22] Parkes, *Their Hands before Our Eyes* and M. B. Parkes, *English Cursive Bookhands, 1250–1500* (Oxford: Clarendon Press, 1969).

[23] See for example: A. I. Doyle, 'Books in and out of Court'; A. I. Doyle, 'The English Provincial Book Trade before Printing', pp. 13–29.

[24] Rebecca Farnham, 'The Manuscripts of The West Midlands Catalogue Project', in Wendy Scase, ed., *Essays in Manuscript Geography: Vernacular Manuscripts of the English West Midlands from the Conquest to the Sixteenth Century* (Turnhout: Brepols, 2007), pp. 231–8, p. 231.

[25] A list is provided in the Appendix. I include a summary of the content and the date usually ascribed to each if them.

quality of material, codicological structure and type of hands. This
resource is ideal to reconsider common assumptions about the making
of medieval books; for instance, theories relating to the codicological
structure of a manuscript can be tested,[26] and a review of scribal labels
can be undertaken.

Analysing the manuscripts

It may now be useful to focus on a few examples to expound upon this
question of scribes, their habits and their environments. Cambridge,
Trinity College, B.14.39 (323), Oxford, Bodleian Library, Digby 86, and
London, British Library, Cotton Vitellius D.iii are three manuscripts
with many features in common. They are miscellanies containing
texts in Latin, English and French datable to the end of the thirteenth
century and are copied by more than one scribe. They are written in
a variety of dialects, but Gloucestershire and the neighbouring borders
of the Worcestershire region are the predominant areas of influence.[27]
They are all unique productions, despite the fact that they are written
in a similar grade of script: an early anglicana featuring double compartment **a** with large bowl and **w** with extended backstrokes. The layout of
verse is in double columns, prose in single columns and capital letters
are tinted in red. Questions here include those concerning the identity
of the scribes: how professional or amateur were they?

Three hands can be found in Digby 86. Scribe 1, who copied the
majority of the manuscript, writes in a hand which 'improves with
experience'.[28] Indeed, the thick ascenders sloping towards the left, the
hairlines and the irregular minim height give the overall impression of

---

[26]   It is striking that some manuscripts are made up by quires of 12 leaves rather
than 8. These manuscripts seem to be clustered by time or by content. See,
for example, Oxford, Bodleian Library, Laud Misc. 108 and Oxford, Bodleian
Library, Ashmole 43, datable to s. xiii/xiv. The first part of Laud Misc. 108 and
Ashmole 43 contain saints' lives, and both manuscripts are made up of quires
of 12. More work on the significance of this type of codicological observation
ought to be carried out. For a description of the manuscripts, see, *A Catalogue
of Vernacular Manuscript Books of the English West Midlands, c. 1300-c. 1475*
(http://www.mwm.bham.ac.uk, 13 October 2009).
[27]   For a description see *A Catalogue of Vernacular Manuscript Books of the
English West Midlands*. On the linguistic profiles of the scribes, see *LALME*, III,
LP7721, p. 558; LP7790, pp. 150–1; LP7130, p. 144.
[28]   Judith Tschann and M. B. Parkes, *Facsimile of Oxford, Bodleian Library, Ms
Digby 86*, EETS, SS 16 (Oxford: Oxford University Press, 1996), p. lvi.

a manuscript perhaps casually written.[29] Scribe 2 of Vitellius D.iii uses a slightly different type of early anglicana with tapered ascenders, minims with serifs, but no hairlines protruding from ascenders and descenders. This is the hand which copies *Floris and Blancheflur* (NIMEV 2288.8), the only English text in the manuscript. It is a less cursive script than the hand of scribe 1 of Digby 86 and is characterised by letter forms of more squarish proportion.[30] Trinity College B.14.39 is copied by several scribes. The scribe who wrote *The Life of St Margaret* (NIMEV 2672) writes in a book hand influenced by textura, using **de** ligatures, diamond-shaped lobes for **d** and closed **g**.[31] Hunt argues that at least six scribes worked on the manuscript and that it reflects activities at the 'Worcester Franciscan convent'.[32] Nothing is known of the Vitellius manuscript. Digby 86, on the other hand, has been associated with Richard de Grimhill (*c*.1263–*c*.1308) and it has been argued that it was copied for his own use.[33] There seems to be here a possible distinction in how these manuscripts were produced, and this reflects a difference in scribal training. It seems likely that Dibgy 86 was produced in a secular environment, while Vitellius D.iii and Trinity College B.14.39 were copied in a religious environment. But the question remains, how can we talk about scribal training when we know so little about it? In *LALME*, the linguistic profiles of these scribes are mapped to the Gloucestershire area, with the exception of Trinity College B.14.39, which is mapped to the Worcester region.[34] Can we start to assume that these scribes were working in this area and trained here?

Similar debates about localisation and language and localisation and training can be seen in other two manuscripts produced in the early fourteenth century. The scribe of British Library, Egerton 1993 and scribe 2 of Edinburgh, National Library of Scotland, Advocates 19.2.1 (Auchinleck), for instance, share a number of palaeographical charac-

---

[29] *A Catalogue of Vernacular Manuscript Books of the English West Midlands*, fol. 127r.
[30] Ibid., fol. 6r.
[31] Ibid., fol. 20r.
[32] Hanna, *London Literature, 1300–1380*, p. 19; see also Hunt, 'Insular Trilingual Compilations', p. 54; James finds twelve hands: see M. R. James, *The Western Manuscripts in the Library of Trinity Cambridge: A Descriptive Catalogue*, 3 vols. (Cambridge: Cambridge University Press, 1900), 1, pp. 438–47.
[33] Judith Tschann and M. B. Parkes, *Facsimile of Bodleian Library MS Digby 86*, EETS, ss 16 (Oxford: Oxford University Press, 1996), p. lvii.
[34] See note 27.

teristics and level of competency.[35] Scribe 2 in the Auchinleck manuscript has been regarded as a conservative scribe probably trained in a
monastic environment.[36] Scribe 2 features a Gloucestershire dialect,
which is shared by the Egerton scribe. It is accepted that the Auchinleck manuscript is a London production. But the place of production
of the Egerton manuscript is still unknown. It is also accepted widely
by scholars that scribes can travel, thus making any dialectal infer-
ence only partially helpful for localising the manuscript.[37] It is not
uncommon to find immigrant scribes in fifteenth-century London,[38]
and the same must have been true in earlier centuries. However, in
order to write in a dialect a scribe must have been trained to write in
a certain way; thus, the issue of training becomes important. One way
forward in disentangling our discussion about different types of copyists and their localisation would be a re-consideration of their training.
This distinction will lead to a discussion about how we can differentiate
between a basic understanding of letter formation and a proficient level
of writing and might assist perhaps in developing new models for how
scribes can be localised.

Where and how

As Petrucci has demonstrated for medieval Italy, certain foundation
scripts were taught in schools – either cathedral or parish schools – or
associated with *stationes* (stations) run by lay notaries to train young-

[35] Both scribes use a type of book hand of squarish proportion; all minims are
traced separately; it is a regular upright body height with very little variation
between ascenders and descenders; and influenced by Textura. They both use a
double compartment **a** with often closed upper lobe; closed **s** and open **w** with
two back-strokes closed with a B-shaped head. See Egerton 1993, fol. 27r, and
Advocates 19.2.1, fol. 39r, available in *A Catalogue of Vernacular Manuscript
Books of the English West Midlands*. Helen Marshall (University of Toronto) is
currently studying the working patterns of these two scribes, and I am grateful
to her for sharing her views on them.
[36] Alison Wiggins, 'Scribes', in *The Auchinleck Manuscript* (http://www.nls.uk/
auchinleck/editorial/physical.html#scribes, 13 October 2009).
[37] Alison Wiggins, 'Middle English Romance and the West Midlands', in
Wendy Scase, ed., *Vernacular Manuscripts of the English West Midlands from the
Conquest to the Sixteenth Century* (Turnhout: Brepols, 2007), pp. 239–55.
[38] M. L. Samuels, 'Scribes and Manuscript Traditions', in Felicity Riddy, ed.,
*Regionalism in Late Medieval Manuscripts and Texts: Essays Celebrating the Publi-
cation of a Linguistic Atlas of Late Mediaeval English* (Cambridge: D. S. Brewer,
1991), pp. 1–52.

sters outside religious life.[39] Scripts were taught in two ways: by teaching or by imitation. The master would write the letter and then the pupil would copy the letters out; these are usually considered the foundation script. With this basic tool any person attending the school would have been able to write.[40] Michael has argued that: 'almost anyone who had been taught to write could be described, or describe him or herself, as a scribe'.[41] However, it is only by further training that scribes would start to master more sophisticated models, and particularly (but not exclusively) ecclesiastical scribes would be directed to imitate models that were 'exercises that were repeated many times and, at least in some cases, under guidance of a master'.[42]

In the West Midlands as throughout England there were numerous schools in which children could learn how to write.[43] But where did these children learn to become copyists or scribes? In these same schools? In London in the late fourteenth century we know that the scrivener trained through a master and apprentice relationship,[44] and the Chancery trained scribes using a similar system,[45] but was it the same in monasteries or in cathedral schools? What about the role of other less investigated writing environments such as medieval households; what was the role of the reeve, for example? Ker has argued that in eleventh- and twelfth-century England there were two types of scribes: *claustrales* and *scriptores*.[46] The *claustrales* were working in the cloister and the *scriptores* moved from place to place, centre to

[39] Armando Petrucci, *Writers and Readers in Medieval Italy: Studies in the History of Written Culture* (New Haven, CT: Yale University Press, 1995), p. 74.

[40] Petrucci, *Writers and Readers in Medieval Italy*, p. 61.

[41] Michael, 'Urban Production of Manuscript Books and the Role of the University Towns', p. 170–1.

[42] Petrucci, *Writers and Readers in Medieval Italy*, p. 62.

[43] Nicholas Orme, *Medieval Schools: From Roman Britain to Renaissance England* (New Haven, CT: Yale University Press, 2006), pp. 189–217.

[44] See, for instance, Peter W. M. Blayney, *The Stationers' Company before the Charter, 1403–1557* (London: Worshipful Company of Stationers and Newspaper Makers, 2003), pp. 9–15.

[45] Malcom Richardson, *The Medieval Chancery under Henry V*, List and Index Society, Special Series 30 (Kew: List and Index Society, 1999).

[46] N. R. Ker, *English Manuscripts in the Century after the Norman Conquest* (Oxford: Clarendon Press, 1960); see also Michael Gullick, 'Professional Scribes in Eleventh- and Twelfth- Century England', *English Manuscripts Studies* 7 (1998), 7–24.

centre.[47] How much of this division could actually be used to understand thirteenth- and fourteenth-century scribal cultures is currently the subject of debate as the roles of scribes naturally evolved over the medieval period, especially with the demand that the increased literacy and the university learning placed on the medieval book trade.[48] But thinking about scribes in these terms, that is considering how scribes could be trained and for which type of copying, be it for legal, secretarial or book-making purposes, may contribute to developing a more sympathetic terminology, which could be used to define typologies of scribes. Terms such as 'amateur' and 'professional' can be misleading and do not provide an objective assessment of the hand itself. Naturally scribes reached different levels of proficiency, and that must be taken into account.[49] Thus Scribe 1 of Digby 86 could be a scribe who had not acquired a proficient level of writing, possibly copying books for his own use, or possibly not. He could have been anyone who had learned how to write without having been trained to copy books. The hand could be associated with clerical training. Scribes trained as clerks or notaries developed a cursive writing system, which was quick and suited to fast copying.[50] A more objective approach to handwriting would remove the judgement on the appearance of the script and re-evaluate the work that is being copied. Indeed, Scribe 1 of Digby 86 is someone who not only copied texts and tinted capitals in red, but also had a clear understanding and knowledge of literature in three languages, which does not correspond, perhaps, with modern expectations of the competencies that this scribe might be expected to have had.[51]

There is much in this paper which ought to be further investigated, and many of the questions posed still remain to be fully explored. This

[47] As Petrucci puts it: 'part-time copyists belonging to the world of documentation, and lay copyists', Petrucci, *Writers and Readers in Medieval Italy*, p. 101. They would fill in duties as required.
[48] *Cambridge History of the Book in Britain*, pp. xvii–xxiv.
[49] For a categorisation of different type of writing in the early medieval West, Petrucci observes that there are mainly four categories: 1. The scribe educated for copying; 2. Competent writers who could imitate certain scripts; 3. Writers educated as clerics or in lay training environments, who would mainly know a cursive script; and 4. Writers who would annotate or copy out partial texts and would develop a personal script. See Petrucci, *Writers and Readers in Medieval Italy*, p. 78.
[50] Ibid., p. 78–9.
[51] Elaine Treharne, 'Vernacular Literatures, 1170–1350', in Andrew Galloway, ed., *Cambridge Companion to Medieval Culture* (Cambridge: Cambridge University Press, forthcoming 2010).

discussion shows the potential that electronic resources might have for research into medieval textual cultures and for formulating research questions. The very research questions which these resources give rise to are at times a direct consequence of the questions underpinning the motivation for the creation of the resource itself. What these resources offer is an ability to quantify data and to consider additional theoretical and socio-historical possibilities. Often qualitative assessments of manuscript production are not based on quantitative analysis of the data; perhaps our perception of the transmission of English texts in relationship to Latin and French may change when we are able to know exactly how many texts written in English survive from this early period. This will lead to a reassessment of early manuscript production of the twelfth, thirteenth and fourteenth centuries in the light of the linguistic and physical contexts. These considerations will also lead to a better understanding of scribal training and localisation. Defining how a scribe is trained will lead scholars to consider different aspects of the transmission of a text and the making of a book, because labels can be defined and understood. I have proposed reconsidering the labels we use when we talk about types of copyists and consider the localisation of a scribe and its dialect. For decades now, we have labelled scribes and manuscripts in particular ways, and expected both the maker and the artefact to behave appropriately, to be boxable and categorisable. What we have neglected to do, until now, is to reappraise the labels themselves in order to contribute to a better understanding of medieval book history and textual cultures.

Appendix: West Midlands manuscripts

Thirteenth-century

1. London, British Library, Royal 12.G.iv: medical treatises, s. xiii,[52] with material included, s. xv
2. Oxford, Bodleian Library, Bodley 652: miscellaneous religious pieces, including Robert Grosseteste's *Castle of Love*, s. xiii[2]
3. London, British Library, Cotton Vitellius D.iii: French, English and Latin texts, including the romance *Floris and Blancheflur*, s. xiii[ex]

---

[52] Dating conventions follow standard practice; thus, s.xiii is thirteenth century; suprascript 1 and 2 indicate first- and second-half of the respective century; 'in' represents the beginning of the century; 'ex' the end; and 'med' the middle.

4. Oxford, Bodleian Library, Digby 86: miscellaneous devotional, didactic, secular and religious texts, s. xiii[ex]
5. Cambridge, Trinity College, B.14.39 (323): miscellany, including macaronic texts, s. xiii[ex]
6. Oxford, Jesus College, 29: miscellany of religious and secular poems, including the *Owl and the Nightingale*, s. xiii[ex]
7. London, British Library, Royal 17.A.xxvii: *Sawles Warde* in the Katherine Group and *Arma Christi*, part 1 s. xiii[in], part 2 s. xiv/xv
8. Oxford, Bodleian Library, Laud Misc. 108: miscellaneous texts, including the *South English Legendary* and *Havelok the Dane*, s. xiii/xiv with material included s. xv
9. Oxford, Bodleian Library, Ashmole 43: *South English Legendary*, s. xiii/xiv

Fourteenth-century

10. Cambridge, Trinity College, R.4.26 (655): Robert of Gloucester's *Chronicle*, Latin prophecy, a French *Brut*, s. xiv
11. London, British Library, Harley 7322: English verses interspersed in Latin text, s. xiv
12. Cambridge, University Library, Dd.6.29: medical tracts and recipes s. xiv, with material included s. xv
13. London, British Library, Harley 2281: *Prick of Conscience*, s. xiv[in]
14. Oxford, Corpus Christi College, 59: miscellaneous texts: xiv[in]
15. London, British Library, Egerton 2891: *South English Legendary*, s. xiv[in]
16. London, British Library, Additional 46919: collection of treatises, poems, sermons in Anglo-Norman, Latin and English copied by William Herebert, s. xiv[1]
17. London, British Library, Egerton 1993: *South English Legendary*, s. xiv[1]
18. London, British Library, Royal 12.C.xii: *Brut* and other religious material, texts in Latin, French and English, s. xiv[1]
19. London, British Library, Harley 2253: miscellaneous secular and religious texts in English, French and Latin texts, s. xiv[1]
20. Edinburgh, National Library of Scotland, Advocates 19.2.1: *Romances*, s. xiv[med]
21. Cambridge, University Library Ee.4.35: miscellaneous texts, including the *Prick of Conscience*, s. xiv[2]
22. Hereford, Hereford Cathedral Chapter Library, P.1.Ix: prose by Rolle, s. xiv[2]

23. Oxford, Bodleian Library, Rawlinson Poet. 139: *Prick of Conscience*, s. xiv^2
24. Oxford, Corpus Christi College, 431: *South English Legendary*, s. xiv^2
25. Charlottesville, VA, University of Virginia, Hench 10: *Prick of Conscience*, s. xiv^2
26. London, British Library, Harley 2398: Religious tracts, s. xiv^2
27. Cambridge, University Library, Dd.3.13: *Piers Plowman* (C-text), s. xiv^{ex}
28. Cambridge, Magdalene College, Pepys 2616: Wycliffite sermons, s. xiv^{ex}
29. Cambridge, Trinity College, R.3.8 (383): *Cursor Mundi*, s. xiv^{ex}
30. Dublin, Trinity College 212: *Piers Plowman* (C-text), s. xiv^{ex}
31. San Marino, CA, Huntington Library, HM 126: Robert of Gloucester's *Chronicle*, s. xiv^{ex}
32. London, British Library, Additional 22283: miscellaneous texts, including the Northern Homily Cycle, *Speculum vitae* and other religious and contemplative texts, s. xiv^{ex}
33. London, British Library, Egerton 2810: *South English Legendary*, s. xiv^{ex}
34. London, British Library, Stowe 949: *South English Legendary*, s. xiv^{ex}
35. London, College of Arms, 57: *Cursor Mundi* and *Prick of Conscience*, s. xiv^{ex}
36. Manchester, John Rylands Library, Eng. 50: *Prick of Conscience* and *Guy of Warwick*, s. xiv^{ex}
37. Oxford, Bodleian Library, Bodley 177, miscellaneous alchemical, astrological, astronomical, and medical treatises in Latin and English, s. xiv^{ex}
38. Oxford, Bodleian Library, Digby 171: *Piers Plowman* (C-text), s. xiv^{ex}
39. Oxford, Bodleian Library, Eng. poet. a.1: miscellaneous religious, didactic and secular texts, s. xiv^{ex}
40. Oxford, Bodleian Library, Laud Misc. 601: *Prick of Conscience* and prayers, s. xiv^{ex}
41. Oxford, Bodleian Library, Rawlinson A.389: miscellaneous texts by Richard Rolle, Peckham, and Richard Maidstone, s. xiv^{ex}
42. London, British Library, Sloane 5: medical treatises, s. xiv^{ex} and xv
43. Oxford, Bodleian Library, Bodley 851: *Piers Plowman*, xiv^{ex} with material included s. xv^2
44. Oxford, Bodleian Library, Douce 78: miscellany, religious texts, medical recipes and *Titus and Vespasian*, s. xiv^{ex}

45. Holkham, Holkham Hall, Library of the Earl of Leicester 668: *Prick of Conscience*, s. xiv/xv

46. San Marino, CA, Huntington Library, HM 125: *Prick of Conscience*, s. xiv/xv

47. Leeds, University Library Brotherton 500: *Prick of Conscience*, s. xiv/xv

48. London, British Library, Additional 37787: collection of mainly Latin texts and devotional and didactic English texts and one French text, s. xiv/xv

49. London, British Library, Egerton 826: prayers, s. xiv/xv

50. Manchester, John Rylands Library, Eng. 90: *Piers Plowman* (C-text), *Prick of Conscience* and Wycliffite material, s. xiv/xv

51. Oxford, Bodleian Library, Laud Misc. 486: *Prick of Conscience* and Gregory's *Pastoral Care* in Latin, s. xiv/xv

52. Oxford, Bodleian Library, Rawlinson B.171: *Brut*, s. xiv/xv

53. Oxford, Trinity College, 16B: *Prick of Conscience*, s. xiv/xv

54. York, York Minster Chapter Library, XVI E 32: recipes and other pieces, s. xiv/xv

55. London, British Library, Cotton Tiberius D.vii: Trevisa's *Polychronicon*, s. xiv/xv

56. London, British Library, Cotton Vespasian B.xvi: miscellaneous verse, including *Piers Plowman* (C – text), s. xiv/xv

57. Worcester Cathedral, Worcester Cathedral Chapter Library, F.10: sermons, c. 1400.

The Ellesmere Manuscript: Controversy, Culture and the Canterbury Tales

A. S. G. EDWARDS

TO BEGIN WITH THE OBVIOUS: Geoffrey Chaucer enjoys a foundational status as 'the father of English poetry' and the *Canterbury Tales*
has been the most popular of his works. Over eighty manuscripts of it
survive, complete, selected or fragmentary; and the earlier existence
of a much larger number can be confidently inferred from a variety
of evidence.[1] No English poetic work occurs in more fifteenth-century
copies. In addition, it was the earliest major such work in English to
be printed and the only medieval English one to have been consistently republished over the centuries since Chaucer's death. In terms of
English cultural and literary history it is a fundamental work.

The Ellesmere manuscript of the *Canterbury Tales*, Henry E. Huntington Library, California, EL 26 C 9 (henceforward 'Ellesmere'),
has become a crucial element in modern awareness of Chaucer. The
general quality of its decoration and the number of its illustrations of
the Canterbury pilgrims have made it the most frequently reproduced
of all his manuscripts. And it has had a central role in modern understanding of the text and transmission of Chaucer's most famous work.

Consequently Ellesmere has come to enjoy a position of great importance in our contemporary perceptions of Chaucer's poem. In such
circumstances it is appropriate to consider why Ellesmere matters to us
as students of the medieval book. How does it contribute to our textual
and cultural understanding of the *Canterbury Tales*?

Before examining such questions, a few facts: Ellesmere comprises
two hundred and forty large (394 x 284 mm), good-quality parchment
leaves. Its principal content is a version of the *Canterbury Tales*, although
there are further additions to it ranging in date from the fifteenth to the
seventeenth centuries.[2] The text is illustrated by twenty-three marginal

---

[1] J. M. Manly and Edith Rickert, eds., *The Text of the Canterbury Tales*
(Chicago: University of Chicago Press, 1940), 8 volumes.
[2] The most detailed and authoritative description of Ellesmere is by C. W.
Dutschke, *Guide to Medieval and Renaissance Manuscripts in the Huntington
Library*, 2 vols. (San Marino, CA: Huntington Library, 1989), I, 41–50. There

miniatures of each of the Canterbury pilgrims placed at the beginning of their respective tales. The manuscript has other elaborate decoration, including over seventy foliate borders, gilt and painted initials of varying size and frequent rubrication. Three artists were employed on the illustrations and possibly others on the borders. It seems certain that the manuscript was produced in London. The hands of some of these decorators have been identified in other London or Westminster-based manuscripts of the early fifteenth century.[3] The overall effect of its quality of production is the creation of a form of *de luxe* manuscript, the lavishness of which is consistently pleasing to the eye.

The scale of Ellesmere's decorative programme is unique among *Canterbury Tales* manuscripts. It raises obvious questions. When was it written, for example? There has been general consensus that it is one of the earliest of the manuscripts of the *Canterbury Tales*. It has been generally assumed that it was prepared after Chaucer's death in 1400, probably at some point in the first decade of the fifteenth century. But recent art-historical research has tended to push the date to 'probably not after c.1405'.[4] Given the complexities that may have been involved in assembling and ordering the text of an incomplete work and the elaborateness of its decoration, including an author portrait (see below), it seems likely that Ellesmere was conceived as an immediate response to Chaucer's death by those eager to commemorate his memory through the appropriate preservation of his work. If this is so, Ellesmere may be the nearest we now have to some 'authorised' form of the text, a form conceived as the basis for both commemoration and for wider circulation.

Tracing Ellesmere's history

Such an assumption raises further questions: who commissioned Ellesmere? From where were copies of Chaucer's texts obtained? And what happened to the manuscript after its completion? There are no satisfac-

---

are helpful observations (and reproductions of all the miniatures) in Herbert C. Schulz, *The Ellesmere Manuscript of Chaucer's Canterbury Tales* (San Marino CA: Huntington Library, 1966).
[3] See further Kathleen L. Scott, 'An Hours and a Psalter by Two Ellesmere Illuminators', in Martin Stevens and Daniel Woodward, eds., *The Ellesmere Chaucer: Essays in Interpretation* (San Marino, CA: Huntington Library, 1997), pp. 87–121.
[4] This is the date given by Kathleen L. Scott in her standard account in *Later Gothic Manuscripts 12390–1490*, 2 vols. (London: Harvey Miller, 1996), II, 140.

tory answers to these questions. It seems certain that the owner was a person of wealth and (quite probably) high social stature, with a keen interest in Chaucer's writings, very likely with some connections to his social and/or familial circle and almost certainly living in London with ready access there to the artistic resources for the manuscript's production. It also seems certain that through this circle the commissioner had access to authoritative forms of Chaucer's work. It could have been some member of Chaucer's family who underwrote the production of Ellesmere. His eldest son Thomas (*c*.1367–1434) was wealthy. But there is no certainty as to the historical agency that may lie behind Ellesmere's creation.

The early, post-production history of Ellesmere is equally unclear. It appears that a little later in the fifteenth century it was in Bury St Edmunds and available to the scribe and decorators of an early manuscript of John Lydgate's *Siege of Thebes*, now London, British Library, Arundel 119, which imitates the Ellesmere layout. Lydgate's poem is a continuation of the *Canterbury Tales*, made in the early 1420s, when he was a monk at the Benedictine abbey in Bury St Edmunds, where the scribe of the Arundel manuscript copied other manuscripts in Middle English.[5] The Arundel manuscript contains the arms of William de la Pole, duke of Suffolk, and his wife Alice, the daughter of Thomas Chaucer. Alice was herself a notable book collector.[6] There are other circumstantial links between Ellesmere and the de Vere family, the earls of Oxford, also notable book collectors, who also had connections with the abbey at Bury St Edmunds and whose achievements are celebrated in a fifteenth-century poem by one 'Rothley', added to Ellesmere. The manuscript seems to have remained within East Anglia, and to have passed to Sir Robert Drury, another book collector, in the sixteenth century. These associations all indicate the ways in which Ellesmere is linked to elite bibliophile circles from its earliest history. The appreciation of the manuscript's quality within such discriminating circles was doubtless a crucial factor in preserving the manuscript intact, when so many Chaucer manuscripts, particularly the more elaborately decorated ones, suffered degrees of mutilation.

[5] See further, R. Hanna III and A. S. G. Edwards, 'Rotheley, the De Vere Circle, and the Ellesmere Chaucer', *Huntington Library Quarterly* 58 (1996), 11–29.
[6] See Carol Meale, 'Reading Women's Culture in Fifteenth-Century England: The Case of Alice Chaucer', Piero Boitani and Anna Torti, eds., *Mediaevalitas: Reading the Middle Ages* (Cambridge: D. S. Brewer, 1996), pp. 81–102.

By the seventeenth century, Ellesmere had passed into the possession of John Egerton, first earl of Bridgewater, coming by descent into the possession of Francis Egerton, Lord Ellesmere, from 1846. It was from this family that it was purchased as part of the Bridgewater Library by Henry E. Huntington in 1917.

Working on Ellesmere

The aristocratic pedigree of the Ellesmere manuscript has had some implications for the history of the study of the text of the *Canterbury Tales*. It has meant that throughout its history the manuscript itself has remained largely inaccessible to those concerned with such matters. The noble environment in which it resided limited awareness of its existence for centuries. It does not figure, for example, in Edward Bernard's great union catalogue of English libraries, *Catalogi librorum manuscriptorum Angliae et Hiberniae* (1697); nor in John Urry's posthumous edition of Chaucer's works (1721), the first to include any descriptions of the manuscripts; nor in Thomas Tyrrwhitt's edition of the *Canterbury Tales* (1775). These were the first editions since the sixteenth century to attempt to consider the evidence of surviving manuscripts.

Ellesmere was initially brought to public attention by the antiquary H. J. Todd (1763–1845), chaplain to John William, 7th earl of Bridgewater, in his *Illustrations of the Life and Writings of Gower and Chaucer* in 1810. This book contains descriptions of a number of *Canterbury Tales* manuscripts, of which Ellesmere is the last: 'I conclude my notices of manuscripts with an account of a copy of the Tales, which in no respect is exceeded, perhaps I might say equalled, by any of those already described.'[7] Todd goes on to describe the manuscript at some length, in what was to remain the most detailed published account of it for more than a century.[8] Later in his volume he prints the 'Rotheley' poem on the de Vere family, the first portion of the manuscript to be printed.[9]

But the text of the *Canterbury Tales* in Ellesmere did not become available for scrutiny until 1868 when it began to be transcribed in the first publication of the Chaucer Society, the parallel six-text transcripts

---

[7] H. J. Todd, *Illustrations of the Lives and Writings of Gower and Chaucer* (London: Rivington, 1810), p. 128.
[8] Ibid., pp. 128–32.
[9] Ibid., pp. 295–301.

of the *Canterbury Tales* edited by F. J. Furnivall.[10] The miniatures were first reproduced in parts III and IV of this series in 1871–2. It was not until 1894 that the Ellesmere manuscript was used as the foundation for a critical edition of Chaucer's text, when it provided the basis for the text of the *Canterbury Tales* in volumes 4–5 of W. W. Skeat's six-volume edition of *The Works of Chaucer* published by the Clarendon Press. Ellesmere is described there as 'the finest and the best of all the MSS. now extant' (IV, xiii) and 'the best in nearly every respect' (IV, xvii).[11]

The recognition by Furnivall's transcript and Skeat's edition of the importance of Ellesmere in the nineteenth century was confirmed in the next generation of editors, when the American scholar F. N. Robinson employed it as the base text for the *Canterbury Tales* in what remains the standard scholarly edition of Chaucer's works, first published in 1933.[12] This edition completed the swift ascent of Ellesmere in little more than sixty-five years from utter obscurity to an unchallenged position as the pre-eminent witness to the text of Chaucer's poem.

Examining Ellesmere

In spite of this rapid establishing of Ellesmere's textual authority and in spite of the publication of a facsimile of the manuscript, partly in colour, in 1911,[13] and of a modern, full colour facsimile in 1995,[14] in some respects Ellesmere has continued to remain aloof from the possi-

---

[10] F. J. Furnivall, ed., *A Six-Text Print of Chaucer's Canterbury Tales in Parallel Columns*, *Chaucer Society Publications*, Chaucer Society (London: N. Trübner, 1868–79). These transcripts, which included both Hengwrt and Ellesmere, were issued in various volumes and formats; for full details see E. P. Hammond, *Chaucer: A Bibliographical Manual* (New York: MacMillan 1908), pp. 523–8.
[11] *The Works of Chaucer*, ed. W. W. Skeat (Oxford: Clarendon Press, 1894), IV, xiii, and IV, xvii, respectively.
[12] *The Poetical Works of Chaucer*, ed. F. N. Robinson (Riverside: Houghton Mifflin, 1933).
[13] *The Ellesmere Chaucer, Reproduced in Facsimile* (Manchester, 1911); the facsimile underwent various forms of retouching and adjustment that mean it was not an exact reproduction; for discussion of them see Daniel H. Woodward, 'The New Ellesmere Chaucer Facsimile', in *The Ellesmere Chaucer: Essays in Interpretation*, pp. 4–5.
[14] *The Canterbury Tales: The New Ellesmere Chaucer Facsimile (of Huntington Library MS EL 26 C9)* (Tokyo and San Marino, CA: Yoshodo and Huntington Library, 1995).

bility of direct examination. It has never passed through the saleroom
and hence has never been subjected to the kinds of commercial assessment that public sale would entail (the Bridgewater manuscripts were
sold *en bloc* to Huntington by private negotiation through the English
auctioneers, Sotheby's, and the American dealer G. D. Smith). Indeed,
the first detailed physical description of it was not published until
1940, in Manly and Rickert's edition (see below). The facsimiles of it
were perforce expensive, beyond the purses of most scholars and many
libraries and issued in limited editions, all factors that restricted access
to such representations of it. Even in its present scholarly home, the
Huntington Library, in California, Ellesmere is physically distinguished
as an artefact, placed on display in a separate case outside the main
reading room.

This relative modern isolation and before this, Ellesmere's recurrent association with bibliophile circles, has meant that direct scholarly assessment of the Ellesmere manuscript and its implications have
proceeded in a rather fitful way. Neither in England nor in North
America has it been straightforwardly accessible and study has not
always been possible in a first-hand, extended way. Editors, and other
students, have perforce had to rely significantly on either the Chaucer
Society transcripts and/or on facsimiles in assessing the significance of
Ellesmere, forms that have themselves posed some problems of reliability.

The point has become of particular relevance in the course of the
twentieth century when new kinds of scholarly questions began to
be asked about Ellesmere. At the forefront of this enquiry were the
American scholars, J. M. Manly (1865–1940) and Edith Rickert (1871–
1938), who produced the fruits of more than fifteen years scholarly
labour, with a team of graduate students at the University of Chicago,
in their eight-volume work, *The Text of the Canterbury Tales*, published
in 1940.[15] The argument of this work, the first (and so far the only)
attempt at analysis of all the witnesses for Chaucer's work, is extremely
dense (and, in parts, possibly not fully intelligible), but its general thrust
is clear. Manly and Rickert challenge the authority of the Ellesmere
manuscript, established over the previous half-century, and suggest that
it is to be treated with great caution:

> Although [Ellesmere] has long been regarded by many scholars as
> the single MS [manuscript] of most authority, its total of unique

---

[15] Manly and Rickert, *Text of the Canterbury Tales*.

variants, many of which are demonstrable errors, is approximately twice that of [Hengwrt] . . . And again, while it has a few lines not in any other MS, and shows some editorial changes that could have been made by Chaucer, it has many others that are questionable and some distinctly for the worst, even involving misunderstanding of the context. Since it is very clear that an intelligent person, who was certainly not Chaucer, worked over the text when [Ellesmere] was copied, the unsupported readings of this MS must be scrutinized with the greatest care. (I, 150)

Instead, they raise another manuscript to a prominent position of textual authority: 'Because of its great freedom from accidental errors and its entire freedom from editorial variants, [Hengwrt] is a MS of the highest importance' (I, 276). The Hengwrt manuscript (Aberystwyth, National Library of Wales, Peniarth 392) had been recognised as an important early witness to the text of the *Canterbury Tales* ever since Furnivall printed it among those manuscripts included in his six-text transcripts, beginning in 1868. Hengwrt is physically very different from Ellesmere. It is smaller in size, and lacks the elaborate decoration so characteristic of Ellesmere; it has only a single border and no miniatures.[16] It is also significantly different textually from Ellesmere, not just in particular readings, but also in larger respects. There are significant differences in the order of the tales and Hengwrt omits one tale that appears in Ellesmere, the *Canon's Yeoman's Tale*, itself anomalous in that it is not told by one of the original pilgrims.

In addition, the relative authority of these two early manuscripts is complicated by the fact that in one significant respect there is a clear relationship between them: they both appear to be copied by the same scribe.[17] It has recently been suggested that this scribe was the 'Adam Scriveyn', apostrophised by Chaucer for his 'necligence and rape' in

---

[16] For a full description, see Manly and Rickert, I, 266–83, and the facsimile of Hengwrt edited by Paul Ruggiers (Norman, OK: Pilgrim Books, 1979).

[17] For details of manuscripts copied by this scribe see A. I. Doyle and M. B. Parkes, 'The Production of Copies of the *Canterbury Tales* and the *Confessio Amantis* in the Early Fifteenth Century', in M. B. Parkes and Andrew Watson, eds., *Medieval Scribes, Manuscripts and Libraries: Essays Presented to N. R. Ker* (London: Scolar Press, 1978), pp. 163–210, especially p. 170. The corpus of this scribe's work is extended by Doyle and Parkes to include other manuscripts of works by Chaucer and Gower; others have attempted to enlarge his corpus, notably Linne R. Mooney (see below).

copying his works,[18] a figure who has often been identified with one Adam Pynkhurst. The accuracy of this identification lies beyond my present concerns. But, if correct, it means that the two earliest manuscripts of Chaucer's work were copied by someone who can be directly linked to Chaucer himself.

In spite of the possible implications of these shared links, before Manly and Rickert's work editors had not placed central editorial reliance on Hengwrt. It had never been used as copy-text for an edition of the *Canterbury Tales*. What is particularly puzzling about the shift in editorial focus proposed by Manly and Rickert are its bases. The opacity of their arguments has meant that there has never been any consensus about what Manly and Rickert actually believed about the transmission of the *Canterbury Tales* – or how they came to believe it. The passages quoted above are the closest they come to declarative clarity, and their opinions are not supported by any coherent assemblage of supporting evidence. And the anomalous order and textual incompleteness of Hengwrt suggest the general likelihood that it preceded Ellesmere and that the latter embodies the nearest we can come to a final intention for Chaucer's work. The implications of Manly and Rickert's arguments seem to divide authority between the two in some way that gives Hengwrt's readings a status that cannot be readily reconciled with other aspects of its surviving form, but an authority which is nonetheless seen as exceeding Ellesmere's. The general logic of such a position (especially when the grounds for such a view are not clearly articulated) remains unclear.

'A splendid manuscript'[19]

It is tempting to speculate about the factors that have led to Ellesmere's elevation, and subsequent devaluation in cultural rather than textual terms. It may be that its protracted, and (to some degree) continuing physical remoteness has had some cultural implications in thinking about Ellesmere, and has served to influence some early editors in social as well as textual terms. Its *de luxe* form and aristocratic association may have seemed to some of those who studied it to offer warranties of its worth, by which social and textual authority were interconnected:

---

[18] See, for the most recent identification with Pynkhurst, Linne R. Mooney, 'Chaucer's Scribe', *Speculum* 81 (2006), 97–138.
[19] *Works of Chaucer*, ed. Skeat, IV, xviii.

so handsome a manuscript descended in ownership through such lines has proved reassuring to editors, particularly British editors, some of whom were doubtless reared secure in the knowledge that you can tell a gentleman by the cut of his coat. And while F. N. Robinson was an American, he was at least from Harvard, and hence capable of appreciating (textual) class. It is not fruitful to attempt to push such arguments very far. But the history of discussion of Ellesmere does seem, in retrospect, to offer some possibilities of interpretation in such cultural terms in which class and nationality may have some role to play.

For certainly the next generations of scholars saw both life and Chaucer's text differently, especially those in North America. Manly and Rickert prepared their work on the *Canterbury Tales*, not under the constraints of the English class system but in the more egalitarian American Mid-West, in Chicago, 'Stormy, husky, brawling, / City of big shoulders'.[20] Did Ellesmere's noble history have any effect on Manly and Rickert's thinking? Certainly George Kane has identified an element of 'irrationality' in their resolute resistance to Ellesmere.[21] In effect, they seem to have been suspicious of the magnificence of its material form, preferring the more modestly presented Hengwrt. Their lead was followed, again in the American Mid-West, by the editors of the Chaucer Variorum, who adopted Hengwrt as the base text for their edition of the *Canterbury Tales*. The general editors' preface to this edition states, however: 'We have never intended in any way to reassess the results of Manly and Rickert's labours except at particular points where correction has become necessary.'[22] Such unexamined trust may seem odd in a major scholarly undertaking. But the canonisation of Hengwrt's authority by the Variorum has proceeded without any critical analysis of its claims to authority.[23] This willingness to accept Manly

[20] Carl Sandburg, 'Chicago', *Chicago Poems* (New York: Henry Holt, 1916).

[21] George Kane, 'John M. Manly and Edith Rickert', in Paul Ruggiers, ed., *Editing Chaucer: The Great Tradition* (Norman, OK: University of Oklahoma Press, 1984), p. 220, where their treatment of Ellesmere is described as 'of such a character as to suggest that it was emotionally based, as if the editors were under some compulsion to discredit the manuscript which clouded their judgement.'

[22] I quote from the this Preface as it appears in the first fascicle of the Variorum *Canterbury Tales* to appear, the *Miller's Tale*, ed. T. W. Ross (Norman, OK: University of Oklahoma Press 1983), p. xv.

[23] F. N. Robinson, in the second edition of his standard *Works of Geoffrey Chaucer* (1957) did make some changes seemingly on the basis of Manly and Rickert's work; for discussion see George F. Reinecke, 'F. N. Robinson',

and Rickert's conclusions without any further testing of their arguments meant it was some time before evidence began to catch up with hypothesis. It was not until 1980 that Norman Blake produced the first modern edition of Hengwrt and followed it with a series of studies designed to press its claims to textual superiority.[24] The shifting and evolving nature of his arguments in a lengthy series of studies introduced new dimensions of complexity into the Hengwrt/Ellesmere debate.[25]

It was more than forty years before any serious challenges were offered to Manly and Rickert's view of the textual superiority of Ellesmere. But when such challenges came they were of great weight. The first was in 1984 when George Kane offered a searching critique of Manly and Rickert's assumptions and methods.[26] And subsequently Jill Mann demolished one of the most enduring fictions created by them: the existence of an Ellesmere 'editor'.[27] In effect, more than half a century of fruitless scholarly debate has now concluded with the state of knowledge about Chaucer's text little advanced. What remains is the probability that both Ellesmere and Hengwrt were almost certainly written by the same scribe[28] and that the order and general content of Ellesmere seem the closest approximation we have to Chaucer's final intentions in these respects.

in *Editing Chaucer: The Great Tradition*, pp. 231–51; he concludes that in his revised edition Robinson was not 'strongly moved by Manly and Rickert's new but still systematic if not mechanical way of establishing the text' (p. 250).

[24] *The Canterbury Tales by Geoffrey Chaucer Edited from the Hengwrt Manuscript*, ed. N. F. Blake (London: Edward Arnold, 1980).

[25] The series of articles by Blake achieved a developed position in *The Textual Tradition of Chaucer's Canterbury Tales* (London: Edward Arnold, 1985). But his views continued to evolve; see for example his 'Editing the *Canterbury Tales*: Preliminary Observations', *Anglia* 116 (1998), 198–214.

[26] Kane, 'John M. Manly and Edith Rickert', pp. 207–29, 289–91.

[27] Jill Mann, 'Chaucer's Meter and the Myth of the Ellesmere Editor of *The Canterbury Tales*', *Studies in the Age of Chaucer* 23 (2001), 71–107.

[28] Only one attempt has been made to challenge this view, by Roy Vance Ramsey, 'The Hengwrt and Ellesmere Manuscripts of the *Canterbury Tales*: Different Scribes, *Studies in Bibliography* 35 (1982), 133–54. His views have not gained much support, but have never been rebutted. He does advance some arguments for orthographic differences between the two manuscripts, but this point (if valid) does not bear on the question of palaeographical identity. For a rebuttal of his arguments see M. L. Samuels, 'The Scribe of the Hengwrt and Ellesmere Manuscripts of the *Canterbury Tales*', *Studies in the Age of Chaucer* 5 (1983), 49–66, reprinted in J. J. Smith, ed., *The English of Chaucer and his Contemporaries: Essays by M L Samuels and J J Smith* (Aberdeen: Aberdeen University Press, 1988), pp. 38–50.

Manuscript authority

This controversy about the relative authority of these two manuscripts and the fluctuating status of Ellesmere's perceived authority is more than just an often overheated academic debate. It also suggests a sense of conflicting notions of what Chaucer's text ought to be and of the editors' role in its restoration and presentation. The material superiority of Ellesmere over Hengwrt ought not, of course, to presuppose any textual critic to identify that superiority with textual superiority; but it does not, of course, preclude it. At times the debate has seemed to involve a scholarly quest to create difficulty, to adopt a process of argumentation that is perverse in its efforts to invest authority in Hengwrt, a version of Chaucer's poem that is both physically and textually incomplete. More than that, the choice between Ellesmere and Hengwrt has at times been presented as a stark one – either one or the other. More helpful is the possibility of greater specific analysis, involving a consideration of all possible readings at points of variation, including, but not limited to, Ellesmere and Hengwrt.[29] It was the significant achievement of Manly and Rickert to assemble a detailed, comprehensive and accurate corpus of variants. Remarkably, no study of the *Canterbury Tales* has used this the full range of this data to establish Chaucer's text. And a significant factor in the lack of interest in the full range of this data has been the preoccupation with Hengwrt and Ellesmere. In effect, it is a controversy that has deflected interest from more detailed examination of specific readings as reflected in the evidence of all the manuscripts. Privileging the readings of Ellesmere, or rejecting them for Hengwrt, in isolation from such evidence, is a strategy of limited editorial usefulness.

Over the past 150 years Ellesmere has come to enjoy an increasingly central role in thinking about the text of Chaucer's most famous work. And if the exact nature of its status in the textual transmission of the *Canterbury Tales* is likely to remain the subject of debate it is clear that its position is always going to be a central one. But its importance extends beyond the debate about the relative authority of different manuscript witnesses in establishing the text of the poem

---

[29] Ralph Hanna proposes something not unlike this in his concept of 'split authority' among the early manuscripts of the poem; see 'The Hengwrt Manuscript and the Canon of the Canterbury Tales', *English Manuscript Studies* 1 (1989), 64–84, 'understanding the transmission of Chaucer's text involves a series of limited decisions on the basis of an item-by-item survey of problematic areas' (p. 79).

and the related issues of canon and tale order. For in both its material form and historical situation it signifies aspects of Chaucer's broader cultural significance in relation to its position in the history of the English manuscript book.

Positioning Ellesmere in the history of the book

One important aspect of Ellesmere's achievement is the artistic. Before its completion only a small number of later medieval manuscripts written in English survive of a comparable degree of elaborateness of presentation. These include the Auchinleck manuscript (Edinburgh, National Library of Scotland, Advocates 19.2.1), a large collection of Middle English verse works, many unique copies of romances, made in London in the 1330s to 1340s, originally with a large number of illustrations and other decoration, much of which is now lost. Also relevant is the enormous vernacular religious compilation, the Vernon manuscript (Oxford, Bodleian Library, Eng. poet. a.1), produced probably in a religious house in Worcestershire towards the end of the fourteenth century; again extensively decorated and illustrated, this manuscript was possibly commissioned by a member of the wealthy book-collecting family, the Bohuns. But it is not possible to point to very many examples of Middle English literary manuscripts before Ellesmere that demonstrate a sustained commitment to producing high-quality forms of such English works and none that lavishes such care on a single work by a named author. The level of artistic commitment in Ellesmere is therefore both highly unusual and highly significant in what it suggests about the early critical esteem of Chaucer the poet.

And Ellesmere differs from these earlier manuscripts in fundamental ways, for it contains a single work of a single author, both identified in the colophon: 'Heere is ended the book of the tales of Caunterbury compiled by Geffrey Chaucer of whos soule Ihesu crist haue mercy' (fol. 232v). This is one of the earliest occasions on which such a title and full name of the author occurs in a Middle English literary work.[30] The form of words here suggests that this was a posthumous assemblage (although, if so, it is unlikely that Chaucer had been dead for

---

[30] Some of the earliest manuscripts of Gower's *Confessio amantis* slightly precede Chaucer in this respect; a few manuscripts of *Piers Plowman* include both title and the author's first name.

very long). It also suggests a concern for the afterlife of his text that is reflected in other elements of Ellesmere's presentation.

For Ellesmere offers a record of Chaucer's poem that is not just textual, but also symbolic. It includes twenty-three marginal illustrations of the Canterbury pilgrims, including for the first time in English literature one of the author, Chaucer himself. The different forms of such character illustrations obviously serve to reflect the diversity of narrative content in the *Canterbury Tales* as well as acting as markers to direct the reader to its various stages. But the inclusion of a representation of the author himself, specifically identified in the rubric accompanying his tale ('heere bigynneth Chaucer's tale of Melibee', fol. 169) is unprecedented in a Middle English literary work. Its significance is underscored by the detail of the penner he carries, emblematic of his creative identity. That such an identity is marked out through his being depicted as part of an elaborate (and very expensive) layout is a crucial element in Ellesmere's claim on our attention as historians of late medieval English culture. It signifies an awareness of authorial identity of an unusually developed kind. The miniature was clearly conceived as one of some importance in the manuscript. An artist was commissioned solely to depict this image. And greater marginal space has been left for it than for other pilgrim portraits, hence giving it greater prominence.

But if the marginal portrait of Chaucer the pilgrim establishes the literal presence of the author within his own work, it is problematic in other respects. For the Chaucer it presents is not Chaucer the poet, the author of the exquisitely comic, incomplete *Tale of Sir Thopas*, but Chaucer the writer of moral prose, a didactic, expository Chaucer, the narrator/author of the *Tale of Melibee*. How the first readers of Ellesmere would have responded to this representation can only be guessed at. Modern readers may be tempted to respond to the perceived ironic wit of the representation of a prolix, prosy Chaucer. Certainly the representation of Chaucer has a latent irony for such readers. It problematises the idea of the poet that is otherwise primarily embodied in Ellesmere, and remains an interpretative crux in the early reception of his work.

More generally the fact that the writings of a contemporary writer of English should be presented in such a systematically elaborate way is equally noteworthy. There is no precedent in English manuscript culture for such an elaborate form of presentation of a single work of imaginative literature by an identified contemporary author, one that insists on the identity of both work and author. The early emergence of a manuscript that signifies in both textual and material terms the status of a 'modern' poet points to the swiftly rising status of the poetic vernacular. It signifies an emergent vernacular literary culture, one in which English works had begun, by the start of the fifteenth century, to achieve a status reflected in the physical forms in which they were presented, a status hitherto afforded chiefly to Latin and French writings.

This fact in its turn reflects another cultural paradox. What is striking is that Ellesmere set a standard in production values that was not to be matched either in the metropolis where it was produced, or elsewhere. No other surviving manuscript of Chaucer's work reflects a comparable lavishness of production. It is possible that one or two others may once have come close had they survived intact.[31] But in the range, quality and systematisation of its decorative design Ellesmere stands apart not just from other Chaucer manuscripts but also from most other fifteenth-century Middle English verse manuscripts by other authors. There are, of course, some indications of wealthy owners, royalty or members of the nobility who clearly did commission or were presented with elaborate copies of particular poetic works. But in relation to the totality of what survives numbers of such manuscripts are quite small.[32]

That such a standard of production was not to be matched again in the history of the transmission of the *Canterbury Tales* is a fact that has implications that seem rarely to have been considered. Does vernacular poetry become so rapidly accommodated as a commercial and cultural medium that only a few readers wish to possess it in *de luxe* forms? Seemingly it did, and hence Chaucer's 'status' was signified quantitatively by the number of copies that were produced, a number that established the *Canterbury Tales* as the most popular surviving fifteenth-century poetic work.

Ellesmere is only one among these witnesses, of course, but its

---

[31] For example, Cambridge, University Library, Gg 4.21 and the surviving fragments of the same manuscript that are now divided between Manchester, John Rylands University Library, Eng. 63, and Philadelphia, Rosenbach Museum and Library, 1084/2. Both these manuscripts are now significantly incomplete and it is not possible to arrive at any clear sense of their decorative programmes.

[32] For some discussion of the numbers and relative quality of the surviving major Middle English poetical works of the fifteenth century see A. S. G. Edwards and Derek Pearsall, 'The Manuscripts of the Major English Poetic Texts', in J. Griffiths and D. Pearsall, eds., *Book Production and Publishing in Britain, 1375–1475* (Cambridge: Cambridge University Press, 1989), pp. 257–78.

importance in the history of Chaucer's text cannot be overstated; nor can its role in the history of the modern editing of his poem. However, its significance extends beyond its role in the complex questions of textual authority that the surviving manuscripts of the *Canterbury Tales* pose. Its form brings us, in some ways, as close as we can get to the figure of its creator and the beginnings of modern formulations of the idea of the author.

Vanishing Transliteracies in Beowulf and Samuel Pepys's Diary

MARTIN K. FOYS AND WHITNEY ANNE TRETTIEN

> To study the institutional identity of a text as well as the function of textual institutions relies, then, on analyzing both the inaugural function of the text, its power to be foundational and to provide a historical beginning, and its monumental function, the strategies whereby it not only testifies to that beginning but also transcends it by serving as a fixed model for specific future (perhaps not only textual) behavior. These strategies gain their authority by strategically 'forgetting' and then recoding in a 'monumental' textual form the historicity of the inaugural moment as a moment beyond and outside history.[1]

THIS ESSAY EXPLORES how media history and the printed book's place within it contribute to the institutional identity of literature, and how the institutional strategies by which these past documents became and maintain their authority as literary artefacts have resulted in various forms of the 'strategic forgetting and recoding' that Jane Newman notes in the quotation above. When we started this essay, we chose two disparate literary works from our respective periods of specialisation, *Beowulf* and Samuel Pepys's *Diary*, for the simple reason that they both were discovered as written documents, became literature through printed editions and scholarship, and now have innovative electronic resources for their reading and study. What we did not expect were the surprising and complicated homologies of transliteracies, alternative media and their dismediation/dematerialisation that arose between them.

As with literary criticism, the field of media studies frequently has, in Timothy Druckery's words, applied a 'lazy linearity' to the historical formation of its subject.[2] For most of their existence, both literary and media studies have espoused an evolutionary model of development,

---

[1] J. O. Newman, *Pastoral Conventions* (Baltimore: Johns Hopkins University Press, 1990), p. 22.
[2] 'Forward', S. Zielinski, *Deep Time of Media: Toward an Archaeology of Hearing and Seeing by Technical Means* (Cambridge, MA: MIT University Press, 2006), p. vii.

where the technological expressive mechanisms of the present day become a proleptic standard, privileging the lineage of their precursors over other forms of communication and information management that may have existed in the past.[3] In general, literary criticism has a hard time imagining any kind of discursive past outside a logocentric progression of the oral to the written to the printed. Up until a century ago, literature by technological necessity had its material origin as a handwritten text, even if at one point it had been oral. Until very, very recently, to be considered literature a text must have been printed, usually in book form, and often as an edition or in an anthology. Then, as canonical status is imagined and/or achieved, it is reproduced in printed criticism and scholarship.

In media studies such straightforward historical schemes have begun to face challenges by theorists such as Siegfried Zielinski, who has argued for a 'deep time' of media that does not limit views of media history to diachronic chains of influence. For Zielinski, 'the history of media is not the product of a predictable and necessary advance from primitive to complex apparatus'.[4] Zielinski draws inspiration from geological concepts that view the relation of time and physical change 'as a dynamic cycle of erosion, deposition, consolidation, and uplifting before the erosion starts the cycle anew'.[5] When studying the operation of historical media, we need to consider the synchronic media ecology of a period, drilling down to a specific moment and studying forms of media that did not survive or immediately influence present media forms.[6]

[3]   See, for instance, M. K. Foys, *Virtually Anglo-Saxon: Old Media, New Media, and Early Medieval Studies in the Late Age of Print* (Gainesville: University Press of Florida, 2007), pp. 19–34, for an exploration of what early medieval discourse becomes canonical and what does not, and why. For a basic overview of the field of media history, see J. Nerone, 'Approaches to Media History', in A. N. Valdivia, ed., *A Companion to Media Studies* (Oxford: Blackwell, 2003), pp. 93–114.
[4]   Zielinski, *Deep Time*, p. 7. See also E. Huhtamo, 'From Kaleidoscomaniac to Cybernerd: Notes toward an Archaeology of the Media', in T. Druckery, ed., *Electronic Culture: Technology and Visual Representation* (New York: Aperture Foundation, 1996), pp. 297–303.
[5]   Zielinski, *Deep Time*, p. 4.
[6]   In his study, Zielinski treats a broad spectrum of forgotten or 'dead' media, from ancient Greek theories of vision and sound that articulate the primacy of interface, to eighteenth-century experiments with electrical writing and beyond.

Because of their perceived irrelevance to modern media, such 'dead end' forms have largely been effaced from the historical record through its own heuristic teleology. But as Lisa Gitelman concisely observes: 'media are historical at several different levels'.[7] Communities of the past were conversant across numerous technologies of expression and communication that remain largely silent or invisible to us today. Such transliteracy (facility in and across a range of expressive platforms) in part defined these communities, and the expressions they constructed in one medium inevitably intermediated with other modes of information discourse.[8] Expressions from the past must be understood as more than records of the past; often they were communication *before* they became records. Hence Zielinski's vaguely Foucaultian call to work through what he terms *anarchaeology*, and in our digging into the past to not so unthinkingly attach meanings to expressions that are entirely different from what they were originally, but instead to find the 'new in the old'.[9]

Such approaches can yield fruitful dividends for literary study. The first parts of each investigation below are anarchaeological, to a degree, in that they examine how a now obsolete communicational discourse – runes in the case of *Beowulf*, and tachygraphy in the case of Pepys's *Diary* – reconfigure the way we understand the operation and historical formation of such canonical literature. Communicating as well as documenting, such texts originally were alive and fully participatory in their past informatic milieu, engaging in what Armand Mattelart has termed a 'communicational configuration'.[10] For Mattelart, communication is not content simply carried by specific forms of media, but a cultural and

---

[7] L. Gitelman, *Always Already New: Media, History, and the Data of Culture* (Cambridge, MA: MIT University Press, 2006), p. 5.
[8] On the relatively recent concept of transliteracy, see S. Thomas *et al.*, 'Transliteracy: Crossing divides', *First Monday* 12.12 (2007), http://www.uic.edu/htbin/cgiwrap/bin/ojs/index.php/fm/article/view/2060/1908.
[9] Zielinski, *Deep Time*, p. 27. Such concepts inevitably recall Michel Foucault's 'archaeological' and 'anti-evolutionary' critique of the history of ideas in *The Archaeology of Knowledge* and elsewhere, though Zielinski's work is less post-structurally determined in his interpretative readings of the past than those of Foucault. For comparison, see C. Tilley, 'Michel Foucault: towards an Archaeology of Archaeology', in C. Tilley, ed., *Reading Material Culture: Structuralism, Hermeneutics and Post-Structuralism* (Oxford: Blackwell, 1990), pp. 281–347.
[10] A. Mattelart, *The Invention of Communication*, trans. S. Emanuel (Minneapolis: University of Minnesota Press, 1996), xiii. See also Gitelman, *Always Already New*, p. 7, who defines media as 'socially realized structures of communication'.

technological *dispositif* that contextualises and enables the dispersal of information, 'encompassing the multiple circulation of goods, people, and messages'.[11] Viewing artefacts of media only as a static record, however, can cut them out of such configurations. In this, expressions not compliant with modern notions of media are rendered foreign and distant, ciphered expressions thought secret, cryptic and alien, and metonyms of the misinterpretation of past organic transliteracies. But the cryptography is modern, not historical, and the present encodings of such approaches to past communication now want decoding. A deep-media approach to *Beowulf* and Pepys's *Diary* reveals these works occupied a liminal place with regard to (now) alternative media, as they looked back to a medium's everyday existence and forward to its inevitable obsolescence. In our dual studies, we were startled to discover close parallels regarding how other media that informed, at times foundationally, these texts had become estranged from them through the process by which text became literature.

The form and function of one particular medium has the capacity to undo others. The second part of each of these case studies explores the role played by the dominant medium of literature, the printed book, in the undoing of past transliteracies, and how the residue of once related media within literature is dematerialised in the critical record. Though the study of print culture has gone far with the materiality of the book (and need not be rehearsed here), there has been far less thought about how economies of writing operate across materials besides the page, and in written forms besides dominant systems of lettering. As Juliet Fleming has argued, our critical disciplines of the aesthetic usually fracture meaning from its physical medium and material form, emptying out what is viewed as only the container and then discarding it as extraneous. But communication can be attached to many other materials besides the page, and through many other systems besides modern alphabets and lexicon. What Fleming terms the *exteriority* of expression places various media in a material continuum 'where there is no difference between painting and writing; no difference, again, between writing on paper, a wall, copper, wood, a body or an axe; and no difference, finally, between writing and other visual patterns'.[12]

[11] Mattelart, *Invention of Communication*, p. xiv; G. Deleuze, 'What is a Dispositif?', in T. Armstrong, ed., *Michel Foucault: Philosopher* (New York: Routledge, 1992), pp. 159–68.
[12] J. Fleming, *Graffiti and the Writing Arts of Early Modern England* (Philadelphia: University of Pennsylvania Press: 2001), p. 25.

Typographic culture largely resists such a continuum and the objects it connects; such resistance is integral to modern notions of literature that the printed medium helps produce. To a degree this is reasonable; at times, one needs to know that a poem is literature and an axe is not. Nevertheless, the communicative symbiosis of weapons and poems that literature like *Beowulf* acknowledges and uses, or the impact of material mobility on Pepys's daily shorthand practices, merit critical attention.

Each study below concludes with an excursus of sorts on the immediate future of these literary texts in the new scholarly digital environment. Modern books may have considerable capacity to accumulate information, but relatively little potential to preserve, as Will Straw puts it, 'the spatializing mutual sustenance through which such artefacts speak to each other' in past and present moments.[13] Straw considers whether new media might be better up to the task of comprehensively archiving historical *dispositifs* of cultural discourse. But so far the digital resource remains a remediated child of print culture, mostly differing from the operation of a book not in terms of quality, but simply in terms of quantity.[14] In literary studies, the effect of earlier dismediation only intensifies as we move from book to computer, and the increasing power of media to accumulate historical granularity creates a backlog of the past within the present, slowing and muddying the historical sequence, and in effect, flattening historical nuance into a single, convergent and visible moment of the present and its always already manufactured past.[15] The promise yet to be realised, Straw argues, is that:

> the abundance of accumulated and discarded artefacts allowed the passage of time to be noted in deeply sedimented and richly resonating clusters of objects. We need large inventories of such objects in order that they may knit together within densely intertextual packages, so that the affinities among [historical objects] start to assume a historical solidity.[16]

Such resonance, simultaneously rooted in expressive technologies of the long past and the imminently present, should be imagined in future literary studies as well. Texts such as *Beowulf* and Pepys's *Diary* were quite different before they became produced as literature. These argu-

---

[13] W. Straw, 'Embedded Memories', in C. Acland, ed., *Residual Media* (Minneapolis: University of Minnesota Press, 2007), pp. 3–15, 15.
[14] See also Foys, *Virtually Anglo-Saxon*, pp. 190–201.
[15] Straw, 'Embedded Memories', pp. 11–15.
[16] Ibid., p. 14.

ments should not be taken as essentialising the content of the past, but rather as more robustly accommodating the traces of its survival.

The runes of Beowulf

For most who study or teach *Beowulf*, the path forward from the murky origins of the poem to its current literary state follows an easy trajectory of media history: orality, either as a source or a stylistic precursor, reformulated as writing in a medieval manuscript, reformatted through modern editions and translations in printed books. While the arguments may be complex about *how* the oral form intersects with the handwritten poem (source? vestige? archaism? inspiration?) within its earliest extant form, the evolutionary skeleton remains a simple, if ultimately misleading one.[17] Nobody thinks much about runes in this poem, and for good reason; when we read *Beowulf* today, there are no specific runes to be found. But runes are present in the Old English poem more than most realise, and what they are doing there has a lot to say about past forms of media and transliteracy, and how these transliteracies themselves are not monolithic and static, but subject to historical change over the long early medieval period that the matter of *Beowulf* spans.

While *Beowulf* may be writing, it is not *about* writing as we would now traditionally recognise it. No physical books or scribbling monks occur in the poem, and the poem makes no allusions to such acts of textual production. As others have pointed out, what 'writing' is referenced in the poem is of a distinctly different kind from the writing that contains it. Versions of the Old English verb *writan* appear exactly twice; in both instances, the term relates not to marks on a page, but to swords and the different kinds of marks they occasion.[18] When Beowulf kills the dragon in the climax of the hero's third battle, the poem uses the past tense of the intensified verb *for-writan* ('to cut through'): 'for

---

[17] For a basic overview of the issues of orality vs. literacy in Old English poetry, see C. B. Pasternack, 'The Textuality of Old English Poetry', in E. A. Joy, M. K. Ramsey and B. D. Gilchrist, eds., *The Postmodern Beowulf: A Critical Casebook* (Morgantown: West Virginia University Press, 2007), pp. 519–45, at pp. 521–8; see R. E. Bjork and J. D. Niles, eds., *A Beowulf Handbook* (University of Nebraska Press, 1997), pp. 5–7, for a brief overview of such debates in relation to *Beowulf*.

[18] A. Frantzen, *Desire for Origins: New Language, Old English, and Teaching the Tradition* (New Brunswick: Rutgers University Press, 1990), pp. 184 ff.

wrat wedra helm wyrm on middan' ('The protector of the Weders cut
through the worm in the middle', line 2705).[19] Such use conveys the
etymological origin of writing as the material act of carving or cutting
a surface, as opposed to a more abstracted act of graphically signifying
language. The other, earlier time writing appears in *Beowulf*, it again
relates to carving, this time not *by* a sword, but *on* a sword. After slaying
Grendel's mother, Beowulf brings back the hilt of the sword he used and
presents it to Hrothgar, king of the Danes. Hrothgar reads the ancient
story inscribed on the hilt (lines 1687–98):

> Hroðgar maðelode.   Hylt sceawode,
> ealde lafe,   on ðæm wæs or **(wri)ten**
> fyrngewinnes,   syðþan flod ofs(loh)
> gifen geotende,   giganta cyn.
> Frecne (ge)ferdon;   þæt wæs fremde þeod
> ecean Dryh(tne).   Him þæs endelean
> þurh wæteres wylm   Waldend sealde.
> Swa wæs on ðæm scen(num)   sciran goldes
> þurh **runstafas**   rihte (ge)mearcod,
> geseted ꞇ gesæd,   hwam þæt sweo(rd) geworht,
> irena cyst   ærest wære,
> w(reo)þenhilt   ꞇ wyrmfah.

> Hrothgar spoke; he examined the hilt,
> the old heirloom; on it was **engraved** the origin
> of ancient strife, from when the flood slew,
> that pouring ocean, the race of giants –
> they fared terribly; that was a tribe foreign
> to the eternal Lord; to them was the end-reward,
> through the surging of waters, by the Ruler granted –
> there was also on the shaft in shining gold
> by **rune-staves** rightly marked,
> set down and stated, for whom the sword
> – the choicest of irons – had been first cast,
> with a bound hilt and serpent-patterned.

If readers ever think about runes in *Beowulf*, it is in this passage. As the

---

[19] All Old English text of *Beowulf* excerpted from K. Kiernan's diplomatic
transcript (relineated to Klaeber's numeration) found in the *Electronic Beowulf*
(CD-ROM, London: British Library, 2004). Emended text (in parenthesis) has
been rechecked against images of Thorkelin's transcripts, found ibid. All translations are modified by Martin Foys from B. Slade's, found on his *Beowulf on
Steorarume* website, http://www.heorot.dk.

extract shows, the hilt contains not one, but two distinct acts of writing – the engraving of the story of the giants and biblical flood, and the runic inscription that records the original owner of the sword.[20] Seth Lerer notes that this passage records the visual process of Hrothgar examining the hilt, ekphrastically registering what his eyes see as it moves down the length of the hilt.[21] Though this hilt is a textual construction, the signified materiality of this moment of the poem is not in doubt. In the past, while the few critics who develop readings of this scene take steps to evaluate these writings within its material context, such evaluations explicitly subsume its alterity under more literary notions of text, and implicitly within a reductive model of media history.[22] Lerer, for example, argues that the hilt's text is consciously alien and distant, contrasting with the shared, social, oral and vernacular performance of the Old English *scop*, and so stands as a figure for the poem as a whole.[23] Allen Frantzen similarly argues that the material engraving is counteracted by Hrothgar's own subsequent oral 'sermon' about moral leadership before performing a neat deconstruction around the notions of the sword as text and the sword as weapon – both the beginning and end of meaning.[24]

This strain of criticism, while valuable, runs the risk of amplifying the metaphoric potential of these moments while obscuring the meto-

---

[20] Though in the past some critics have argued that the depiction of the flood is pictorial, and not a runic inscription, the material evidence of surviving swords does not support the former, and the argument for both episodes as runic is generally accepted. See R. D. Fulk *et al.*, *Klaeber's Beowulf*, 4th edition (Toronto: University of Toronto Press, 2008), pp. 211–12, for discussion.

[21] S. Lerer, 'Hrothgar's Hilt and the Reader in *Beowulf*', in *The Postmodern Beowulf*, pp. 587–628, at p. 593.

[22] Cf. Fulk *et al*, *Klaeber's Beowulf*: 'Regardless of what is precisely inscribed on the hilt, this is the sole reference in the poem to writing and reading, and as such it has attracted repeated notice as a site of tension between encroaching literacy and the historically oral genre of the poem' (p. 212, and subsequent critical references). G. Overing's treatment in 'Swords and Signs: Dynamic Semeiosis in *Beowulf*', in *The Postmodern Beowulf*, pp 547–86, at pp. 572–6, of the iconicity of this hilt as material object, and her position that the object and the text exist in parallel to each other, remains a notable exception to such literalising effects. Though Overing begins with the observation that the hilt can function as 'an icon of the text' (p. 573), her argument develops further with the idea that such objects and texts exist together in a semiotic network of meaning inside and outside the poem.

[23] Lerer, 'Hrothgar's Hilt', p. 589, pp. 601–5.

[24] Frantzen, *Desire for Origins*, p. 188 and p. 189.

nymic qualities of the systems of communication they function within. As Gillian Overing describes it:

> The narrative progression of the poem foils logical or linear attempts to sum up, to stand back and conclude that *this*, after all, meant *that*. The poem is essentially non-linear, describing arcs and circles where persons, events, histories, and stories continually intersect. This poem requires a critical confrontation with difference.[25]

To Overing's list, we need to add *material media*. In the poem, artefacts of communication (inscribed or not) cycle through a dense interstice of signification that defies the unified and linear notions of media progression that traditional interpretations of the poem impose. Runic inscription functions culturally within the poem, even if the poem never reproduces the exact content of these runes.

Significantly, both Frantzen's and Lerer's readings of Hrothgar's hilt rely on the perception that these engraved characters are clandestine, exotic and removed from the central world and public expression of the poem, and by implication, its audience. Frantzen translates *runestafas* as 'secret letters', though the practice of runic inscription of ownership suggests just the opposite – that the owner's name on the hilt was not meant to be a secret.[26] Lerer claims 'the *Beowulf*-poet describes a cryptic text or an alien writing of restricted usage and professional skill', that does not 'deploy the language of *runica manuscripta* [the scribal practice of using runes in writing] but of runestones' – a practice further distantiated from the manuscript writing which records it.[27] Certainly this kind of writing is arcane to *us* – it falls well outside the historical scheme of writing that constructs the medieval past through the modern present. Runes were probably arcane, in a different mode, to the Old English scribe of the poem we have surviving. But while the Old English word *run* can mean secret, it can also just denote the character of a rune, as analogous to 'letter'.[28] As R. I. Page has argued, modern scholarly misconceptions of runes suffer from a 'magico-religious' bias that derives

---

[25] Overing, 'Swords and Signs', p. 549, emphasis original.
[26] Frantzen, *Desire for Origins*, p. 185. Cf. S. C. Hawkes and R. I. Page, 'Swords and Runes in South-East England', *The Antiquaries Journal* 47 (1967), 1–26.
[27] Lerer, 'Hrothgar's Hilt', p. 595.
[28] J. Bosworth and T. N. Toller, *An Anglo-Saxon Dictionary Based on the Manuscript Collections of the Late Joseph Bosworth* (Oxford: Oxford University Press, 1898, 1921), accessed through David Finucane's searchable, digital version at http://www.davidfinucane.com.

largely from contemporary unfamiliarity.[29] We simply need to recall the secretive utility of Tolkien's Dwarvish runic system in *The Hobbit* to have a sense of how medievalesque runes are viewed in the popular imagination today.[30]

While some aspects of runic epigraphy promote the secret or the otherworldly, throughout the first several centuries of the early Middle Ages, quite likely the majority of such inscriptions and the objects they marked were less strange than common. The material form of runes suggests an origin designed for ease of cutting against the grain of wood, so providing a convenient (and in the long view ephemeral) medium for communication and/or documentation.[31] Though surviving evidence is minimal given the relative fragility of the base material, that widespread wood carving of runes for informal purposes continued throughout Europe for the eight or nine centuries of their use is a reasonable conjecture.[32] In England and in other parts of north-western Europe, runes were used for hundreds of years on a wide variety of objects, from monumental stone sculpture to small wooden footstools, and including weapons, jewellery, coins, furniture and animal and even human bone – the scale and scope of the surviving evidence represents only a tiny percentage of rune usage in Anglo-Saxon England.[33] While inscribed objects move from the clearly arcane, such as formulae for protection against dwarf-stroke or bleeding incised on a human skull, to

[29] R. I. Page, *An Introduction to English Runes*, 2nd edition (Woodbridge: Boydell Press, 1999), pp. 11–12. Page is responding in part to a hypothesis of runic arcana set forth in R. Elliot's influential *Runes: An Introduction* (London: Philosophical Library Inc., 1959).

[30] As J. R. R. Tolkien wrote in his forward to *The Hobbit*, 'At the time of this tale only the Dwarves made regular use of [runes], especially for private or secret records', *The Hobbit* (New York: Houghton Mifflin, 2001 [1937]), p. 1.

[31] J. Graham-Campbell and D. M. Wilson, *The Viking World*, 3rd edition (London: Frances Lincoln, 2001), p. 156.

[32] T. Looijenga, *Texts and Contexts of the Oldest Runic Inscriptions* (Leiden: Brill, 2003), p. 14 and p. 22; R. Derolez, 'The Runic System and its Cultural Context', *Michigan Germanic Studies* 7 (1981), 19–26, at pp. 20–1.

[33] Page, *English Runes*, p. 14. Runic objects range from the Feddersen Wierde footstool (5th century, German), the Ramsund Stone (11th century, Sweden), an 'Æthelbert' runic coin (England, 8th century), the Kingsmoor ring (9th century, England), and the Ribe Skull (9th century, Jutland), to the Thames scramasax blade (9th century, England), the Chessel Down sword and scabbard mouthpiece (6th century, England), and Ash-Gilton Pommel (6th century England). Fittingly, many runic items such as these are reproduced in *Beowulf: An Illustrated Edition*, trans. S. Heaney, ed. J. D. Niles (New York: Norton, 2008); see also pp. 94–95 below.

the clearly utilitarian, such as runic names on minted coins, it is safe to say that runes for most of the early medieval world were as much if not more 'known' than chirographic writing, a medium rarely encountered outside of monasteries or aristocratic and legal *scriptoria*.

By the time *Beowulf* was written down in its surviving form, in the late Anglo-Saxon period, the medium of engraved runes was gradually moving towards obsolescence after centuries of use. It is only at this point that we find the emerging attitude that runes *as a system* functioned more cryptically than other forms of writing. Unsurprisingly, such attitudes are codified within manuscripts, at a time when monastic writing in Anglo-Saxon England was increasingly viewed as the technology of cultural preservation.[34] Beginning in the ninth century, continental and then English monastic writers began to record *runica manuscripta* – lists of Anglo-Saxon (and other) runic alphabets, perhaps at first as reference, but later as esoteric systems of ciphers and codes.[35] At the end of the Anglo-Saxon period, such lists grew more arcane and alien, though their recording continued, as attested in the twelfth-century list of Anglo-Saxon and Norse runes from a monastery in Thorney (Fig. 1).[36] Here the now-dominant form of writing records the dying of another media form, encoding it twice over – first within the context of the manuscript, and second as a code itself. In this form, the runes *are* exotic, alien, and arcane – they have been ported to literary curiosity by a medium contributing to their obsolescence. But literary scholars who consider runes within early medieval writings seldom understand that this tradition is not so cleanly divorced and distinct from the material practices of runes during the majority of the Anglo-Saxon period.[37]

In *Beowulf*, applying only a latter-day 'secret life' of *runica manscripta* to Hrothgar's reading of the engraved hilt distorts a deeper historical reality of the medium, and likewise re-inscribes the poem's use of runes within the reductive tradition of literary media. To do so flattens the use of runes within Anglo-Saxon England to a point of critical singularity, and mutes their earlier cultural significance. *Beowulf*, a poem about a sixth-century south Swedish hero, survives as a text in an early-

---

[34] E. Christie, 'The Image of the Letter: From the Anglo-Saxons to the Electronic *Beowulf*', *Culture, Theory and Critique* 44 (2003), 129–50, at pp. 133–5.
[35] See Page, *English Runes*, pp. 60–79, for an overview of *runica manuscripta*.
[36] F. Wallis, *The Calendar and the Cloister: Oxford-St. Johns MS 17* (commentary for fol. 5v), http://digital.library.mcgill.ca/ms-17/folio.php?p=5v.
[37] Page, *English Runes*, p. 62.

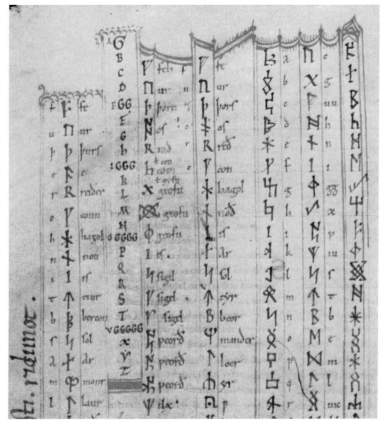

Figure 1: Oxford, St. Johns College Library, MS 17, fol 5v (*ca.* 1110): section of a *runica manuscripta* chart, among other esoteric letter sets. Reproduced with permission: President and Fellows of Saint John Baptist College in the University of Oxford.

eleventh-century manuscript that has cultural and linguistic forms compatible with anywhere from an eighth- to a tenth-century milieu.[38] Even taking into account the wide disparity of claims for dating the piece, *Beowulf* is a poem which begins in and travels through times, places and cultures of functional runes, but survives in a document recorded when such media forms were on the cusp of obsolescence. Given the work's own deep *historia*, the poem's episode of Hrothgar's reading of the engraved sword hilt needs also to be read liminally, and as accommodating both configurations of Anglo-Saxon runic reception.

The runes on the hilt Hrothgar reads twice encode the transitional state of the epigraphic medium. The hilt contains two inscribed discourses – one that accesses an ancient, mysterious and typological spiritual strife, and one that publicly witnesses the original owner of the sword. These twinned incidences of inscription make the material space they share both mystical and common: one leans towards the magico-religious, but the other plainly does not. And while the arcane epigraphy of the great flood eons ago might dominate the scene for the late Anglo-Saxon composers and/or scribes of the poem (along with the modern critics who follow them), the *runestafas* of everyday use still inhabit the poem as cultural residue – not magical, and pointing to a past and more quotidian nature of such media.[39]

An inscribed hilt need not have writing on it, runic or otherwise, to participate within a system of communication.[40] *Beowulf* is full of objects that convey specific information without writing – weapons, armour, necklaces and treasure circulate through the poem's societies, often carrying more meaning than the purely symbolic. Space here does not permit a full study of such objects in the poem, such as the named swords (*Hrunting, Naegling*), Wealhthrow's necklace (lines 1192–1214) or the Heathobard weaponry (lines 2032–56).[41] Such weapons and

---

[38]   Fulk *et al. Klaeber's Beowulf*, pp. clxii ff. See also J. Niles, *Beowulf, Poem and Tradition* (Cambridge, MA: Harvard University Press, 1983), p. 564, for a discussion of the poem's own internal temporal complexities, which then mirror and augment its historicising substrata.

[39]   The term 'cultural residue' is borrowed from R. Williams, *Marxism and Literature* (Oxford: Oxford University Press, 1977), p. 122.

[40]   For broader treatments of Anglo-Saxon swords and the poem's use of them, see C. Brady, 'Weapons in *Beowulf*: An Analysis of the Nominal Compounds and an Evaluation of the Poet's Use of them', *Anglo-Saxon England* 8 (1979), 79–141; and H. R. Ellis Davidson, *The Sword in Anglo-Saxon England* (Woodbridge: Boydell Press, 1962).

[41]   These objects, among others, are the subject of a chapter-length study in a

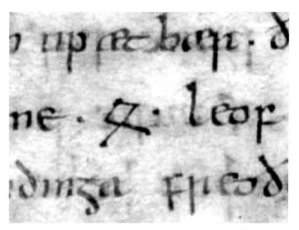

Figure 2: London, British Library, Cotton Vitellius A. xv, fol 141, l.18: use of the rune *eþel* in *Beowulf*. © British Library Board. All Rights Reserved.

Figure 3: Oxford, St. Johns College Library, MS 17, fol 5v (*ca.* 1110): detail of *runica manuscripta,* showing *eþel* for the rune ᛟ. Reproduced with permission: President and Fellows of Saint John Baptist College in the University of Oxford.

treasure do not seek to be texts; but they do perform communication additionally, as metonyms invested with a figure's identity or a
society's enculturating past through their exchange and ownership.[42]
These objects operate in an ill-defined space between recognised media
and material implements, reminiscent of Mattelart's communicational
configuration and Juliet Fleming's continuum of exteriority, in which
Hrothgar's hilt is only more likely to be recognised because it carries
with it the more familiar mode of written signification.[43] Writing
itself is absent in most of this material communication, but in the
Old English *noesis*, such alternative forms of communication closely
relate to the material, cutting acts of 'writing' (*writen, forwrat*) found
within the poem, and to the cultural performance of the poem's own
written text. Such mobile media parallel and help produce the essential 'wandering' nature of the poem's narrative that is so resistant to
traditional critical desire for structural unity,[44] and suggest that we need
new critical heuristics that recognise no functional difference between
linguistic and non-linguistic expressions of materiality.

Today the *de facto* medium through which the surviving Old English
version of *Beowulf* is understood remains the printed book, whether it
is a scholarly edition, a careful critical analysis, or a popular translation
or guide. The books of *Beowulf* have replaced weapons and treasure
as the centrally circulating objects of *Beowulf*, while the exteriority of
this modern medium (both in the sense of its formal logic and the fact
that books do not appear in *Beowulf*) has now become central to its
understanding. Books and the conventions of the modern, agglomer-
ating edition produce a new, yet curiously static, version of the poem
that continues to dilute the residue of earlier media, dismediating forms
of communication not viewed as historical precursor.

It is not widely known that the Old English text of *Beowulf* itself
contains runic characters (albeit not very many). Three times, in fact,
the first scribe of the poem uses the runic character ᛟ as a substitution
for *eþel* (Fig. 2), an Old English word for homeland (lines 520, 913,
1702). In his seminal edition Frederick Klaeber (and now Fulk *et al.*)
notes this fact in passing in his discussion of the poem's orthography,

planned book by Martin Foys on the nature of Anglo-Saxon media.
[42] Cf. S. Viswanathan, 'On the Melting of the Sword: *wæl-rápas* and the
Engraving on the Sword-Hilt in *Beowulf*', *Philological Quarterly* 58 (1979),
360–3; and Ellis Davidson, *Sword in Anglo-Saxon England*, pp. 211–12.
[43] See pp. 77–78 above.
[44] Overing, 'Swords and Signs', pp. 547–8; Frantzen, *Desire for Origins*, p. 175.

520 ðonon hē gesōhte   swæsne ēþel,
    lēof his lēodum,   lond Brondinga,
    freoðoburh fægere,   þǣr hē folc āhte,
    burh ond bēagas.   Bēot eal wið þē
    sunu Bēanstānes   sōðe gelǣste.
525 Ðonne wēne ic tō þē   wyrsan geþingea,
    ðēah þū heaðorǣsa   gehwǣr dohte,
    grimre gūðe,   gif þū Grendles dearst
    nihtlongne fyrst   nēan bīdan.'
    Bēowulf maþelode,   bearn Ecgþēowes:
530 'Hwæt, þū worn fela,   wine mīn Unferð,

505ª *MS.* ge/hedde ; *Holt.*¹ gehēde. *Cf. Siev. ZfdPh. xxi 357* ; *T.C.* § *16.* — 516ª *MS.* wylm ; *Tho.*, (*Ric. Zs. 387, 404,*) *Siev. R. 271, Schü., Cha.* wylm[e] ; *Mü. 131, Holt., Sed.* [þurh] w. w.; *Klu.* (*in Hold.*¹) wylm[um] ; *cp. Andr. 451 f.* — 519ª *MS.* heaporæmes ; *Munch Samlede Afhandlinger ii (1840–51) 371,* (*cf. E.tr.*), *Müll. ZfdA. xi 287, Holt., Schü., Sed.* Rēamas; *Gr.*¹, *Cha.* -Rēmas. *See Lang.* § *9.1* ; *T.C.* § *16.* — 520ᵇ *MS.* . ⚕ . (= ēþel). *So 913ª, 1702ª.* — 523ᵇ *Fol 142ª* beot. — 524ª *Bu.Zs. 108* (?), *Krüger Beitr. ix 573* Bānstānes; *Bu.Zs. 108* Bēahstānes (?). — 525ᵇ *Kr. ii* pinges (?) ; *Kie. Germ. ix 303, Ric. Zs. 389, Sed.* geþinges. — 530ᵇ *MS.* hun ferð. *See 499ª.*

Figure 4: replacement, without editorial formatting, of the rune ⚕ as 'eþel' (line 520, and note) in Fr. Klaeber's edited transcription of *Beowulf* (third edition, p. 20).

but for most scholars and teachers of the poem, it is likely forgotten as a curiosity of little or no consequence.[45] The use of ⚕ in *Beowulf* derives from the conventions of the *runica manuscripta*, where rune lists often came with corresponding word-names, likely used as mnemonic aids for the characters (Fig. 3).[46] In turn, runes at times replaced these words in Old English writing.[47] Their presence in the poem shows the first scribe of *Beowulf* also understood runes as functional and not yet wholly alien (though subscribing to a literary mode of signifying alterity quite different and reduced from runes' original materiality and operation).

[45] F. Klaeber, ed., *Beowulf and the Fight at Finnsburg*, 3rd edition (New York: D. C. Heath, 1950), p. xcvii.

[46] Page, *English Runes*, pp. 60–79.

[47] For a list of runes that occur in this mode in the Old English corpus, see D. Fleming, 'Eþel-weard: The First Scribe of the *Beowulf* MS', *Neuphilologische Mitteilungen* 105 (2004), 177–86, at p. 179, nn. 14–15.

In modern scholarship, these runes have been quietly redacted out of printed transcriptions and editions that serve as the new foundation of study and criticism. Klaeber's edition of the poem, as with many other editions, replaces each rune with the word 'eþel', with no brackets, italicisation or any other formatting usually employed to indicate these letters are not original to the text (Fig. 4). To discover a rune was used, readers must look (unprompted by the silent emendations in the central text) through the mass of textual annotations at the bottom of the page.[48]

One might argue that such substitution is trivial, and that what matters is not the container of the linguistic meaning, but the meaning itself. But media always have the capacity to contribute to the message. One of the times ᛟ occurs in the text comes within the very episode of Hrothgar examining the runic hilt. Immediately following his reading of the runes, Hrothgar turns to Beowulf (and everybody else in the hall) and proclaims (lines 1700–3):

> Þæt, la, mæg secgan,   se þe soð ᚾ riht
> fremeð on folce,   feor eal gemon,
> **eald** ·ᛟ· wea(rd),   þæt ðes eorl wære
> geboren betera.

> That, indeed, may say he who truth and right
> performs among the folk, remembers all from far-back,
> that **old homeland's** warden that this hero was
> born a better man.

The transcription above is modified from Kiernan's transcription, which retains the pointing originally around the rune ᛟ, but like all

---

[48] See, for example, the Old English text of G. Jack, ed., *Beowulf: A Student Edition* (Oxford: Clarendon, 1994), of H. D. Chickering, ed., *Beowulf: A Dual-Language Edition* (New York: Anchor Books, 1977) and of S. Heaney, trans., *Beowulf: A New Verse Translation* (New York: Norton, 2000). As editions, Chickering and Jack provide no note in the text to indicate the rune ever existed. Remarkably, the facing-page transcription of J. Zupitza, ed., *Beowulf Reproduced in Facsimile*, EETS, os 77, 2nd edition (Oxford: Oxford University Press, 1959) also replaces the rune with *eþel*, though italicises it to indicate emendation, but does not provide any other information for the emendation or the nature of the runic character ᛟ. A notable exception to this trend is E. V. K. Dobbie's Anglo-Saxon Poetic Records edition, *Beowulf and Judith* (New York: Columbia University Press, 1953), which retains the rune in the text. In his editorial notes (p. xxix), Dobbie groups the use of this rune in with roman character abbreviations used by the manuscript's two scribes.

modern editions silently rewrites it as *eþel*. But here, as elsewhere, the Old English text points the rune on the right and the left, as if at pains to distinguish it from the roman characters around it. Though set apart, the rune here links back to the runes of old, a graphologic bridge from the present to the past history of the poem and its matter. As Damian Fleming contends, the runes of *Beowulf* appear at precise moments that emphasise the ancient Germanic past.[49] In the scene of Hrothgar's hilt-reading, the Germanic ᛟ represents the *eald eþel* (the 'old homeland'); it is at once the record of an outmoded medium in vestigial form, and the active communication through this form of an imagined origin for the Anglo-Saxon community who produced and read it. We never see the runes on the hilt, of course; they are long gone. But the written rune surviving in the text routes through *Beowulf* the visible connections of Hrothgar's reading of the Germanic past to an immediate Anglo-Saxon sense of the historical past, in transit through *Beowulf*; in short, the rune tracks its own function from communication to record, from the runes no longer visible to those now (barely, today) on the page.

In an oral formulation or performance of *Beowulf*, of course, the rune's written form probably did not exist, so its presence here is an artefact of the poem's exteriority. Appropriately, the connection between the new and old runes of *Beowulf* was also not discovered by us through study of conventional printed editions of the poem, but through Grímur Jónsson Thorkelín's eighteenth-century handwritten transcription of the poem from London, British Library, Cotton Vitellius A.xv, which faithfully records its writing as a visual, not a logocentric phenomenon.[50] Thorkelín's transcript A was made before the *Beowulf* manuscript was seriously damaged in the Cotton Library fire of 1731, and we scanned through images of this transcription (available in the *Electronic Beowulf*) to check the evidence for modern textual emendations of the scene of Hrothgar's reading of the runic hilt. In the A transcript, as in the original manuscript, the image of the runic ᛟ stands out on the page, pointed, distinctive, and immediately noticeable among the Old English characters.[51]

[49] D. Fleming, '*Eþel*-weard'. See also I. Senra Silva, 'The Rune *eþel* and Scribal Writing Habits in the *Beowulf* Manuscript', *Neuphilologische Mitteilungen* 99 (1998), 241–7. Note that Silva's title itself elides the form of the rune.
[50] On early Anglo-Saxon scholars' liminal status between pre-modern and modern logics of textuality, see Foys, *Virtually Anglo-Saxon*, pp. 9–16.
[51] Kiernan, *Electronic Beowulf*: 'Thorkelin Transcript A', p. 51, line 2 (fol. 167r) and 'Manuscript', fol 167r, line 15.

One place we do not see runes, however, is on the cover of the recently published fourth edition of Klaeber's edition of *Beowulf* (2008), substantially and vitally updated by a new generation of editors, which prominently displays the Snartemo sword hilt.[52] While its gold-patterned 'disjected zoomorphic and anthropomorphic writings' are pretty to look at, the sixth-century Norwegian hilt contains no runes, and so the cover of the new edition of Klaeber references and absents the iconic and runic hilt that Hrothgar reads in the poem.[53] Such modern visual paratexts emphasise how central the materiality of objects continues to be for modern conceptions of what the textual poem is about, even if those conceptions differ drastically from Old English ones. In part this kind of the poem's graphic 'rewriting' derives from the process of print culture, one that has substantially influenced the way in which the visual and material within the poem now operate.[54] In his discussion of the effect of early print culture's enabling of scientific specificity through the innovation of mass-produced and precisely rendered images, Walter Ong notes that 'technical prints and technical verbalization reinforced and improved upon each other. The resulting hypervisualised noetic world was brand new'.[55] Ong's sense of the hypervisual conveys how print technology accommodates the modern production of hypervisualised texts from preprint and premodern, medieval expression unobsessed with such visual precision; one can follow, as Siân Echard has, the growth of illustrations in seventeenth-century volumes of antiquarian material as more and more representations of objects were sought to 'help create the picture of the Saxon past'.[56] But the Old English *Beowulf* is arguably more about the silence and space between the written than it is about a specificity of detail within it. The text on

[52] Reproduced also in *Beowulf: An Illustrated Edition*, p. 146.
[53] M. Swanton, *Beowulf* (Manchester: Manchester University Press, 1997), p. 199.
[54] This is not to argue here or elsewhere in the article for a pure brand of technological determinism. Rather, as Lisa Gitelman argues, while media are not intrinsically 'social and economic forces . . . [but] more properly the results of social and economic forces . . . at certain levels, media are very influential, and their material properties do (literally and figuratively) *matter*, determining some of he local conditions of communication amid the broader circulations that at once express and constitute social relations' (*Always Already New*, p. 10, emphasis original).
[55] W. J. Ong, *Orality and Literacy: The Technologizing of the Word* (London: Methuen, 1982), p. 126.
[56] S. Echard, *Printing the Middle Ages* (Philadelphia: University of Pennsylvania Press, 2007), p. 44.

Hrothgar's hilt, like the monstrous bodies of Grendel, his mother, and the dragon, is explicitly excluded from the text; it is not meant to be read by the audience, but only imagined. For modern readers, the status of the unknowable diminishes in face of the hypervisualised, while for modern scholarship, there is no point in trying to read a text that is not really there.[57]

Another modern book of *Beowulf*, the 'illustrated edition' of Seamus Heaney's best-selling translation of the poem, demonstrates the particular qualities of modern hypervisualisation found in modern media. For this award-winning translation, John Niles assembled one hundred images, one for each page of Heaney's text. Ironically, the images supplant the facing pages of the edited Old English text of the entire poem included in the original American publication of his translation. Niles, who possesses a deep and careful understanding of the poem, cultivated through decades of study, understands the stakes in such a project. As he explains in his afterword: 'the fundamental principle that has therefore guided the making of the present book is that *all individuals have the inalienable right to visualize the action of Beowulf in whatever manner they prefer*'.[58] Niles continues, in a passage worth quoting at length:

> The purpose of this illustrated edition of Seamus Heaney's translation of *Beowulf* is to enhance modern readers' experience of that poem – while not confining that experience in any way – by putting on display a gallery of images that have a meaningful relation to the objects and settings of which the poet speaks. The images are meant first and foremost for visual delight, so as to augment one's pleasure in reading the text . . . Of course, many of the poet's themes and scenes could not possibly be illustrated except through an artist's fantasy. No attempt has here been made, for example, to illustrate Grendel's mother because there is nothing like her in nature . . . Moreover, there are times when efforts to illustrate the text must fail because even the poet may not have known exactly what he was speaking about, given the archaic words that were an inherited part of his vocabulary . . . The images included here are meant to provide a visual counterpoint to the text, then, rather than to illustrate it in the usual sense. After a good deal of research and reflection, these particular images have been chosen from among a nearly infinite

---

[57] See also Frantzen, *Desire for Origins*, pp. 187–8.
[58] 'Afterword: Visualizing *Beowulf*', in *An Illustrated Edition*, pp. 213–48, at p. 214 (emphasis original).

number of possibilities. Any other person who compiled a similar picture gallery might come up with different results that would be equally valid.[59]

From one perspective, the (very well-chosen) images Niles includes of swords, jewellery, landscapes, engravings, reconstructions and manuscript pages do the reader a great service, rendering what may have been known to an early medieval audience, and what otherwise could only be very poorly imagined today. These images help fill in visual and mental gaps that would not have existed for earlier experiences of the poem.

Yet in spite of the affirmation of modern readers' rights of interpretative freedom, the images included in effect hypervisualise the Old English text in a very pointed manner. In a sense, the illustrated edition enacts Will Straw's argument that the power of modern media to accumulate and simultaneously present historical granularity also creates a backlog of the past within the present, slowing and muddying the historical sequence and, in effect, flattening historical nuance into a single, convergent and visible moment of the present.[60] In the illustrated edition of *Beowulf*, the media-assemblage of such pan-spatio-temporal material, from many geographic areas across hundreds of years in the medieval period and thousands of years to the present, at such specific levels of detail, is a representational phenomenon only possible in modern media. Graphically it recalls the temporal flattening of runic literacy by modern practices of media and criticism explored above, inverting the relationship of the unknowable between medieval and modern individuals, and translating the act of material knowing that would have been originally interior to a medieval audience into an act of exterior signification of materiality for the reader – one that 'fixes' the general knowledge of early medieval objects to explicit, static and contained images and the modes of interpretation they engender.[61]

While providing valuable referents for material objects described within the poem, the photographs of objects, like the *runica manuscripta* before them, circulate as part of the contemporary books of *Beowulf* that contain them, and mute earlier communicative qualities. For the past eight decades or so, students of Old English usually learned to translate *Beowulf* using Klaeber's edition of the poem, a book that has

---

[59] Ibid. p. 215.
[60] See p. 79 above.
[61] Overing, 'Swords and Signs', p. 556.

remained 'the' edition to use if one is studying *Beowulf* – most using his 1950 expansion and revision of the original 1922 work. This edition contains a precious passage. At the end of his introductory section on the poem's tone, style and metre, Klaeber writes:

> If a practical word of advice may be added for the benefit of the student, it is the obvious one, that in order to appreciate the poem fully, we must by all means read it aloud with due regard for scansion and expression. Nor should we be afraid of shouting at the proper time.[62]

Klaeber believes that an oral, dynamically so, production of the text is both essential and obvious to experience the poem as written. In the heavily revised and updated fourth edition of 2008, such performative advice has been redacted. In other places the new editors assess the 'verbal surface' and 'residual traces of orality' of the poem,[63] as well as the hoary oral-formulaic debate,[64] and their consensus is that 'the language of most of the verse represents a κοινή (Gk), a literary dialect . . . just as [early West Saxon] is now generally understood to be an artificial literary dialect'.[65] While still present, the aural qualities of *Beowulf* in the fourth edition of Klaeber have diminished from the third, continuing a subordination to the visually oriented medium of print, and attendant critical practices.[66]

The scholarly weighting of the written/literary quality of the poem over other material qualities is understandable, and for literary study, even necessary. Modern books of *Beowulf* have slowly silenced the auralities/oralities of preprint expression it now re-presents – the words to the modern user remain frozen and mute on the homogenised page – typeset, mechanical, a new kind of textual exteriority. Klaeber felt the need to remind the modern student that this poem needed to be voiced – that there was something more than what was read on the page. Doubtless the editors and many users of the fourth edition would

---

[62] Klaeber, *Beowulf*, p. lxxi. My thanks to Allen Frantzen, who introduced me to this passage in his own graduate seminar on *Beowulf*.

[63] Fulk *et al.*, *Klaeber's Beowulf*, p. cix and p. cxx.

[64] Ibid. p. cxiii.

[65] Ibid. p. cliv

[66] The scholarly notion that print is a visually obsessed medium that subjugates all other senses to it essentially begins with Marshall McLuhan's seminal argument and continues as a *leitmotif* through studies of print culture. See his arguments in *The Gutenberg Galaxy: The Making of Typographic Man* (Toronto: University of Toronto Press, 1988 [1962]), pp. 124–7 and pp. 159–61.

agree, but the fact remains that this scholarly update has left no explicit room for shouting the poem out loud as Klaeber encouraged. Funny, yes, but also telling – books of *Beowulf* shift its meaning further away from the earlier poetic forms of orality and handwritten grapholect – still somewhat organic forms – and the 'obvious' point Klaeber made becomes considerably less obvious.

The purpose of these books of *Beowulf* is to reaffirm the poem as literature and literature mostly – they continue Tolkien's famous and influential call to move the poem from a historical quarry to the literary summit – and use or absent other aspects of media in making this point.[67] Material culture can serve the poem (somewhat), but in between the covers, the re-presentations of the poem do not usually serve it. Books of *Beowulf* are predicated upon the preservation and recovery of the single surviving instance of the Old English poem – itself the only material artefact of this medieval expression. But the these books in turn also encourage a modern, isolating notion of the literature – one that, in part due to the physical limitations of their medium restricts its subject's convergence with other forms of media, past and present. In a sense, these books are incapable of effectively connecting to Will Straw's vision of media's new frontier for studies of the past as not only accumulating, but accommodating 'deeply sedimented and richly reso-nating clusters of objects'.[68]

Straw views electronic media as repositories of accretion which fail to realise their potential. But such failure occurs because new media still remediates the older logic and function of print media, which as we have already seen accumulate historical materials but flatten their resonance. Both print and new media exhibit a great capacity to collect, and the excitement about new media thus far has centred on simply an *increased* capacity to collect and index. Consequently, scholarly electronic resources to date largely lack the ability to create deep networks of meaning between the historical data they gather.[69] In regards to *Beowulf*, Kevin Kiernan's pioneering and award-winning *Electronic Beowulf*, first published in 2001 and upgraded in 2003, stands as a case in point, functioning more like a digital extension of the printed

[67] J. R. R. Tolkien, '*Beowulf*: The Monsters and the Critics', *Proceedings of the British Academy* 22 (1936), 245–95.
[68] Straw, 'Embedded Memories', p. 14.
[69] The same criticism, it must be noted, must be levelled at the co-author's own early digital resource, M. K. Foys, *The Bayeux Tapestry Digital Edition* (CD-ROM, Scholarly Digital Editions, 2003).

book than anything else. The boon of digital projects such as *Electronic Beowulf* is that they are able to marshal a stunning number of material resources surrounding their subject into readily accessible form. The edition contains high-resolution images of every manuscript page of the poem, and of the rest of Cotton Vitellius A.xv (thus providing a 'virtually' comprehensive manuscript context for the work), of Thorkelin's and other early transcriptions of the poem, and of copies of the 1815 first edition with early-nineteenth-century collations of the manuscript, in addition to a comprehensive glossarial index, a new edition and diplomatic transcript of the poem, and search facilities throughout. Images of individual folia of *Beowulf* are scalar, up to 300% magnification, and come provided with infra-red readings of damaged characters, as well as the ability to collate original gatherings of the manuscript by reconstructing sheets. One can arrange most of the resources for study and convenient comparison (though only two at a time).

As a resource for the study of the Old English poem, the *Electronic Beowulf* is a massive accomplishment, creating as it does the materials by which to assemble the literary *dispositif* of centuries of the surviving text's transmission and study. Still, the heuristic mechanisms of the edition remain resolutely anchored in the recovery of the single text, and nothing more. And even then, we find it furthering the mono-literate logic of its printed predecessors. In the digital texts of the transcription and edition of the poem contained within, the rune ᛟ has faded even further from current view, with no obvious (and little other) indication in the scholarly text that it ever existed. We only have in the glossary entry for *eðel* the note: 'runic .eðel. 141v18:519, 149v16:912'. In this entry, the indication of the character ᛟ is merely *a record of a rune*.[70]

Here the electronic medium falls in line and lockstep with the reductive media trajectory of oral to written to print.[71] The 'new' media may

---

[70] Doubtless this is because the 2001 edition was pre-Unicode in its digital typography. Further, the third incidence of the rune, in the scene of Hrothgar's runic hilt reading, has been omitted entirely from the glossary entry.

[71] For a more rigorous analysis and critique of the remediation and limit of *Electronic Beowulf*, see Christie, 'The Image of the Letter', pp. 142–8. Christie argues that 'In Anglo-Saxon writing the letter saves the past from oblivion, and in the Early Modern typographical remediation of Old English documents, the letter is represented as a material encryption of the past. The digital letter, like these predecessors, makes an impossible promise to provide unmediated access to the past.' In doing so, Christie both participates in the basic linear model of media and literary history, but sounds cautionary concerns about modern schol-

come after print, but currently stay on the same path of lazy linearity, reaching back towards the vanishing point of an originary chirographic text. Such resources provide a more powerful storehouse of visual materials, but promote pre-existing and proleptic heuristics of study that preserve only what they have already remade in their own 'image'.

De-coding Pepys's Diary

While *Beowulf*'s material history may be easily (if misleadingly) located on a simple line of orality to writing to print, the tachygraphic medium of Samuel Pepys's daily notebooks disappears long before they begin their new life as printed volumes. Written in a seventeenth-century form of shorthand over a nine-year period (1660–9), the manuscript was not transcribed, edited and published until 1825, and then in a severely bowdlerised form that retained only one quarter of the transcribed text and rewrote large portions. Since this original 'travesty' (as Robert Latham and William Matthews call it), the *Diary* has undergone multiple revisions, each claiming to rectify, while in fact often amplifying, the errors of previous editions.[72] In fact, an unbowdlerised critical edition was not available to scholars until 1970, when Latham and Matthews published the first volume of their transcription. This now standard scholarly edition – coupled with the fact that Pepys serendipitously began his *Diary* on the first day of 1660, a date increasingly (if artificially) viewed as the start of literary modernity[73] – has launched Pepys from a relatively obscure figure in British naval history to a member of the literary canon, anthologised and taught in the Norton and Longman surveys of English literature.

It is perhaps no surprise that Pepys's path into the canon aligns neatly with his path into print. Compared to the imposed coherence of the scholarly edition, Pepys's shorthand, like the runes of *Beowulf*,

arly exuberance for the idea 'that high-technology reproduction of manuscripts conflates photographic transparency with historical transparency' (142), and that such technology can help recover a pure(r) text of the medieval past.

[72] R. Latham and W. Matthews, eds., *The Diary of Samuel Pepys, 1660–1669*, vol. I (Berkeley: University of California Press, 1970), p. lxxix. Hereafter, *Diary* entries will be cited from the Latham and Matthews edition by date, volume and page numbers.

[73] On the artificially inflated importance of 1660 for literary history, see S. N. Zwicker, 'Is there such a thing as Restoration literature?', *The Huntington Library Quarterly* 69.3 (2006), 427–8.

seems esoteric and inaccessible – a secret code to be cracked, eluci-
dated, made legible – while the chirographic diversity present in the
manuscript seems a problem to be solved. Pepys's occasional longhand
only magnifies the illusion, since, in the words of his most recent
biographer, proper names not easily translated into shorthand 'lea[p]
out' from the manuscript like 'small packets of meaning surrounded
by the elegant, impenetrable shorthand'.[74] By effacing Pepys's handwritten tachygraphy, the printed book implicitly confirms what modern
readers, through our own ignorance of shorthand, suspect of the myste-
riously absent symbols; and a form of writing actually quite common
during Pepys's lifetime comes to serve as a metonym for the *Diary* itself,
ciphered and secretive.

Although long warned against, this perception of shorthand as
cryptic has nonetheless left a deep imprint on the critical literature.[75]
Consider Francis Barker's contentious reading of the *Diary*'s now notorious *L'escholle des Filles* incident, in which Pepys buys, reads, mastur-
bates to and then burns a book of erotica:

> We sang till almost night, and drank my good store of wine; and
> then they parted and I to my chamber, where I did read through
> L'escholle des Filles; a lewd book, but what doth me no wrong to
> read for information sake (but it did hazer my prick para stand all the
> while, and una vez to decharger); and after I had done it, I burned
> it, that it might not be among my books to shame; and so at night
> to supper and then to bed.[76]

Relying on Henry Wheatley's bowdlerised transcription that omits
the phrase 'it did hazer my prick para stand all the while, and una
vez to decharger', Barker believes that Pepys represses his sexual urges
during this scene – that he 'says sing when he means fuck, . . . enjoys
sex and calls it reading', but never succumbs to his desires.[77] In this
way, Wheatley's Victorian-era edition, extracted and anthologised in

---

[74] C. Tomalin, *Samuel Pepys: The Unequalled Self* (New York: Knopf, 2002), p.
80.
[75] As early as 1934, Matthews writes of scholars arguing that shorthand 'was
too popular in the seventeenth century to appeal to anybody as a secret cipher'.
See W. Matthews, 'Samuel Pepys, Tachygraphist', *Modern Language Review* 29.4
(October 1934), p. 397.
[76] 9 February 1668, IX, 59.
[77] F. Barker, *The Tremulous Private Body: Essays on Subjection* (New York:
Methuen, 1984), p. 9.

1957, shapes the contour of Barker's argument, pushing him to presume Pepys less sexually frank than the manuscript shows him to be. Once Barker adopts this interpretative approach, Pepys's use of shorthand serves as further proof of his bourgeois repression by seeming to displace his guilt onto ostensibly strange symbols that are 'ciphered and partly coded, hidden in secret and kept locked away'.[78] Thus the silences of the printed text force (and reinforce) a critical interpretation of the manuscript based largely on its absence, manufacturing the past from our present moment.

Barker has been censured for citing an outdated edition. As James Nielson puts it, the bowdlerised text 'severely jeopardize[s] the soundness of his reading for anyone who does not utterly scorn the factual':

> His very view of the strangely transparent, publicizable text of Pepys's private self (a view shared by most or all modern readers) is one based upon the already falsified accessible versions of his diary we have in print, including those of the impressive and self-conscious scholarly edition. Indeed, the accessibility and transparency of public personality which Barker attributes to Pepys's writing and its historical moment may in fact be more the effects of nineteenth- and twentieth-century editorial intervention than of Pepys's own situation in the history of subjectivity.[79]

Note that Nielson's complaint is not with Barker's interpretation of Pepys's masturbatory habits, but with his failure to choose and appropriately use a printed scholarly edition. In other words, whether or not Barker's claims are valid – and here we are inclined to agree with Aaron Kunin that 'several readings of this passage, including Barker's, are still possible, even when the text of the diary is expanded to include the sixteen additional words'[80] – his very use of a 'falsified' text vitiates

---

[78] Ibid., p. 6.
[79] J. Nielson, 'Reading between the Lines: Manuscript Personality and Gabriel Harvey's Drafts', *Studies in English Literature, 1500–1900* 33.1 (Winter 1993), 48. Turner takes Barker to task most relentlessly; see J. Turner, 'Pepys and the Private Parts of Monarchy', in G. MacLean, ed., *Culture and Society in the Stuart Restoration: Literature, Drama, History* (Cambridge: Cambridge University Press, 1995), pp. 96–7. See also H. Berger, 'The Pepys Show: Ghost-Writing and Documentary Desire in *The Diary*', *English Literary History* 65.3 (Fall 1998), 563–4. For a more balanced approach to and summary of the Barker debates, see A. Kunin, 'Other Hands in Pepys's Diary', *Modern Language Quarterly* 65.2 (June 2004), 195–219.
[80] Kunin, 'Other Hands', p. 200.

his interpretation. As James Turner concludes, 'his larger thesis thus collapses'.[81]

There is a certain danger in dismissing an entire thesis on the basis of the quality of the edition it cites, particularly since all printed transcriptions of Pepys's notebooks are by definition already radically remediated. While Latham and Matthews is no doubt superior to the Wheatley edition by contemporary standards, these standards – particularly those relating to textual integrity or appropriateness – change according to the values attached to scholarship and the printed book at any given time, as the preface to the much-maligned Wheatley edition itself shows:

> Although the Diary of Samuel Pepys has been in the hands of the public for nearly seventy years, it has not hitherto appeared in its entirety. In the original edition of 1825 scarcely half of the manuscript was printed. Lord Braybrooke added some passages as the various editions were published, but in the preface to his last edition he wrote: – 'there appeared indeed no necessity to amplify or in any way to alter the text of the Diary beyond the correction of a few verbal errors and corrupt passages hitherto overlooked' . . . [T]here was therefore a general feeling of gratification when it was announced some eighteen years ago that a new edition was to be published by the Rev. Mynors Bright, with the addition of new matter equal to a third of the whole. It was understood that at last the Diary was to appear in its entirety, but there was a passage in Mr. Bright's preface which suggested a doubt respecting the necessary completeness. He wrote: 'It would have been tedious to the reader if I had copied from the Diary the account of his daily work at the office'. As a matter of fact, Mr. Bright left roughly speaking about one-fifth of the whole Diary still unprinted[.][82]

With apparently no sense of irony, Wheatley then promises the public that *his* edition is complete – 'with the exception of a few passages which cannot possibly be printed'.[83] Here, print not only helps to elide determining characteristics of the original shorthand but motivates editorial decisions regarding what is appropriate for the medium,

---

[81] Turner, 'Pepys and the Private Parts', p. 96.

[82] H. B. Wheatley, *The Diary of Samuel Pepys* (New York: Croscup and Sterling, 1892), pp. v–vi.

[83] Ibid., p. vi. He continues: 'It may be thought by some that these omissions are due to an unnecessary squeamishness, but it is not really so, and readers are therefore asked to have faith in the judgment of the editor.'

thereby framing the critical discourse – a pattern not resolved by but
repeated in our dependence on Latham and Matthews. By rewriting the
Diary's varied and discontinuous editorial history as one of 'falsifiable'
evolutionary progress toward an ever more perfect text, we run the risk
of losing the very context we aim to restore, neglecting the cultural
and social embeddedness of *all* mediated literatures, even (and perhaps
particularly) those that present themselves as a definitive, corrective or
complete edition of an absent original.

In a final irony, most of Barker's critics – even those who, like
Nielson, carefully attend to the printed edition's abridgements –
are themselves guilty of omitting a footnote from the Latham and
Matthews transcription: 'garbled s[hort]h[and]'.[84] As the note explains,
the sixteen bowdlerised words used to 'correct' Barker's reading are not,
as assumed, written in legible longhand, but in a mixture of shorthand
and longhand laced with extra syllables, such that (for instance) the
word assumed to be 'prick' is actually written in a shorthand that could
be literally rendered 'primick'.[85] Although Latham and Matthews note
the apparently intentional garbling that occurs in the last two years of
Pepys's notebooks, the editors transcribe the words as they interpret
them without the extra syllables, thereby foreclosing the hermeneutic
possibilities inherent in Pepys's use of shorthand. Thus without a more
thorough explanation, images of the manuscript or, better yet, the
funds to travel to the Pepys Library at Magdalene College, Cambridge,
scholars are left to parse static, abstracted transcriptions, mere shells of
Pepys's playful, polysemic medium (Fig. 5). In fact, here we are relying
on Turner's authority, since unlike with *Beowulf*, high-quality facsimiles
of Pepys's manuscript simply *do not exist*.[86]

The lesson is not that printed editions are unreliable, but that *media
matters*. As we shall see, tachygraphy was not, as Barker supposes, arcane
or transgressive during the second half of the seventeenth century;
in fact, it was only one node in a dense network of graphologies (a
'communicational configuration', to return to Mattelart) that included

---

[84] Here, Turner is the exception.

[85] As Latham and Matthews point out in an earlier note, during the last two
years of the *Diary*, Pepys uses less shorthand and begins adding extra letters and
syllables to some shorthand passages. See Latham and Matthews, XIII, 245na.

[86] Turner, 'Pepys and the Private Parts', p. 97. Turner includes an image of
the manuscript page in question, but it is of low quality and it is difficult to
make out individual marks. Latham and Matthews also include several black-
and-white images of the manuscript, and The Pepys Library has made a low-
resolution digital scan of a single opening available online. See Fig. 5.

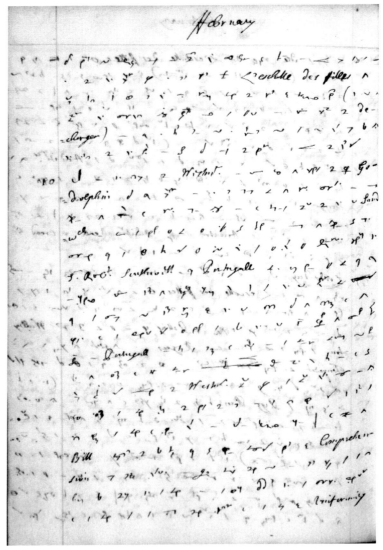

Figure 5: 9 February 1668 entry from Pepys's *Diary*, showing the notorious *L'escholle des Filles* passage. By permission of The Pepys Library, Magdalene College, Cambridge.

codes, ciphers, encryption technologies and universal languages, all used, mentioned or studied by Pepys throughout his *Diary*. Rather than emerging from a single convergent moment or motive, Pepys's shorthand circulated within a messy, energetic and highly visual writing culture that was actively questioning what it means to signify, communicate and record meaning. Understanding shorthand as a *medium*, then – as a historically situated writing practice that does not encode longhand but is itself text – not only challenges our printed caricature of Pepys but more broadly helps to excavate the layers of media forms that have accreted (and eroded) in the *Diary*'s journey from shorthand manuscript to longhand transcription and, eventually, printed book.

Understanding tachygraphy, or 'rapid writing', as a medium means understanding how it operates as a system of written signification. Pepys's form of shorthand is neither a cipher nor a code. By its very nature, the process of encryption – of feeding a string of characters through an algorithm (a cipher) or substituting it for another string (a code) – requires that the target message remain the same both before encoding and after decoding, with the simple substitution ciphers of the seventeenth century treating each letter as a discrete unit.[87] Pepys, however, employs an idiomatic version of Thomas Shelton's shorthand, a quasi-phonetic system that uses the positioning between consonant symbols to record vowel sounds. Shelton's shorthand does not rely on a one-to-one relationship between letters and symbols – to do so would make tachygraphy pointless – but instead uses a simplified mark to represent multiple consonant clusters. Unlike the largely mechanical processes of encryption, then, shorthand typically leans on context to resolve potential ambiguities between (for instance) 'bite' and 'bit', or 'bit' and 'bat'.[88] These ambiguities are infrequent but not insignificant, and are rarely marked as equivocal in any printed edition.

[87] Although substitution ciphers date back to Caesar's code and the *notae Tironianae* of Marcus Tullius Tiro in the first century BC, Johannes Trithemius's *Steganographia*, written at the end of the fifteenth century but not published until 1606, describes perhaps the most well-known early modern example. *Steganographia* was printed with nesting volvelles used to encode and decode messages. For a discussion of ciphers versus tachygraphy contemporaneous with Pepys, see for example J. Wilkins, *Mercury, or the secret and swift messenger* (London: J. Norton, 1641); T. Powell, *Humane industry, or, A history of most manual arts deducing the original, progress, and improvement of them* (London: H. Herringman, 1661), pp. 52–4.

[88] As Latham and Matthews point out, the only difference between 'bat' and 'bet' would be the position of the 't' next to the 'b'. For more examples, see

As Michael Mendle has shown, this form of rapid writing 'became in England something of a national craze' during Pepys's time, with hundreds of shorthand systems circulating.[89] During a visit to England in 1641, Comenius noted the 'large number of men and youths [who] copy out the sermons with their pens' using 'an art which has now come into vogue even among the country folk', while in the same year, John Wilkins described shorthand as 'now so ordinary in practice (it being usuall for any common Mechanick both to write and invent it) that I shall not need to set downe any particular example of it'.[90] Court proceedings, too, were transformed from ephemeral communications to public record by tachygraphy: in 1679 John Evelyn wrote of his reluctance 'to be often present at any *Capital Trials*, we having them commonly, so exactly published, by those who take them in short hand'.[91] Pepys himself frequently uses Shelton's system of shorthand (taught to all students at Cambridge University, where Pepys was a student) in his professional capacity as a naval administrator,[92] so much so that his superior Sir Coventry 'insists' upon a clerk who 'may write shorthand if it may be'.[93] Thus by the time Pepys began his *Diary* in 1660, tachygraphy in general and Shelton's system in particular was standard practice in England, thoroughly institutionalised in the government, the Church and the academy.

Shorthand had a private use as well, described by Shelton in his *A Tutor to Tachygraphy* (1642): 'sometimes a man may have occasion to write that which he would not have every one acquainted with, which being set downe in these Characters, hee may have them for

Latham and Matthews, Vol. I, li–liii. In his *A Tutor to Tachygraphy* (1642), of which Pepys owned a copy, Shelton admits that it may 'breed some confusion, to have one Character stand for two severall things', but explains that 'they may be differenced thus' because 'it is a part of a word, and is alwaies joyned with some other mark or letters'. See Shelton, *A tutor to tachygraphy* (London: S. Cartwright . . ., 1642), p. 25.

[89] M. Mendle, 'News and the Pamphlet Culture of Mid-Seventeenth Century England', in S. Baron and B. Dooley, eds., *The Politics of Information in Early Modern Europe* (New York: Routledge, 2001), p. 63; see esp. pp. 63–7.

[90] Wilkins, pp. 98–9; Comenius is quoted in J. Simon, *Education and Society in Tudor England* (Cambridge: Cambridge University Press, 1979), p. 385. See also L. Potter, *Secret Rites and Secret Writing: Royalist Literature, 1641–1660* (Cambridge: Cambridge University Press, 1989), p. 43.

[91] E. S. de Beer, ed., *The Diary of John Evelyn*, vol. IV (Oxford: Clarendon Press, 2000 [1955 1]), p. 175 (18 July 1679.).

[92] 17 Nov 1663, IV, p. 385; 8 Jun 1664, V, 174.

[93] 9 May 1667, XIII, 207.

his owne private use onely'.[94] Given our own illiteracy in early modern shorthand, it is tempting to interpret Shelton's 'private use' as a form of ciphering; yet, importantly, 'privacy' here implies only an individual and personal, as opposed to official or public, interest, with a suggestion of concealment but not necessarily seclusion or surreptitiousness – characteristics sometimes viewed with suspicion in seventeenth-century England.[95] For Shelton, then, a 'private use' was simply any writing done (as we might say) off the public record.[96]

Whether acting as a form of institutional transcription or a private script for personal correspondence, shorthand did not hinder or encrypt communication but rather facilitated it, helping to give rise to administrative and secretarial methods that lasted long into the twentieth century (including, as Mendle points out, those of news reporters).[97] In other words, shorthand does not merely cipher, condense or transliterate longhand writing but *is itself* a form of writing. As such, it carries particular affordances that motivate, shape and interact with the writing culture of a given historical period, as well as its own signifying force as a media form. For instance, in its public capacity shorthand captures the spontaneous moment of speech in writing, creating a record of otherwise transitory acts, and in doing so encourages a collaborative model of authorship in which the speaker and writer jointly construct a text. In this sense, shorthand acts as an intermediary between speech and its written record without ever becoming a fixed archive of either. Pepys himself uses shorthand in this way to dictate letters to his clerks,[98] as well as draft notes and letters that he later rewrites in longhand.[99]

---

[94] Shelton, *Tutor to Tachygraphy*, p. 1.

[95] 'privacy, n.', *Oxford English Dictionary*, 2nd ed., *OED Online*, http://www.oed.com; see also C. Jagodzinski, *Privacy and Print: Reading and Writing in Seventeenth-Century England* (Charlottesville: University of Virginia Press, 1999), pp. 2–4.

[96] Jagodzinski, *Privacy and Print*, p. 3. See also Turner, 'Pepys and the Private Parts', pp. 96–7; M. S. Dawson, 'Histories and Texts: Refiguring the Diary of Samuel Pepys', *The Historical Journal* 43.2 (June 2000), 419–20. The topic of privacy in early modern English has a rich and growing literature; see for example R. Chartier, ed., *Histoire de la vie privée: de l'Europe feudale à la renaissance* (Paris: Ed. du Seuil, 1999); C. Abate, ed., *Privacy, Domesticity and Women in Early Modern England* (Brookfield, VT: Ashgate Publishing, 2003); M. T. Crane, 'Illicit Privacy and Outdoor Spaces in Early Modern England', *Journal for Early Modern Cultural Studies* (Spring/Summer 2009), 4–22.

[97] See Mendle, 'News and the Pamphlet Culture', esp. pp. 63–5.

[98] 1 Jan 1666, VII, 1; 18 May 1667, VIII, 221.

[99] 17 Nov 1663, IV, 385; 8 Jun 1664, V, 174.

Yet the same rapidity that allows one to record speech as it occurs also allows writers to jot down their thoughts in an impulsive, non-deliberative manner, creating a (more) direct link between an individual's mind and the page. Thus even as the shorthand systems of the seventeenth century circulated within a communal, public culture of writing, they also encouraged the kind of solitary, silent textual production that would become the predominant form of literacy by the end of the eighteenth century; indeed, that would become the framework through which we read Pepys's *Diary* today.

From Pepys's staccato style to his vocabulary and phrasing, these features and affordances of tachygraphy pervade the *Diary*, producing textual ambiguities that are unavoidable and irreconcilable once transliterated into longhand. Although careful editors, such as Latham and Matthews, often note these inconsistencies, the printed critical edition as a medium pushes foreign literacies into footnotes, endnotes or, as we've seen with the Barker debates, completely off the page, constructing an illusion of stability around an inherently dynamic and variable text. In fact, this illusion is practically a prerequisite for canonisation: to be literature, the original form must disappear. The *Diary* must be translated from an abbreviated, quasi-oral form of written English into the longhand language of the translator, with punctuation and period-specific colloquialisms added for smooth reading. Thus the transcribed Pepys we read is always/already a modern Pepys, and an immortal Pepys – a man who speaks the dialect of our time, and who is only ever as old as his last transcription.

Although less discussed in the critical literature, the changing material circumstances of writing in the 1660s influences Pepys's text as much, if not more than, his use of shorthand. Until 1670, England produced no white paper, and government officials like Pepys had to negotiate for cheaper imports, as he records in his *Diary*.[100] By condensing writing to about one-third the length of longhand, shorthand and other logographic systems conserved paper; thus aside from questions of speed or secrecy – neither of which seems wholly responsible for Pepys's choice – it makes economic sense for Pepys to use shorthand in a daily diary. In fact, whether intentionally or not, Pepys carefully constrains his text

---

[100] P. Gaskell, *A New Introduction to Bibliography* (New Castle, DE: Oak Knoll Press, 1995), p. 60. Pepys writes on 15 July 1660: 'Captain Stoeks came to us and so I fell into discourse of buying paper at the best hand in my office, and the Captain promised me to buy it for me in France', I, 201.

to the boundaries of his material medium, wasting no marginal space and ending each entry neatly at the bottom of a page.[101]

Moreover, while the quill pen and inkhorn generally required a stationary location, modern tools such as erasable wax tablets, cleaner lead pencils and 'fountain inkhorns', self-contained metal tubes of ink, spurred the growth of writing as a more mobile and spontaneous activity.[102] Traces of these new practices are found throughout the *Diary*, when, for instance, Pepys receives his first fountain pen: 'This evening came a letter about business from Mr. Coventry, and with it a Silver pen he promised me, to carry inke in; which is very necessary';[103] or 'This day I begun to make use of the Silver pen (Mr. Coventry did give mee) in writing of this sermon, taking only the heads of it in Latin; which I shall I think continue to do'[104] – or when Mr Lovett gives Pepys a writing tablet:

---

[101] Latham and Matthews, I, xliv.

[102] While the fountain pen as we know it today did not come into widespread use until the nineteenth century, a self-contained 'silver pen' is found mentioned throughout the second half of the seventeenth century. Latham and Matthews point out that at the time Coventry gifts Pepys his implement, 'pens which carried their own ink had been made in Paris for some years' (IV, 264 n.1; see A.-P. Faugère, ed., *Journal du voyage de deux jeunes hollandaises à Paris en 1656–1658* (Paris, 1899), 11 July 1657). Other traces can be found: Hester Dorsey Richardson, in her obscure 1913 history of Maryland families, tells of finding an entry in the criminal records of the English local courts during the reign of Charles II that mentions the robbery of 'three silver fountain pens, worth 15 shillings' (*Side-lights on Maryland History*, vol. I (Baltimore: Williams and Wilkins Co., 1913), p. 216); in *A Journey to Paris* (1698), Martin Lister mentions a 'very curious . . . Writing Instrument of thick and strong Silver-Wire, wound up like a hollow bottom or screw' (p. 126); and by 1700, Roger North writes to his sister using a French-made metal pen (Augustus Jessopp, ed., *The Lives of the Norths*, vol. III (London: George Bell and Sons, 1890), p. 247). Unfortunately, these citations have yet to be collated into a comprehensive history of writing implements during the seventeenth and early eighteenth centuries. On Renaissance writing instruments, see R. Chartier, J. Franklin Mowery, P. Stallybrass and H. Wolfe, 'Hamlet's Tables and the Technologies of Writing in Renaissance England', *Shakespeare Quarterly* 55.4 (Winter 2004), 403–4; on material (and materially mobile) writing practices during the early modern period, see A. Blair, 'Reading Strategies for Coping with Information Overload ca.1550–1700', *Journal of the History of Ideas* 64.1 (2003), 11–28.

[103] 5 Aug 1663, IV, 263–4.

[104] 9 Aug 1663, IV, 268. Pepys's silver pen does not seem to have lasted him long; on 28 November 1665 he writes: 'there thinking of some business . . . by help of a candle at a Stall where some pavers were at work, I wrote a letter to

Lovett and his wife . . . have brought me some sheets of paper varnished on one side, which lies very white and smooth and, I think, will do our business most exactly, and will come up to the use that I intended them for, and I am apt to believe will be an invention that will take in the world. I have made up a little book of it to give Sir W. Coventry to-morrow, and am very well pleased with it.[105]

Presumably using these new writing implements, Pepys jotted down notes throughout the day on a folded leaf of foolscap using a hypermediate amalgam of shorthand, longhand and account tables, as we know from two periods later in the *Diary* when he pasted the loose leaves directly into his notebooks. Characteristic of Pepys, the notes show the same matter-of-fact mingling of public business and private philandering for which the *Diary* is known, as when on 10 April 1668 he kisses his bookseller's wife just before purchasing a book of saints:

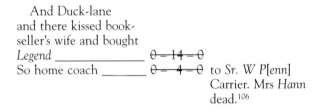

The numbers woven into his routines show his expenses – here, fourteen shillings for the *Legenda aurea* and four for a coach home. Most likely, he later transferred these to his account book, while the details of his day were copied to and expatiated in his daily journal or perhaps another by-book for drafting or other forms of recordkeeping.[107] As Mark Dawson points out, the *Diary* cross-references additional notebooks as well as 'other more specific records of sermons, personal transactions

Mr. Hater; and never knew so great an instance of the usefulness of carrying pen and ink and wax about one' (VI, 312).
[105]   9 Jul 1666, VII, 198.
[106]   10 Apr 1668, IX, 160–1. The transcription is Latham and Matthews'; italics represent words written in longhand.
[107]   On two occasions late in the *Diary*, one cited in part above, Pepys pasted notes directly into the journal, using pages left blank for the more complete entries. Latham and Matthews use these notes to argue that the *Diary* represents fair copy of earlier drafted editions which have not survived (Latham and Matthews, Vil. 1, xlv). See 10–19 Apr 1668, IX, 160–8; 5–17 Jun 1668, IX, 224–43.

and official dealings, table talk, and household expenditure which were also maintained by Pepys'[108] – all in some way the product of a material writing practice that transformed mundane, spontaneous communications into a personal archive with flexible time stamps.[109]

Pepys himself never referred to his manuscript as 'Diary', a term first used when the notebooks were printed. Rather than textualising any one representation of Restoration-era sexuality, writing or privacy, Pepys's daily notebooks link together multiple textual practices, both individual and collaborative. In short, they enact a moment of media in transition. Written two centuries after the printing press began to spread across Europe but nearly a century before social standards for print were codified in England, the *Diary* remixes private cryptography and public institutions, remediating a life lived in the flow of time as a quasi-phonetic transcription, then a fixed fair copy. Although Pepys, perhaps influenced by the printed books he loved to collect, bounds his monospaced shorthand symbols within the limits of the page, bits of longhand or paste-in notes continually take root, drawing Pepys's self-consciously bookish form back to the mobile, scribal practices from which it emerged. When read from a media-historical perspective, Pepys's negotiation between the spoken and the written, instantiated materially as shorthand, has less in common with the diary as a transhistorical literary genre of record (or even diaries of the same period, such as John Evelyn's, with which it is often paired) than it does with the dynamic Restoration-era account ledgers, commonplaces and journals of natural philosophers and physicians conducting experiments.

If our investigation into Pepys's material context, brief and incomplete as it is, underscores the relevance of shorthand to any literary analysis of his notebooks, it also hints at how far the printed *Diary* is from the manuscript it re- and dis-mediates. Indeed, as we have already seen with the books of *Beowulf* or the Barker debates, our own media ecology frames the 'deep time' of any literary artefact, often positioning the text's present form as its teleology. In the process, the communicational configuration of a text's material past is not only effaced, but reduced to a simple narrative of correction and refinement – a fact particularly evident in the *Diary*. To understand how Pepys's shorthand notebooks became canonical, then, we must step back to the

[108] Dawson, 'Histories and Texts', p. 415.
[109] On the relationship between time and Pepys's writing practice, see S. Sherman, *Telling Time: Clocks, Diaries, and English Diurnal Form, 1660–1785* (Chicago: University of Chicago Press, 1996).

published edition's beginning (or forward to the end of Pepys's short-hand, depending on your historical perspective), tracing the myths, some now deeply embedded in the critical literature, surrounding the *Diary*'s 'discovery'.

A *tale of publishing*

In 1819 (the tale goes) George Neville commissioned a nineteen-year-old John Smith – then a 'poor sizar', we are told, 'already cumbered with a wife and child'[110] – with the task of transcribing Pepys's note-books, recently found in Magdalene Library at Cambridge University. According to a series of letters published in the *Illustrated London News* in 1858, Neville's uncle supplied Smith with a key to Pepys's symbols and paid him £200 for the job, leaving the task of editing and finding a publisher to Lord Braybrooke, another Neville. In his reply of 1858, Smith mocked the gift, claiming to have worked twelve to fourteen hours a day for three years on a task 'very trying and injurious indeed to the visual organs', with the result (stated several times throughout his letters) that the *Diary* was 'brought into its *legible* state by my sole exertions'.[111] Smith's story – written forty years after the fact, and by a clearly bitter man – has been recited without question in most retell-ings, sometimes dressed with the comic (though not quite believable) twist that Smith never realised that Shelton's shorthand tutorial was sitting on a shelf in Pepys's library all along.[112] In another version, Smith finds Shelton's textbook but cannot crack the ciphers within the shorthand;[113] in yet another, Smith is himself a shorthand reporter.[114] In all versions, an impoverished but hard-working underclass hero accom-plishes an 'impossible' feat (as the stenographer William Brodie Smith told him at the time), bringing an 'impenetrable' secret to light, and to print.

Something has never fitted with this narrative: David Macpherson cites a passage from the *Diary* in his *History of the European Commerce*

---

[110] Latham and Matthews, I, lxxvi.
[111] J. Smith, letter to the editor, *Illustrated London News* (23 March 1858; 13 April 1858).
[112] Tomalin, *Unequalled Self*, p. 375.
[113] F. Pratt, *Secret and Urgent: The Story of Codes and Ciphers* (New York: Blue Ribbon Books, 1942), p. 151–3.
[114] D. Kahn, *The Codebreakers: the Story of Secret Writing* (New York: Scribner, 1996), p. 779.

with India, published in 1812, seven years *before* Smith began tran-scribing the manuscript. Latham and Matthews venture that some scholar was 'led to the passage', which records Pepys's first drink of tea, 'a China drink',[115] 'by the words "Cupp" and "Tee" in longhand'; but 'who he was remains a mystery'.[116] Yet how did she or he come across this passage, if the notebooks lay in secret until 1819? And how did she or he decipher it, if no one knew Pepys's shorthand prior to the mid-nineteenth century?

The September 1807 volume of the journal *The Literary Panorama* contains a clue. In it, editor Charles Taylor relates the following anec-dote:

> I have been favoured by Mr. Twining of the perusal of the poem written on Tea by Nahum Tate, referred to in one of the preceding notes. This book originally belonged to Dr. Lort, and on the blank leaf at the beginning, is an entry in the Doctor's handwriting, as follows: 'Mr. Samuel Pepys, in his manuscript diary, in the Pepysian Library at Cambridge, says, September 25, 1661, I sent for a Cup of Tea (a China drink) of which I had never drank before, and went away'.[117]

Michael Lort was a professor of Greek at Cambridge and a pre-eminent book collector well known in eighteenth-century literary society. He, along with Sir Lucas Pepys, Samuel Pepys's great-nephew, helped to edit Hester Lynch Piozzi's *Anecdotes of the late Samuel Johnson during the last twenty years of his life* (1786) and was also known to Sir William Weller Pepys, Lucas Pepys's brother and the subject of Alice Cecilia Caroline Gaussen's 1904 study, *A Later Pepys*. Within this published collection of W. W. Pepys's letters, Gaussen includes two 'specimens' found among his papers after he died in 1825 (coincidentally, the same year the first edition of Pepys's *Diary* was published): a sample transcrip-tion of several entries, including the 25 September 1660 entry on tea, and an estimate for the cost of printing the *Diary*. The estimate states that 'T. Cunningham offers to translate the M.S. at 2 per sheet, which is the price he has always received for <u>compiling</u>' (Fig. 6).[118]

115   25 September 1660, I, 253.
116   Latham and Matthews, I, lxxiv.
117   C. Taylor, ed., *The Literary Panorama* (1807), p. 569.
118   A. C. C. Gaussen, *A Later Pepys: The Correspondence of Sir William Weller Pepys, Bart., Master in Chancery 1758–1825*, Vol. 2 (London: John Lane, 1904), p. 52. Emphasis in original.

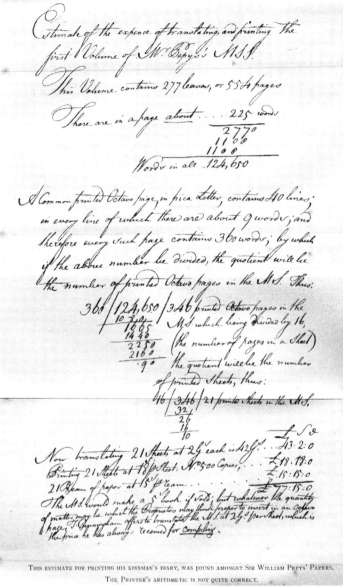

Figure 6: Evidence of a plan to publish Pepys's *Diary* that presumably predates the Braybrooke edition; found among the papers of William Weller Pepys and printed in A. C. C. Gaussen's *A later Pepys*, vol. 2 (London: John Lane, 1904), p. 52.

Although Gaussen's 'specimens' went largely unnoticed (and are now all but forgotten), she seems to have stumbled upon a plan to publish the *Diary* that predates Braybrooke's first edition, inadvertently confuting what would in the latter part of the twentieth century become the dominant history of Pepys's manuscript: namely, that it lay dusty and forgotten in Pepys's library until it was 'discovered' and then tragi-comically 'deciphered' by a struggling young husband and father who never knew the *Diary*'s 'key' was in the library the entire time. In fact, given that shorthand systems remained popular for more than a century after Pepys's death, and that Pepys's family continued to live among shorthand authors and diarists who published their personal papers (including Samuel Johnson, John Byrom and Hester Lynch Piozzi), it seems highly unlikely that Pepys's notebooks would *not* have been known prior to 1819. Only when shorthand systems (at least of the kind popular in the seventeenth and eighteenth centuries) cease being a popular writing medium do Pepys's symbols look secret; and only the singular publishing event of the printed edition demands a prior narrative of secrecy to legitimise (and capitalise on) its 'discovery'.

Thus in our increasingly complicated history of Pepys's notebooks, John Smith's transcription nullifies the manuscript; the Wheatley edition nullifies the first transcription; and the Latham and Matthews nullifies all before it. Each new edition presents itself as a radical rupture from its predecessors, so much so that the very notion of historical rupture underlies our experience of the *Diary* qua literature, justifying its place along the timeline of literary history. For if Pepys's first entry (1 January 1660) retroactively marks the beginning of literary modernity, the Latham and Matthews edition now represents the final correction of a text long travestied by bowdlerisation and backwards Victorian values – indeed, has become *the* text of Pepys's *Diary*. (While serious students of *Beowulf* learn Old English, and can now consult high-resolution images of the manuscript, no university offers seminars on Shelton's shorthand system, and no edition of the *Diary* is also a facsimile.) Yet, as we have seen through the Barker debates, Latham and Matthews may share more in common with the now disparaged earlier editions than Pepys's notebooks. Thus the experiences, stories, speech, notes and acts of reading that the *Diary* remediates, the print edition unmediates, funnelling the heterogeneous streams of literacies experienced and performed by Pepys into a homogenised, standardised and normalised text; that is, a set of words that float free of their medium, remote from matters of script, materiality or form. Excavating both the original layers of media and (sometimes more interestingly) the artificial stories that build up around them tells us much about not only Pepys's *Diary* as a historical artefact but also our own textual practices.

Mediating anew

New media have inevitably complicated our present ecology. With the coalescence of an (inter)discipline calling itself Digital Humanities, the print edition has loosened its grip over the academic study of texts and textual cultures, translating old documents into new spaces that challenge progressionist paradigms. Although we regrettably have no facsimile version of the *Diary* comparable to Kiernan's *Electronic Beowulf*, Pepys has been blogging since 1 January 2003, when British programmer Phil Gyford began to post each entry of the *Diary* in chronological order exactly 343 years after its original timestamp.[119] Each post allows readers to comment on (or 'annotate') the text and links to an encyclopedic database that tracks the people, places, events, even food and clothing mentioned in the *Diary*, with some readers contributing longer articles. Thus the unwieldy collection of footnotes, indices, annotations and cross-references accumulated in the eleven-volume Latham and Matthews edition has become an inter-operable database, allowing readers to search across a wide variety of Pepys-related materials.

Although Gyford is not himself a scholar of Pepys, his project quickly became a space for scholars, students, amateur historians and fans to reconsider the meaning and relevance of Pepys's *Diary* today, mingling historical insight with contemporary debates. In one representative entry for 22 December 1665, annotators pick over the phrase 'making up my Journall for 8 or 9 days' for clues as to Pepys's writing process; revisit the seventeenth-century definition of the word 'gloss(e)'; ponder the now lost tradition of the twelve days of Christmas; and, in response to Pepys calling Lord Brouncker's mistress a 'mad jade', argue the merits of the term 'arm candy' (can a feminist accept its use?). Quite a few comments light-heartedly banter with Pepys's writing ('Ah, Sam!', annotator Eric Walla writes; 'if only life were as neat and tidy as Lord Brunckner's watch!'), while one contributor in particular, Robert Gertz, annotates many entries with fan-fiction that rewrites the *Diary*

---

[119] P. Gyfird, ed., *Pepys' Diary*, http://www.pepysdiary.com.

in humorous dialogue. From a portion of Gertz's annotation on the same entry:

> 'Mr. Pepys, I have to tell you that yesterday Sir William Warren's man actually handed me a note which listed the prices we would be paying for his masts.'
> 'Really?'
> 'Indeed, sir. And further, the man winked at me and actually asked if I expected to do well out of the business.'
> 'He did?'
> 'Yes, sir.'
> 'And what did you do?'
> 'Well, sir, I told him this being the office of Mr. Samuel Pepys, Clerk of the Acts of the King's Navy we would stand for no such things here and gave him a bloody how-dee-do out the door, sir.'
> 'Did you?'
> 'Yes, sir. Should I have called for help, sir?'
> 'Oh, no . . . You did quite right. Hmmn . . . Yes . . . Uh, Poynter? Did the man . . . By any chance . . . Leave anything behind? Say a glove or a box? Perhaps a bag?'
> 'Actually, you mention it, sir, he did try to. But I told him to take it along with him and be off. I do suspect, sir, he sought to leave something behind, perhaps to incriminate the office, sir.'
> 'Right . . . Well, very good, Poynter.'[120]

Gertz's revisionary fan-fiction serves as a metonym for the blog's activity, highlighting the multiple levels at which users both serious and casual can engage the remediated text. Thus even as the digital medium invites fresh analysis of old texts, it encourages scholars and non-scholars alike to participate in creating and exchanging new meaning, constructing dynamic clusters of communication around a static record.

Yet it would be a mistake to tell the story of the blog as another tale of rupture and rediscovery, as if new media is bringing us closer to the original by dint of its accumulatory potential. While web-based digital media can easily and powerfully network a rich variety of widely dispersed resources – one can imagine entries linked to Pepys's account ledgers, his 'bye-book', maps or digitised versions of the texts he mentions – Gyford's blog culls together relatively little reference material, with Pepys's shorthand no less effaced than in the

---

[120] R. Gertz, annotation no. 7 on 'Friday 22 December 1665', *Pepys' Diary*, posted 23 December 2008, http://www.pepysdiary.com.

Diary's printed edition. Battered between institutional forces, including but certainly not limited to copyright law and the significant cost of digitising fragile notebooks, the online Pepys actually highlights how difficult it is for hypertext to fulfil the hype for an infinitely expansive docuverse. Contrary to what Matthew Kirschenbaum dubs our 'medial ideology', which sees digital texts as pure 'light, reason, and energy unleashed in the electric empyrean',[121] online editions often clunkily re- and dis-mediate texts as much as, and in some cases more than, a corresponding print edition. For Pepys's *Diary*, the blog's source text is none other than a Project Gutenberg text file of Wheatley's 1893 edition – the same 'twice-bowdlerized' text that led Barker to misread the *L'escholle des Filles* incident. While the openness of the blog format allows vigilant scholars to correct errors and annotate entries with bowdlerised passages, as often happens, a new generation of students and fans is becoming familiar with Pepys solely through a discredited edition over a century old. In other words, to return to Straw's argument, even as new media provide greater access to a wider variety of historical materials, the build-up of residual texts in repositories like Project Gutenberg allows discredited information to reassert itself with much less transparency than in the printed book; indeed, restrictive copyright laws encourage the use of outdated materials online.[122]

On the one hand, then, the hybridity of the online space reflects the overlapping literacies of Pepys's *Diary*, providing a model for thinking of Pepys's *Diary* not as a coherent history, as in its printed edition, but as one star in a constellation of written records. Thus, like *Electronic Beowulf*, the blog can spark new readings of the primary text, its historical context and its relationship to Pepys's entire library and corpus. Yet by drawing on and even decontextualising the discredited Wheatley edition – and a stripped down version at that – the blog gives new authority to old transcription errors without reinstating the long-elided tachygraphic transliteracies of Pepys's notebooks. Thus like its print precursors, Pepys's new remediation is not a true restoration but a translation, expunging obsolete textual practices even as it deposits new forms not yet fully understood.

[121] M. Kirschenbaum, *Mechanisms: New Media and the Forensic Imagination* (Cambridge, MA: MIT Press, 2008), p. 39.
[122] See above, p. 116.

Coda

What remains wanting in new media technology and new(er) media textual studies is a historical and cultural dimensionality addressing the transliteracies and silenced media that came before – a *dispositif* of practice, materiality, media, and time that enables networking beyond the indexical heuristics that dematerialise its past in the establishment and propagation of literary study. In his study of video game media and narratology, Henry Jenkins suggests that perhaps stories need to be understood less as temporal and linear structures, and more as bodies of information. For Jenkins, a video game for a film series 'exists in dialogue with the films, conveying new narrative experiences through its creative manipulation of environmental details. One can imagine games taking their place within a larger narrative system with story information'.[123] Jenkins's transmedial vision/version of narratives outside texts again echoes Will Straw's call to reconfigure new media's accumulatory potential. Critical awareness of media and their histories help emphasise how the relation of objects and texts (circulating as objects of communication themselves, as books or otherwise) *both* inside and outside texts has become more and more significant for interpretation; in short, what in relation to *Beowulf* Overing defines as 'words, things, and the space between'.[124] A lot more is happening in the space between words and things than current scholarship and media (print or its remediating electronic scions) are thus capable of accommodating or envisioning. Perhaps we need to stop thinking in terms of this *Beowulf* or that *Beowulf*, or this or that material redaction of Pepys's *Diary*, and more in terms of such larger narrative systems – call them *Beowulf+* and Pepys's *Diary+*. The circulating objects of *Beowulf+* or Pepys's *Diary+*, from runic hilts and tachygraphic notes to transcriptions and printed critical editions, by their nature remain both metaphors of textuality and metonyms of extra-textual, extra-temporal sign systems that defy reductive, linear progressions of both literary study and media history.

Such movement itself is both metaphoric and metonymic of the circulation that occurs in this *deep time* of media, not only in past media ecologies of these works of now canonical literature, but also among the constellation of their present and future synchronisms as well. As

---

[123] H. Jenkins, 'Game Design as Narrative Architecture', in *First Person: New Media as Story, Performance, and Game* (Cambridge, MA: MIT Press, 2004), pp. 118–30, at p. 124.
[124] Overing, 'Swords and Signs', p. 555.

with the Old English *Beowulf*'s liminal relationship to runic expression, or with the strange kinship between Pepys's blog, his tachygraphic notebooks, and editions of his *Diary*, the literary forms emerging from the latest media are already looking back to what is fading into obsolescence, and forward to what mechanisms of expression the new technology will foster. Expressions of the past and the media that generate them are always in a transition of some sort. Our critical capacity must do more than acknowledge this fact; it must keep pace with it.

Descriptive Bibliography
and Electronic Publication[1]

DAVID L. GANTS

AS PART OF A SESSION at the 1977 Annual Meeting of the Association
of American University Presses, five scholarly publishers prepared business plans for an imagined work entitled *No Time for Houseplants*, by
Purvis Mulch. The University Presses at Chicago, MIT, North Carolina, Texas and Toronto each presented detailed procedures for the
acquisition, editing, design, production and marketing of this made-up
book. Published as *One Book / Five Ways* a year later, the results of the
experiment illustrate how the physical embodiment of a single verbal
text can display quite different stylistic and bibliographical characteristics. Each press brought to the experiment a wealth of expertise
based on decades of successful publishing. The University of Chicago
Press, founded in 1891, had the longest track record of the group, while
the University of Texas, created in 1950, was the relative newcomer.
Considered together, the exercise provides an opportunity, as Joyce
Kachergis observes, to 'see the differences and similarities between
equally valid and startlingly different solutions'.[2]

Recent scholarship on the history of printing and publishing, and
the concurrent growth of interest in material culture, especially the
impact of books on society, all underscore the integral part played by
physical characteristics in our perception of a text. The MIT edition of
No Time for Houseplants would be a fundamentally different work from
one issued by Texas or Toronto. Furthermore, had the participating
presses taken the experiment to the next step and actually published
No Time for Houseplants, the editorial processes in each establishment
would have necessarily generated textually distinct editions: individual
editors have different ideas on how to make problem passages clearer;
house styles dictating form vary from press to press; punctuation and

---

[1]   An earlier version of this essay was presented at the 2007 Modern Language
Association Meeting in Chicago as part of a panel on Editing and Interpreting
in the Digital Age.
[2]   *One Book/Five Ways: The Publishing Procedures of Five University Presses* (Los
Altos: William Kaufmann, 1978), 'Foreword'.

spelling conventions change when crossing the Atlantic or the US–Canada border; even the book's title would be subject to revision.[3]

Books, as material manifestations of and durable witnesses to, verbal texts, make available to the scholar a dizzying array of complex systems of meaning. Yet any research that considers these systems of meaning must depend first and foremost on physical evidence that is at times confusing and contradictory. In the English-speaking realms, making sense of books and book forms has been a focus of scholarly concern for nearly 300 years. G. Thomas Tanselle notes that in 1715, the British clergyman Thomas Bennet 'used typographical evidence (such as the spacing and damage of types) to order several sixteenth-century editions (the variously titled 1571 editions of the "thirty-nine articles of religion")'.[4] Early editors of Shakespeare often relied on the circumstances surrounding the first printings of his works when fashioning a new edition. Codifying the disciplines that would become descriptive and analytical bibliography began in earnest in the 1860s with the work of Henry Bradshaw, librarian of Cambridge University. Tanselle outlines the achievements of Bradshaw:

> His approach to books and manuscripts was founded on a study of their physical structure, of the way sheets had been folded to form the conjugate leaves that made up the sewn gatherings in them; he explored the relation of this structure to the texts on the pages thus formed, and in the early 1860s he developed a collation formula to express concisely the number of conjugate leaves in each gathering of a book and the number of sheets (or part-sheets) required to make up those leaves . . . . He also demonstrated that one could classify incunabula as to source and date by examining the characteristics of the typography in them, not only the types themselves but also the peculiarities in their deployment, and in this activity he foreshadowed some of the compositorial studies of later analytical bibliographers.[5]

---

[3] In a letter to the author dated 16 December 1976, Gwen Duffey of the University of North Carolina Press proposed an emendation to the title. 'At a recent staff meeting', she writes, 'it was suggested that the present title of your book is somewhat negative in tone. Our sales manager suggested that the addition of a question mark would give it more appeal . . . How does <u>No Time for Houseplants?</u> strike you?' (*One Book*, p. 159).

[4] G. Thomas Tanselle, 'A Description of Descriptive Bibliography', *Studies in Bibliography* 45 (1992), p. 9.

[5] Tanselle, 'Description', p. 10.

Later scholars like A. W. Pollard, R. B. McKerrow, W. W. Greg and Fredson Bowers continued to develop the bibliographical disciplines, in the process illuminating 'the connection between the physical and intellectual aspects of books'.[6] Thanks to the work of these and other students of print culture, descriptive and analytical bibliography now provide a fully formed system for investigating the book as a material object.

However, the transmission of verbal texts no longer takes place solely in the press rooms of publishing houses. With the widespread adoption of networked digital technologies has come a new order of textual creation and reproduction. A reader can now encounter a work through a number of electronically mediated forms: word processor, Web page, mobile phone, e-book reader, even aurally through a text-to-speech translator. Each new form creates its own unique set of interpretative signals, much in the same way the five presses developed distinct editions of *No Time for Houseplants* from the same raw materials. New types of evidence require new approaches to their description and analysis as well as new methods of research into the meanings they create. This is not to say we must begin from a fresh set of first principles to generate a completely independent discipline; the history of intellectual inquiry is littered with warnings about the dangers of competing standards and incompatible technologies. Rather, any initiative that seeks to understand the expansion of texts into the digital domain should build upon the existing methodologies designed for the study of physical books.

How useful such methodologies will prove depends upon where the object of inquiry lies on the broad continuum of electronic forms. Matt Kirschenbaum is currently pursuing research into the editorial implications of 'born-digital objects', that is, texts created in an electronic domain with no physical precursors.[7] Writers now compose with a word processor, leaving few if any physical witnesses to their imaginative labours, and video games are built exclusively in a computer environment. Focusing on digital and media art, Richard Rinehart is

---

[6] Ibid., p. 11.

[7] See in particular 'Editing the Interface: Textual Studies and First Generation Electronic Objects', *TEXT* 14 (2002), pp. 15–51; and *Mechanisms: New Media and the Forensic Imagination* (Cambridge: MIT Press, 2008). Kirschenbaum is also heading an NEH-funded project at the University of Maryland, whose goal is to develop procedures for archiving born-digital literary materials.

exploring the challenges surrounding the preservation and documentation of digital works of art. Like word-processed fiction or an Xbox
first-person shooter, new media constructions leave no corporeal traces.
When dealing with objects such as these, with materials that have no
real analogues in the printing and publishing of books, the tools of the
bibliographer provide few applicable models.

The physical–digital event horizon

Computer-based works with a closer relationship to traditional
publishing offer greater possibilities for intellectual cross-fertilisation,
and that is the subject of this essay. Electronic editions have emerged
only recently as an attractive commercial proposition, but their roots
extend back to the early days of post-war computing. The first efforts
to create electronic texts centred on the compilation of word lists and
research collections, such as the concordance to the works of Thomas
Aquinas begun in 1949 by Fr Roberto Busa. This was followed by
national corpus initiatives such as the *Brown Corpus of Standard American English* and the *Lancaster–Oslo/Bergen Corpus of British English*, both
released in 1961. Lou Burnard founded the Oxford Text Archive in
1976 with the aim of collecting full-text works for scholarly research.
The bulk of the materials deposited with the Archive were simple texts
keyboarded from print sources with little or no structural or semantic
mark-up, which served the needs of literary and linguistic scholars but
not casual readers. A more fully realised digital tool emerged in 1992
when the Oxford University Press released the second edition of its
Oxford English Dictionary on CD-ROM. All of these resources were
digital, but they derived directly from existing print materials and thus
retained many of the organisational, rhetorical and aesthetic characteristics of their physical ancestors.

   The development of sophisticated mark-up and display systems,
along with the commercialisation of the World Wide Web, has
prompted serious work into the possibilities of complex electronic
editions. While fully formed examples are as yet rare, the editorial and
humanities computing communities have laboured for over a decade to
generate guidelines for scholars embarking on digital enterprises. Peter
Shillingsburg distributed his 'General Principles for Electronic Scholarly Editions' at the 1993 MLA convention in Toronto. Four years later
the Committee on Scholarly Editions folded those insights into the first

instantiation of its 'Guidelines for Editors of Scholarly Editions', the latest revision of which was published in the autumn of 2007.[8]

Efforts by the CSE and others have gone a long way to help ensure that the intellectual standards underpinning computer-based works will match those of earlier codex editions. However, they do not address the deeper mistrust of digital materials held by many, a suspicion rooted in the fear that electronic files are inherently unstable and unreliable. Because of the relative ease with which texts can now be altered and the seeming lack of evidence left behind when such changes occur, we feel we must view any electronic text with native scepticism.

Tanselle addressed this view in his 2001 article, 'Thoughts on the Authenticity of Electronic Texts'. In it, he points out that the generation of text on the page or the screen involves 'a two-stage process: the forme of type, the negative for a photolithographic plate, the pasted-up document, and the electronic file are not what one finally reads, but rather intermediate objects from which the objects to be read are derived'.[9] Conscious changes can occur at either end of the printing process: at the source, where they are for all intents and purposes invisible; and in the output, where altering the text often generates evidence of tampering. Concern over authenticity usually arises when we mix the two stages, when we compare 'the ease of altering an electronic file with the difficulty of altering a text that has been printed on a piece of paper. But the relevant comparison would be with switching pieces of type in a forme, altering a photographic negative, or pasting new words or passages over or between others for xerography, not with the attempt to change the text inked onto a piece of paper.'[10]

Thus any attempt to establish the veracity of an electronic resource must focus on authenticating the source files, in much the same way that traditional editors collate multiple copies of books to uncover changes to the original formes of type or stereotyped plates. And just as traditional editors rely upon insights into the physical properties of the codex structure provided by descriptive bibliographies, users of digital editions can apply many of the same bibliographical principles to interrogate the accuracy and reliability of the materials on their screen or print-outs.

---

[8]   Committee on Scholarly Editions, 'Guidelines for Editors of Scholarly Editions', http://www.mla.org/cse_guidelines.
[9]   Tanselle, 'Thoughts' *Studies in Bibliography* 54 (2001), pp. 133–4.
[10]   Ibid., p. 134.

This is not to say that authentication is the only goal of descriptive work. In his landmark *Principles of Descriptive Bibliography*, Fredson Bowers summed up its basic function as to 'present all the evidence about a book which can be determined by analytical bibliography applied to a material object'.[11] The results can then be used for a variety of scholarly purposes across many fields. In characteristically incisive fashion, Bowers ends his discourse on the discipline by asserting, 'A true bibliography is primarily an analytical bibliography'.[12]

The scholar describing and analysing a physical book has at hand an embarrassment of evidentiary riches: careful examination of paper, type, binding, illustration and other corporeal phenomena can provide significant forensic data; tools such as optical collators, digital microscopes, beta radiography and even the lowly ruler allow us to uncover information almost invisible to the unaided eye; and an array of primary and secondary documentary collections help us put our evidence in context. A descriptive bibliography of an electronic edition must exploit the same classes of data, tools and resources. The challenge, then, is to find the digital equivalent of paper, type, collators and documentation.

First descriptive principles

A little over a decade ago, John Lavagnino delivered a paper entitled 'The Analytical Bibliography of Electronic Texts' at an annual conference of computing humanists. In it, he pointed out that like their physical analogues, digital files do retain traces of their origins, their transmission and their transformation, although those able to discern such traces are 'more likely to be found in your university's computer center than in any academic department'.[13] An informed examination of an electronic text's container and internal conventions reveals a significant amount of information about its life. An 8-inch, 5.25-inch, or 3.5-inch disk each falls within a specific time frame and set of manufacturing constraints – for example, Macintosh computers never had 8- or 5.25-inch drives. Operating systems often differ in the digital

---

[11] Fredson Bowers, *Principles of Descriptive Bibliography* (Princeton: Princeton University Press, 1949), p. 34.
[12] Ibid., p. 34.
[13] John Lavagnino, 'The Analytical Bibliography of Electronic Texts', *ALLC-ACH '96 Conference Abstracts* (Bergen: Norwegian Computing Centre for the Humanities, 1996), p. 180.

codes used to represent formatting characters such as spaces, line feeds and hard returns. They also employ different file naming rules based upon system needs: older MS-DOS files had to observe the eight-dot-three convention,[14] while UNIX-based protocols discouraged the use of spaces in file names. When an electronic file moves from system to system or application to application, incomplete or inaccurate translation of platform-specific phenomena such as soft hyphens or line breaks occurs. And most of us have encountered the problems arising from the often conflicting encoding schemes employed by the various popular word-processing packages. The difficulty older systems have reading Microsoft's latest Office Suite XML-based format is only one in a long line of technological mismatches.

The core elements of a descriptive bibliography, as codified and elaborated by scholars such as Bowers and Tanselle, help scholars collect and present in an organised fashion specific aspects of a book in order to aid identification and support analysis. Each section of a description asks certain carefully constructed questions of an object, and the larger intellectual impetus behind those questions can serve as a model for a bibliographical examination of electronic materials. Using the table of contents to Bowers's *Principles*, we can tease out the bookish issues raised to determine how they might illuminate similar digital problems.[15]

State, issue, and edition.[16] Different copies of the same book can vary among themselves in many ways. Leaves can be added, deleted or replaced, sections of type can be reset, copies can be printed but held back for later issue, and the same setting of type or Linotype slugs can be stored and used for subsequent impressions at later dates. Such variation is not solely a phenomenon of the hand-press period, however. After an initial print run, contemporary publishers are often forced to emend errors that slipped past during the editing phase by correcting the plate or photographic negative.[17] Differentiating among distinct

---

[14] Because of early design constraints, a file name could consist of no more than eight characters, followed by a dot (or full stop), followed by no more than three characters. For example, 'filename.doc' would conform to these rules.

[15] Bowers, *Principles*, pp. xiii–xvii.

[16] Ibid., pp. xiii–xiv.

[17] For a classic piece of scholarship detailing modern press variants, see Matthew J. Bruccoli, 'Textual Variants in Sinclair Lewis's Babbitt', *Studies in Bibliography* 11 (1958), pp. 263–8. Of course, such variation is not limited to works printed from metal type. For an example of press variation occurring in a book printed from photographic negatives, see Jerome J. McGann's *A*

physical versions is crucial to understanding a book's printing history. Likewise, large Web-based editorial and archival projects usually publish materials in stages rather than in a single release, a reflection of the administrative and financial constraints under which they work. Scholars need to know the stages of an electronic project and how the contents changed from one release to the next.

Title page.[18] A book reveals important information about itself on its title page, not just author and publisher identification but larger aesthetic and cultural announcements as well. So too does an electronic edition prepare readers for what they will encounter within via a front page or portal.

Format.[19] In hand-press books, format describes the relationship of the sheet to the leaf, that is, how many times were the sheets that make up a book's gatherings folded (a folio sheet is folded once to produce two leaves, a quarto sheet folded twice to produce four leaves, etc.). Describing the format of a modern book is a little trickier since what constitutes a sheet when using machine-made paper can be difficult to determine.[20] Nevertheless, the crucial question here concerns the structure of the book-machine onto which the text is impressed. The structure of the digital machine through which one apprehends data and the media on which information resides is perhaps the most important information a scholar requires, for they dictate the circumstances under which an electronic edition may be used and raise important issues of preservation.

Collation formula.[21] This element is an abstracted symbolic representation that describes how the gatherings of leaves that make up a book are named, collected, and ordered. For example, a four-gathering quarto with the gatherings identified (or 'signed') A, B, C, and D respectively would have this collation formula: $A–D^4$. A–D is a compression of the sequence A-B-C-D and the superscript '4' indicates each gathering contains four leaves. This formula is similar to representations

Critique of Modern Textual Criticism. The original 1983 University of Chicago Press hardback edition varies in many places from the corrected 1985 paperback impression (see lines 18–28 on p. 30 and line 31 on p. 38). Adding to the confusion, the 1992 University of Virginia Press edition, which was printed from the original Chicago negatives, reinstates the initial uncorrected readings.

[18] Bowers, *Principles*, p. xiv.
[19] Ibid., p. xv.
[20] See G. Thomas Tanselle, 'The Concept of Format', *Studies in Bibliography* 53 (2000), pp. 67–116, for a discussion of the issues involved.
[21] Bowers, *Principles*, p. xv.

of directory structures containing data on a server hard drive. Because functioning hyperlinks in an electronic edition depend upon accurate location names of files, a map of its directories is essential both to a developer and to a scholar seeking to understand its nexus of materials.

Statement of signing.[22] Related to the collation formula, the statement of signing details how the gatherings are identified. For example, the first leaf of each gathering might be signed ('$1 signed') or the first and fifth ('$1, 5 signed', typical of nineteenth-century American duodecimos). Computer files, the gatherings in an electronic text if you will, also follow specific naming conventions. Knowing the scheme a developer followed when naming files alerts a scholar to possible changes signalled by non-standard or conflicting directory and file designations.

Pagination.[23] Printers and publishers number pages for readers (but they sign gatherings for the binder). Citing page numbers is common to nearly all activities involving texts, from book reviews to scholarly articles. This allows others to track down references to check for accuracy or context, or just to investigate a text for their own enjoyment. One should also be able to cite electronic texts for the same reasons.

Bowers goes on to examine many other descriptive elements, from headlines and direction lines to typography and paper. These sections are either too print-specific to apply to digital works or reiterate matters already explored in one of the components just discussed. Taking these six core items as a starting point, then, we can begin to build a set of descriptive questions for digital works.

Digital descriptive principles

Media. How are data in the edition physically embodied? Is it on a static storage device such as a floppy disk, CD or DVD? Is it on a dynamic external storage device such as stand-alone hard drive or thumb drive? Is it on a networked server? If so, what is the machine's architecture and operating system? Just as a text must conform to the physical limits of the codex – page dimensions, margins, binding requirements – so too must an electronic text conform to the strictures of the media on which it is encoded. An accurate description of media enables both

---

22 Ibid., p. xv.
23 Ibid., p. xv.

authentication and analysis (recall Lavagnino's observation about the forensic traces of creation left at the machine level).

Delivery applications. Does the file come with its own self-contained software? Does the file rely on large public network protocols such as the World Wide Web? If so, are there intermediary applications translating data for display on the Web (e.g. database search-and-display routines or HTML stylesheets)? Does the file employ commercially available, stand-alone software? On what operating systems do these applications run? A book is a delivery application, taking information encoded on formes of type or photolithographic plates and presenting it to the reader in an intelligible fashion. The mechanisms through which digital information is made intelligible serve the same purpose and reveal a great deal about the interpretative intentions of author and publisher.

Data forms. Is the information stored as a text-based file? Is the information contained within a database? Is it compiled in binary form? A Blake poem printed from one of his engraved plates functions differently at the perceptual level from a plain-text poem often found in anthologies, in part because they are contained in different forms. The experience of electronic information shifts as the form shifts, from plain text to encoded text to digital image to database inquiry result.

Data types. How is the textual information encoded? ASCII?[24] If so, what level? What other data types are there and what encoding schemes are used? JPEG,[25] TIFF,[26] MP3,[27] F4V?[28] Related to the above data form element, an accurate description of the specific ways information has been digitised is crucial to an understanding of how the edition works as a whole.

---

[24] American Standard Code for Information Interchange, a character-encoding routine developed for computer and communications equipment, first published in 1963.

[25] Joint Photographic Experts Group, a digital image compression routine developed by an international committee and recognised as an ISO standard in 1994.

[26] Tagged Image File Format, a routine for digitising images published by Aldus in 1986.

[27] MPEG-1 Audio Layer 3, a routine for digitising audio information developed by a team of US and German engineers, approved as an ISO/IEC standard in 1991.

[28] Flash Video, introduced by Micromedia in 1996 and currently distributed by Abode Systems; a protocol for embedding multimedia text, image, audio and video presentations in Web pages.

Text encoding. Has an encoding scheme been added to the plain-text files? COCOA,[29] GML,[30] SGML,[31] HTML,[32] XML?[33] If so, are the associated protocol files provided? Has any encoding information been added to the basic files of other media? What level of semantic meta-data has been included? Encoding has become increasingly important to electronic works with the development of XML protocols such as CSS[34] and XSLT.[35] Knowing how a text is encoded and what mediating routines are attached allows a scholar to determine how that text has been designed for display as well as what levels of digital analysis are supported.

Internal documentation. Does the edition have a separate editorial rationale? Do the files contain editorial metadata describing changes, standards, and so forth? Access to the stated intentions of an edition's editor or editors provides crucial insights into its structure and contents. More important for electronic editions are complete change logs that detail what modifications took place during development and after initial publication.

Data source. Not directly addressed by most descriptive bibliographers, questions of source are usually the primary concern of editors. Nonetheless, when dealing with electronic editions derived from print materials, one must scrutinise a work's origins. Where did the material making up the work come from? How was it remediated? What quality control and error check routines were employed? In translating information from print to digital media, many opportunities for error, erasure and distortion arise. The MLA's Committee on Scholarly Editions addresses this problem at a number of points in its 'Guidelines for Editors of Scholarly Editions', especially section 1.2.1. Any descrip-

---

[29] Count and Concordance Generation on Atlas, an encoding scheme introduced by Atlas Computer Labs of England in 1967.

[30] Generalized Mark-Up Language, developed by an IBM research team led by Charles Goldfarb and released in 1969.

[31] Standard Generalized Mark-Up Language, an improvement of GML addressing certain structural concerns and recognised as an ISO standard in 1986.

[32] HyperText Mark-up Language, an improvement of SGML designed specifically for the nascent World Wide Web by Tim Berners-Lee in 1990.

[33] An HTML/SGML hybrid developed by the World Wide Web Consortium and published in 1998.

[34] Cascading Style Sheets, a mechanism for communicating Web page display and format to a browser, adopted by the World Wide Web Consortium in 1998.

[35] eXtensible Style Language Transformation, a language for transforming encoded documents according to a set of rules and published in 1999.

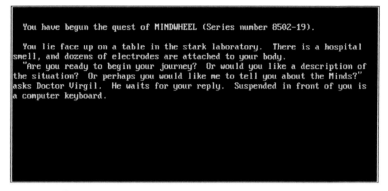

Figure 1: The opening screen of the MS-DOS version of Mindwheel, running in the OpenDOS emulator on a MacBook Pro.

tion of an electronic edition must address the source of the text and images it contains as well as the method employed in translating those materials into digital form.

These six preliminary categories provide a starting point for uncovering the circumstances of an electronic resource's creation and distribution. They are by no means definitive answers for immediate application but rather interrogative questions for further development. To test these categories, I would like to apply them to three electronic works either derived from print materials or containing a significant print component.

Mindwheel

Written by Robert Pinsky and developed by Synapse Software in 1984, and published by Synapse and Brøderbund[36] in 1985, *Mindwheel* advertises itself as an 'electronic novel'.[37] It employs a hybrid physical-digital structure in which both media (codex and computer) act as literary complements, although functionally the physical book plays a secondary role to the primary interactive fiction narrative unfolding on the screen. Like similar text-based adventure games of the period, users step through the narrative by following prompts posed by the software.

---

[36] Brøderbund bought Synapse Software in late 1984.
[37] Synapse went so far as to trademark the term 'electronic novel'.

The 96-page codex companion volume contains preliminary background text, black-and-white artwork, various poems by Pinsky and answers to copy-protection questions the software regularly poses. The publishers also included a tri-fold 'Electronic Novel Reference Card' with the disks, designed to help users start, navigate and troubleshoot the software.

Describing the codex part of the package is fairly straightforward, following the established protocols of the discipline. The beginning of a description might look like this:

16.5 x 23.5 cm: [unsigned: 1^4 2^{12} 3–4^{16}]; 48ll., pp. [1–12] 13–93 [94–6]

followed by sections on content, typography, paper and so on. Describing the electronic piece poses more problems. Unlike the printed material, five versions of the software package were created and published. Initially the package was compiled to run on MS-DOS machines, Apple II, the Commodore 64 computer and the Atari 8-bit and ST systems. Descriptive bibliographers generally consider a distinct edition as any work in which a majority of the pages were printed from the same setting of type. Using this definition as a guideline, the five software packages might constitute impositions rather than editions. For example, data for the DOS issue of the electronic novel come on a single 5.25-inch, double-sided floppy disk with a 128Kb capacity, contained in three binary source files (ADISK.OBJ, Clear.com, and Go.exe) and one ASCII batch file (MndWheel.bat) for the game programmed by Steve Hales and William Mataga in BTZ (or Better than Zork[38]), an authoring system created by Mataga. For its day, BTZ offered a fairly robust environment with a simple notion of distance, real-time reactions and a recognition lexicon of over 1200 words. However, when the same BTZ code was compiled for the Commodore 64 operating system and hardware, it resulted in three disks, each containing a piece of the overall program (MINDWHE0.D64, MINDWHE1.D64, and MINDWHE2.D64). This holds true for the other platform-specific packages: each separate instantiation derives from a single parent. If we consider the source BTZ code as a single setting of type and the process of compiling for multiple operating systems analogous to the

[38] Zork refers to a series of early interactive computer adventure games written in the late 1970s at the Massachusetts Institute of Technology. They were released commercially in the early 1980s by Infocom.

act of reimposing the plates for different formats, then all five versions
are the same edition imposed separately.

Documentation for the work is spotty and mostly out of date,[39]
although some outside information can shed light on certain design
aspects of the packaging. A presentation copy from the author to the
literary critic Hugh Kenner contains an autograph note from Pinsky
that comments briefly on what the poet, who appreciates the aesthetic
potentials of technology, thought of Synapse's handling of the project.
'The *package* for *Mindwheel*', he writes, 'as you will see, is a (rather silly)
hard cover book. They wanted some highbrow patina.'[40]

The OETL Chaucer

The second electronic publication for testing digital descriptive principles is the *Oxford Electronic Text Library Edition of The Riverside Chaucer*
(*OETL*). Published in 1992, it is a translation into digital media of
the 1987 third edition of the *Riverside Chaucer* and part of a series
that includes works by a number of canonical authors.[41] The package is
housed in a plastic shell mimicking the dimensions of a standard univer-
sity-press book, while the text files are stored on two write-protected,
low-density 3.5-inch floppy disks each with a 720Kb capacity formatted
for PC (the Macintosh version was distributed among five disks).

The first disk of the PC version contains the zipped files (in PKZIP)
for *Canterbury Tales*, *Troilus and Criseyde* and the system files required
to use the texts, along with a copy of PKUNZIP[42] for uncompressing
them. The second contains zipped files for the *Consolation of Philosophy*
and the *Treatise on the Astrolabe*, the *Romaunt of the Rose* and shorter
poems, with another copy of PKUNZIP. When uncompressed, the
entire collection consists of 39 separate text and system files totaling
approximately 3.5 Mb:

---

[39] Nick Montfort has some astute observations on technical obsolescence in
general and *Mindwheel* specifically. See 'Condemned to Reload It: Forgetting
New Media', http://nickm.com/writing/essays/condemned_to_reload_it.html.

[40] From an autograph note dated 20 April 1989 in the possession of this essay's
author.

[41] Other authors in the series include Jane Austen, Samuel Taylor Coleridge,
David Hume and John Locke.

[42] PKZIP and PKUNZIP are file compression and uncompression utilities first
released in 1989 and widely employed to make maximum use of the limited
storage capacity common to early floppy disks.

IBMENTS.DTD, a subsection of the OET document type defini-tion[43] declaring the required special character entities,[44] mapped to the IBM system;

OETHDR.DTD, a subsection of the OET document type definition for the *.DVF files;

OETLIB.DTD, a subsection of the OET document type definition of the *.OET files.

Six master files, CT.DVF (*Canterbury Tales*), PR.DVF (prose works), ROM.DVF (*Romaunt of the Rose*), SP.DVF (shorter poems including the F Prologue of *The Legend of Good Women*), and TR.DVF (*Troilus and Criseyde*), SPA.DVF (shorter poems including the G Prologue of *The Legend of Good Women*) and TR.DVF (*Troilus and Criseyde*), containing the document type declaration,[45] header information, tag counts, a revision log and a list of entities which enables a user to open the whole work or collection in one document;

Twelve files containing the text of *Canterbury Tales*, named CT01. OET to CT12.OET;

Four files containing the text of the prose works, named PR01.OET to PR04.OET;

Three files containing the text of the *Romaunt of the Rose*, named ROM01.OET to ROM03.OET;

Six files containing the text of the shorter poems, named SP01. OET to SP05.OET (including two versions of *The Legend of Good Women*, SP04.OET with the F Prologue and SP04A.OET with the G Prologue);

Five files containing the text of *Troilus and Criseyde*, named TR01. OET to TR05.OET.

The Macintosh edition comes with the same number of files uncom-pressed on five disks with a different entity DTD to deal with the way Macintosh machines represent special characters.

---

[43] A set of formal rules declaring the grammar, syntax and vocabulary of a specific text mark-up scheme. The XML language initially relied upon DTDs, but in 2001 the World Wide Web Consortium published XML Schema, a more highly abstracted and flexible tool for accomplishing these tasks.

[44] Variables that define abbreviations which in turn are used by a text proc-essor to insert things such as special characters or large storage objects.

[45] The first lines of any SGML file in which the document type definition is identified as well as all required entities.

All the data comprising the *OETL Chaucer* are in plain 7-bit ASCII, the standard for encoding the 128 basic machine and alpha-numeric characters used by computers. Thus no special software is required to view or manipulate the texts, and none is included in the edition. In order to do anything more than look at the plain text, as the sample in Diagram 1 demonstrates, one needs an application that will interpret SGML, the structural and semantic tagging system that provides the backbone for the edition. When the work first came out in 1992, SGML was established as the favourite protocol for creating sophisticated electronic scholarly editions. Since then, XML has supplanted the prior scheme, and most contemporary applications designed for marked-up texts no longer fully support SGML. Anyone wishing to use the *OETL Chaucer* today must convert the original files into XML before processing.

The opening lines of 'The General Prologue' encoded
in *OETL* SGML

```
<GROUP ID=CTA N='Fragment I (Group A)'>
   <PB N='23'>
   <FRONT>
      <HEAD>Here bygynneth the Book of the Tales of Caunterbury.</HEAD>
   </FRONT>
   <TEXT ID=GP N='The General Prologue'>
      <BODY>
         <DIV1 TYPE='para'>
            <L N='1' PART=N>Whan that Aprill with his shoures soote</L>
            <L PART=N>The droghte of March hath perced to the roote,</L>
            <L PART=N>And bathed every veyne in swich licour</L>
            <L PART=N>Of which vertu engendred is the flour;</L>
            <L N='5' PART=N>Whan Zephirus eek with his sweete breeth</L>
            <L PART=N>Inspired hath in every holt and heeth</L>
            <L PART=N>The tendre croppes, and the yonge sonne</L>
            <L PART=N>Hath in the Ram his half cours yronne,</L>
            <L PART=N>And smale foweles maken melodye,</L>
            <L N='10' PART=N>That slepen al the nyght with open ye</L>
            <L PART=N>(So priketh hem nature in hir corages),</L>
            <L PART=N>Thanne longen folk to goon on pilgrimages,</L>
            <L PART=N>And palmeres for to seken straunge strondes,</L>
            <L PART=N>To ferne halwes, kowthe in sondry londes;</L>
            <L N='15' PART=N>And specially from every shires ende</L>
            <L PART=N>Of Engelond to Caunterbury they wende,</L>
            <L PART=N>The hooly blisful martir for to seke,</L>
            <L PART=N>That hem hath holpen whan that they were seeke.</L>
         </DIV1>
```

Fortunately, the electronic editor David Edmonds and technical consultant Lou Burnard employed the Text Encoding Initiative's guidelines (TEI)[46] when preparing the edition. Included in the package is a 48-page staple-bound manual, a basic description of which might read:

14.5 x 20.5 cm: [unsigned: 1^{24}] 24*ll*., pp. [i–v] vi, [1] 2–10 [11] 12–32 [33] 34–7 [38] 39 [40] 41 [42]

Documentation within the manual details the SGML implementation, and system files contain metadata that describe changes or modifications not covered in the printed manual. The choice of TEI encoding and accompanying documentation supports the SGML-to-XML migration procedure developed and freely distributed by the TEI, thus extending its life.

Mindwheel and the *OETL Chaucer* illustrate how initial design choices inform the descriptive bibliographer's job. In the former, an outdated proprietary delivery application restricts our ability to view the edition in its original intended state. Analysis is further restricted because the source data is compiled in a binary form that resists detailed investigation. In the latter, we have access to the complete source files accompanied by copious documentation. We can also refer to the *Riverside Chaucer* third edition from which the text derives for detailed editorial information. In both cases, however, careful examination of the editions following some of the core avenues of inquiry employed by print bibliographers reveals a mass of valuable data for a new digital description.

The William Blake Archive

The final work for consideration presents many more and diverse challenges than *Mindwheel* or the *OETL Chaucer*, both of which exist in static, stand-alone form. This is not the case with the electronic scholarly archive, which occupies an area along the digital continuum much closer to that explored by Kirschenbaum and Rinehart. Begun in 1994 at the University of Virginia's Institute for Advanced Technology in the Humanities with an initial public release in 1996, the *William Blake*

---

[46] http://www.tei-c.org. Established in 1987, the Text Encoding Initiative is a consortium of institutions, projects and individuals that develops and maintains guidelines for the encoding of humanities texts.

Archive has, with the help of a number of funding agencies, created a vast collection of digital facsimiles and transcriptions of Blake's work as well as a significant amount of secondary documentation. Not a born-digital object, the electronic primary materials descend from original or facsimile print sources and currently reside on three Linux servers at the University of North Carolina, Chapel Hill, with a mirror site at Oxford University. Delivered via the World Wide Web, it consists of a mixture of HTML front-ends following different standards depending upon the date of creation, Javascript[47] extensions to those pages, XML-encoded text files employing two different mark-up protocols, a text-search routine built on the eXist open source software,[48] high-resolution JPEG facsimiles derived from various sources, and image-delivery software written in Java[49] and developed for the archive.

Attempting to describe this sprawling resource poses a number of methodological and theoretical challenges, beginning with the question of publication. Like many networked literary projects, the *William Blake Archive* has evolved through a series of cumulative releases, the latest of which was announced on the 28 May 2010. According to the archive's update pages, over sixty new texts have been added to the original release in the past fifteen years. As a distribution mechanism, periodic release closely resembles the serial publication of novels in magazines and newspapers popular in the nineteenth and twentieth centuries. In addition, a number of significant large-scale improvements took place: in January 2001, a major revision of the site's front-end as well as the re-organisation of some of its contents was announced; in December of that year, the Oxford mirror site went on-line; and in May 2006 the original SGML encoding and underlying framework was replaced by an XML structure.

We can use the bibliographer's concepts of state, issue, and edition to help make sense of the Archive's history so far. The work began in 1996 as a serial publication with cumulative back issues available on demand. The January 2001 upgrade involved rearranging the contents for a new framework, much like the nineteenth-century US printing-industry practice of imposing the same stereotype plates in different

---

[47] A client-side, object-oriented scripting language first released in 1995 and used for manipulating materials within a Web page.
[48] A native XML database employing the W3C XQuery protocols and created in 2000 by Wolfgang Meier.
[49] A programming language designed and released by Sun Microsystems in 1995.

formats. The Oxford mirror site might be considered a type of joint operating agreement, with one printer supplying content for two publishers. Finally in 2006 the entire contents were re-encoded for a new 'setting' of digital type. As noted above, bibliographers often define an edition as a work printed mostly or wholly from a new setting of type. If we extend Tanselle's correlation between a printing plate and an electronic source file, then transforming a document from SGML to XML is analogous to resetting a page. In other words, the serialised archive up to May 2006 constitutes a separate edition from the one released at that point and currently available.

Viewed this way, the Blake Archive has had four bibliographical states:

1. 1996–2001, the first serialised edition;
2. January–December 2001, a second imposition of the first edition;
3. December 2001 – May 2006, the second imposition, first edition, published in two identical states in the US and UK;
4. May 2006 – present, the second edition of the *William Blake Archive*.

Fleshing out this broad conception of an electronic serialised work in two editions requires a great deal of detective work. With a little technical probing one can locate the current Blake Archive Description DTD (or BAD), based on the TEI standards used in other publicly available documents. The BAD change log outlines fifteen revisions to the original DTD, beginning in January 1998. Examining the encoding of the front-end pages reveals they were built at different times, the chronology of which can be inferred from the HTML standards employed. The Internet Archive's search tool provides snapshots of the site files going back to at least 1997, where we can see that many front-end pages have been significantly modified or completely replaced – cancels, if you will.

Although the editors have supplied copious amounts of technical and historical documentation concerning the site's development (in addition to file-level change logs and comments not shown in the public interface), it is difficult to dig much deeper without access to the servers and archive files themselves. The first pre-2006 SGML edition is no longer available publicly and presumably resides only on server back-up directories and tapes. Users call up notes, transcriptions and descriptions of Blake's prints through eXist, which converts the native XML into HTML for display while keeping the source files secure. And of course digital image facsimiles are protected for copyright reasons. The only way to create an accurate and thorough descriptive bibliography of the Blake Archive is to do what scholars have done for centuries – go to the original materials. Nevertheless, this exercise in digital bibliographical description demonstrates the possibilities for analytical insight that emerge when one applies traditional print methodologies to digital objects.

Conclusion

In their 1989 *An Introduction to Bibliographical and Textual Studies*, William Proctor Williams and Craig Abbott posed a series of questions designed to guide the creation of a description: What is the book? What does the book say about itself? How was the book put together? What does the book dontain? What is the book made of? How was the book packaged? What is known about the printing and publishing of the book? These queries, a rephrasing of some of the issues addressed in this essay, serve as a valuable framework for designing bibliographical descriptions of electronic editions. The requisite tools for the digital bibliographer are much different from the student of the book – XML editors and UNIX utilities rather than collators and flat-light sources – but the scholarly goals are the same: collecting, organising and presenting all the evidence which can be determined through the application of analytical bibliography to a book, whether that book is on vellum, paper or hard drives.

Oxford, Bodleian Library, Bodley 647 and its Use, c.1410–2010

RALPH HANNA

I

OXFORD, BODLEIAN LIBRARY, BODLEY 647 has always been central to forming perceptions of vernacular Lollardy; indeed, until just over twenty years ago and publication of a broader conspectus, this book stood as the primary example of Lollard polemical texts.[1] The book was a major source of information for the founder of modern studies, Walter W. Shirley (1828–66), after a spell as maths tutor at Wadham College, Regius Professor of Ecclesiastical History from 1863. Shirley had planned the contents, and received the endorsement of Clarendon Press, for several volumes of what he took to be the central texts, *Select English Works of John Wyclif*. However, owing to his premature death, these seminal volumes were only produced and finished by his amanuensis Thomas Arnold (see I: i–ii). Between them, Arnold's third volume and two items included in F. D. Matthew's later collection put into print nearly all of the book's English texts (the one exception is item 7 in the descriptive appendix below). The early publication and continued availability of these writings has always provided the primary evidence for vernacular Lollard interests.[2]

---

[1] This is, of course, Anne Hudson, *The Premature Reformation: Wycliffite Texts and Lollard History* (Oxford: Clarendon Press, 1988). Subsequent notes will amply demonstrate Hudson's inestimable and continuing influence on this study, and I am additionally grateful to her for many kindnesses and suggestions in the preparation of this paper. A good description of Bodley 647 appears at R. W. Hunt *et al.*, *A Summary Catalogue of Western Manuscripts in the Bodleian Library at Oxford*, 7 vols. in 8 (Oxford: Clarendon Press, 1895–1953), II, 582–3 (no. 3072); I supplement this in an appendix with additional modern bibliographical references, mainly from R. E. Lewis *et al.*, *Index of Printed Middle English Prose* (New York: Garland, 1985).

[2] See Shirley, *A Catalogue of the Original Works of John Wycliffe* (Oxford: Clarendon Press, 1865) – and note his edition of *Fasciculi Zizaniorum Magistri Johannis Wyclif cum Tritico*, Rolls Series 5 (London: Longman, 1858). For the editions, see *Select English Works of John Wyclif*, ed. Thomas Arnold, 3 vols. (Oxford: Clarendon Press, 1869–71), esp. vol. III, *passim*; F. D. Matthew, *The*

I have treated this book before, somewhat peripherally in that context. I then associated the volume's production with that of two other important Wycliffite manuscript anthologies, Cambridge, Corpus Christi College 296 and Dublin, Trinity College 244. All of them, I argued, showed access to a common Lollard copying centre or 'library'. There, a variety of materials, especially vernacular ones, were available, probably in thematically linked fascicles; from these, interested parties might produce further combinations of texts, to meet specific needs and interests.[3]

Date and Origin of Bodley 647

The Bodley manuscript is, in the main, the work of two scribes, whose hands one would date s. xv[in]. The first is responsible for nearly all of Booklets 1–2, fols. 1–65[v], text items 1–5, written in informal textura; the second, initially, for nearly all of Booklets 3–4, fols. 71–106, items 10–13, written in anglicana formata. The two scribes are, given similarities of format, probably partners: the first uses a writing area 150 x 95–100, with 29 or 30 long lines; the second, a writing area 142–4 x 97, with 31 long lines.

The book may also provide additional evidence that this pair were joined in an ongoing collaboration. At the opening of his stint, scribe 2 appears originally to have left the first leaf, fol. 70, blank. This behaviour may imply that the two scribes had originally planned to effect a smooth join between two stints proceeding independently. But in the event, the first scribe concluded after filling only half his final quire. Scribe 2 then appears to have copied additional texts onto his blank opening leaf, but he did so in a unique page format designed to handle the texts he had at hand, not that of the remainder of his stint (see further the appendix below).

The two scribes are also linked with one another by their rather surprising language. *LALME* places the first scribe's language north-

---

English Works of Wyclif Hitherto Unprinted, EETS, os 74 (London: Trübner, 1880, 1902). For one outstanding instance of Bodley 647's inspiring later scholarship, see Margaret Aston, 'Caim's Castels': Poverty, Politics and Disendowment', in Barrie Dobson, ed., *The Church, Politics and Patronage in the Fifteenth Century* (Gloucester: Sutton, 1984), pp. 45–81. Aston's title phrase is well attested in the manuscript; see *Select Works* III, 241, 368–9 (three times), 398.

[3] 'Two Lollard Codices and Lollard Book-Production', *Studies in Bibliography* 43 (1990), 49–62, including descriptions of Corpus and Trinity. With both of these Bodley shares three texts, here items 10 and 13.

east of Kirk Ireton, Derbyshire.[4] Although I have not fully surveyed it, the second scribe's language (and those of added texts, to which I will turn in a moment) appears comparable. Such language would apparently challenge the general assumption, especially prevalent since M. L. Samuels's influential comments on 'central Midland standard', and supplemented by provocative materials associated with Braybrooke (Northamptonshire), that a manuscript centre like that I imagine should have been located somewhere within the central south-east Midlands. Certainly supportive of such a theory, Hudson has adduced some information suggesting a Huntingdonshire locale, a placement that finds echoes in the language of several copies of the interpolated prose Psalter. Further support might be drawn from the access to some materials variously shared between the Bodley, Corpus and Dublin manuscripts, in Bodley 938, copied by a locally trained scribe, writing either Huntingdonshire or Ely language (although, on the basis of other work, perhaps operating in London, c.1450).[5]

But whatever the coherence of this information, the best evidence for the investment of Derbyshire persons in Lollardy turns out to be contemporary with the book. This is associated with the wave of persecutions that followed the Oldcastle Revolt, from 1414 to the later 'teens of the fifteenth century. Although he is described in other documents concerning the affair as a resident of London, John Purvey was alleged to have been engaged in Derbyshire activities at this time. But the locals scarcely required the presence of external agitators, and the ringleader in the Derbyshire disturbances appears to have been a chaplain from Aston-upon-Trent, William Ederyk. Certainly, the authorities uncovered a fair nest of suspects (and persons willing to stand bail for their future lawful behaviour); these individuals were concentrated in villages ringing Derby from the south around to the east: Hartshorne, Findern, Sinfin, Littleover, Aston and Chaddesden.[6] The atlas's

[4] See *LALME*, LP 61, described III, 68–9.
[5] See M. L. Samuels, 'Some Applications of Middle English Dialectology', *English Studies* 44 (1963), 81–94 at pp. 84–5; for Braybrooke, and its long-time Lollard priest/book-distributor, Robert Hoke, see Hudson, *Premature Reformation*, pp. 90, 200, 206–7. For her discussion focusing on Huntingdonshire language, see A. Hudson, ed., *The Works of a Lollard Preacher*, EETS, OS 317 (Oxford: Oxford University Press, 2001), pp. xxvii–xxx. Lollard psalters in appropriate dialects include Harvard University Library, Richardson 36; Bodleian Library, Bodley 288; and Oxford, University College 74.
[6] See especially John A. F. Thomson, *The Later Lollards, 1414–1520* (Oxford: Oxford University Press, 1965), pp. 13, 96–7, 99–100; A. Hudson, *Lollards*

suggested placement of Bodley 647's scribal language is fifteen or so miles to the north-west.

Although removed from the expected, the language of the manuscript might solidify the view of a well-known textual centre. Information concerning the availability of books suitable for consultation and copying would have spread through the 'bush telegraph' in which sectarians participated. At such a centre, those of suitable sympathies and discretion could select, from a broad range of materials, texts suitable for the patrons who had sent them. The model is well known, again from contemporary sources, through the 1407 Bohemian pilgrimage, in which Mikuláš Faulfiš and Jiří Knĕhnic were guided, perhaps by Peter Payne, to appropriate dispersed locales where copies of Wycliffe's Latin might be obtained for continental transmission.[7]

At least one additional feature of Bodley 647 may lend further support to such a hypothesis. Unlike the comparable Corpus and Dublin manuscripts, with only English versions of Francis's rule and testament (item 10), scribe 2 here provides the Latin originals as well. This might imply this scribe's access to the translator's original. Certainly, the decision to include this material accords with the interest, in this volume, in mixing in Latin materials to provide unimpeachable precedents for Wycliffite opinions. The tendency is perhaps especially marked in the theological excerpts that form item 12, which scribe 2 supplemented a quire to add in, immediately following his supply of the Franciscan *originalia*.

II

Whatever the original scribes were doing, a topic to which I will return as a post-modern reading at the end, certain aspects of Bodley 647 proved unusually attractive to very early readers/users. The original work has been supplemented, and a great many originally blank leaves

---

and their Books (London: Hambledon, 1985), pp. 88–9. I have also profited from information in Maureen Jurkowski's unpublished paper, 'The Career of Robert Herlaston, Lollard Preacher', and there is further relevant material in Jurkowski's unpublished dissertation cited therein.

[7] See Hudson, *Premature Reformation*, pp. 90–1, 100–1, 106 n. 280, 457; and 'Which Wyche? The Framing of the Lollard Heretic and/or Saint', in Hudson, *Studies in the Transmission of Wyclif's Writings* (Aldershot: Ashgate, 2008), XIV, 233–7.

filled, first by further activities of scribe 2, already noted above, and subsequently by at least two further hands writing early-fifteenth-century anglicana (fols. 65–8, 68ᵛ–69). In both cases, these individuals appear to have been stimulated by existing contents. Further, these original texts to which later hands responded are disposed in such a way that they imply that both scribes' portions of the volume were present together from an early date.

These additions, filling as many blank leaves as possible, might be described as 'associative', consonant with the argument I will later suggest that Bodley 647 forms a 'thematic miscellany'. Scribe 2's provision of items 8–9 and 14 follows from the unique free copy (all other examples of the text are associated with Knighton's *Chronicle*) of item 5. This text, of course, appears *in scribe 1's portion*, further evidence for the early juncture of the book's parts. Scribe 2's additions constitute an early effort to see the book as providing ancient Wycliffite testimonies, memorials of the founders – and the founders before their recantations. These texts certainly imply very close access to materials associated with the founders of the sect. They could well have been supplied *in situ* (although perhaps implying a sequence of visits to some text-centre?), in whatever context one imagines production. Analogously, item 6, a series of Latin excerpts, added later on blank leaves at the end of the first scribe's stint, will have sought to mirror *the second scribe's work in another booklet*.

A similar analysis would explain the latest of these additions, item 7, on its other appearance in the manuscript identified as 'Documentum Roberti Grosehede'. It thus answers item 4, but, interestingly, proves to be a fragmentary excerpt. Indeed, its scribe ceased once it is clear that Grosseteste is only invoked in the *incipit* (although the text, on clerical abuse of the right to tithes, might be construed a relevant counterpoint to various materials, both Latin and English, original to the volume). In addition to these inserted texts, the volume is equipped with a partial medieval foliation (not very readily datable), a sign of some interest in ready consultation.

Yet other fifteenth-century readers were not so enthusiastic. The volume includes two cautionary notes of the late fifteenth century, both very faded, and the first nearly defaced: 'Liber venenosus in anglico' (fol. i, the third front flyleaf) and 'Explicit Malicia facta contra fratres' (fol. 107ᵛ). From their fading and their position (at top and tail), these conceivably date from a time when the book remained unbound. But although certainly critical, these readers did not destroy the book, and it was indeed in well-disposed hands after their activity. Although one critical reader added what appears under ultra-violet light, following Wycliffe's name at the head of item 5 (fol. 63ᵛ), the parodic identification 'hereticus ewangelicus' (the first word mostly indistinct, but certainly beginning 'h.r'), this has been vigorously erased.

The volume appears to have received its first binding in the medieval period. The first two front and the two rear flyleaves, each set a conjoint bifolium, come from a book written in formal anglicana, s. xiv²/⁴ or med., the text completely surrounded by glosses. At least three of these leaves indicate that this was an important, now-lost book, a copy of Rolle's *Melos amoris*, probably made during the hermit's lifetime. Staining on the first front flyleaf and the first rear one (indicating the reversal in the current binding of inherited materials) implies that only one leaf of each bifolium was originally 'free', the outer one being used as a pastedown.[8]

III

Bodley 647 remained in active use well into the sixteenth century. One sign of continuing interest in the book is provided by the current binding. This is of blind-stamped leather over millboard, re-backed in brown calf, sewn on four thongs, s. xvi. The roll on the binding is London work of the 1530s.[9] There are holes near the top and foot of each board, originally with string ties to hold the book closed.

John Bale certainly handled Bodley 647, *c*.1548–52, and described in detail its contents. These he identified as works of Wycliffe, and

[8]   The script shows features generally removed from central booktrade hands by mid-century, e.g. hooked ascenders and unevenly inked strokes. In order, leaf 4 (the second at the rear) has *The Melos Amoris of Richard Rolle of Hampole*, ed. E. J. F. Arnould (Oxford: Blackwell, 1957), 31/7–32/10; leaf 1 (the first at the front) follows, with 32/10–33/13, and leaf 2 (the second at the front) bears 44/14–45/23. The current recto of the remaining leaf, written almost entirely in red ink, has sustained too much damage from pasting down to be readily legible, and I have been unable to identify the text on its verso, although it does not appear to be from *Melos*, but is probably text from whatever was introduced by the materials in red.

[9]   The Bodleian repair is not limited to refurbishing the spine, but seems also to have beenresponsible for the current pastedowns and the supply of single modern paper flyleaves at either end of the volume. For the stamps, see J. Basil Oldham, *English Blind-Stamped Bindings* (Cambridge: Cambridge University Press, 1952), HM (a) 12 (no. 781, plate xlvii).

he gives their *incipits* in Latin translation.[10] In these procedures, Bale essentially offers a secularised version of longstanding medieval behaviours.[11] The works he takes as his predecessors formed finding guides to theological truth, instructions for those seeking the most authoritative early writers on persistent theological issues (often, including information where to find copies of these works). In contrast, Bale was engaged in gathering up anew a now dispersed national glory, in preserving, following the Henrician despoliation of monastic Britain, any still-extant record of the insular intellectual past. Although in other contexts, he often voices strenuously anti-Catholic sentiments, in his bibliographical work, Bale exhibits a form of archaising historical nostalgia, a pursuit of early sources of national intellectual glory.[12]

At the time Bale saw it, the manuscript belonged to John Stokes, a fact known only from Bale's notation, not from anything in the volume itself. Stokes was a don; he came up to Queens' College, Cambridge, in 1538, apparently from Bedfordshire, and was a fellow (and eventually president) from 1543 until his death in 1568. In addition, he was University chaplain and librarian (conventionally a joint appointment), 1556–68, and also served a term as vice-chancellor.

Bale saw two other manuscripts in Stokes's house, both chronicles. One of these was clearly an English prose *Brut* (489), and probably still survives, as London, British Library, Harley 53, with Stokes's arms.

---

[10] See Reginald L. Poole and Mary Bateson, eds., *Index Britanniae Scriptorum . . .*, 2nd edition, intro. Caroline Brett and James P. Carley (1902; repr. Cambridge: D. S. Brewer, 1990), pp. 270–1. For John Stokes, see p. xxxiii.

[11] See Richard H. and Mary A. Rouse, 'Bibliography before Print: The Medieval *De viris illustribus*', in Peter Ganz, ed., *The Role of the Book in Medieval Culture*, 2 vols. (Turnhout: Brepols, 1986), I, 133–53; and their two contributions to the *Corpus of British Medieval Library Catalogues*, vols. II and XI, *Registrum Anglie* (London: British Library, 1991) and *Henry of Kirkestede, Catalogus de libris autenticis* (London: British Library, 2004).

[12] Bale, of course, has attracted a considerable literature; see recently Cathy Shrank, *Writing the Nation in Reformation England, 1530–1580* (Oxford: Oxford University Press, 2004), pp. 18–19, 63–4, 67–9. Some hint of his nostalgia still survives in the writings of Thomas James, whom I will consider in a moment. Cf. James's *Apologie*, pp. 45–6 (a full reference in the text below), where he argues that 'Wycliffe's "Lollard disendowment bill"', A. Hudson, ed., *Selections from English Wycliffite Writings* (Cambridge: Cambridge University Press, 1978), pp. 135–7, 203–7, was a more constructive approach to 'Reformation' than that adopted by Henry VIII. However, as we will see, James is considerably estranged from Bale's sense of medieval English glories, e.g. his reference to the 'Romish or rather Diuelish opinions' of 'Antichrist and his deerest Minions, the Moonks & Friars' (*Apologie*, p. 10).

For the second, which I have not traced, Bale provides a Latin incipit, 'Postquam vero de inclytorum gestis' (486). This book, which Bale indicates ran from Vortigern to William the Conqueror, may well have been a second *Brut* (beginning mid-chapter 55?), but could equally have been Latin.[13]

We have further information about Stokes's library from his post-mortem inventory. This includes 94 entries, comprising at least 148 volumes, virtually all printed Reformation theology (although no. 92 was a copy of Bale's printed *Scriptores*, valued at 20 *d.*). Any surviving manuscripts were presumably part of the final entry in the inventory, 'certayne other old bokes', valued at vj *s.* viij *d.* (the same value assigned to no. 4, a one-volume Paris works of Ambrose, probably either the 1549 or 1551 edition). Stokes's will contained no mention of books.[14]

A single detail from the sparse biographical information that survives suggests that Stokes might have had an interest in topics germane to Wycliffism. On 9 August 1564, he was one of four divines who argued before Elizabeth, then on a Cambridge progress, the proposition whether civil magistracy conferred authority in ecclesiastical matters as well. For such a subject, obviously, certain Lollard writings, although mainly Wycliffe's Latin and not texts of this manuscript (although cf. item 12 [d] here), might have provided food for thought.[15]

The book later apparently belonged to one 'Wyldsley' (s. xvi/xvii?), who signs on fols. i[v], 68, and 107[v]. The name does not occur among alumni of either university, in Prerogative Court of Canterbury wills before 1610, the British Library manuscript catalogue index or the index to Ker's *Medieval Manuscripts*. Fol. i has a pre-Bodleian shelfmark 'B.7', likely one of these owners.

[13] See C. E. Wright, *Fontes Harleiani: A Study of the Sources of the Harleian Collection* (London: British Library, 1972), p. 318; Lister M. Matheson, *The Prose Brut: The Development of a Middle English Chronicle* (Tempe, AZ: MRTS, 1998), p. 297. I would imagine that a search of Harleian chronicles might turn up Stokes's second manuscript.

[14] See E. S. Leedham-Green, *Books in Cambridge Inventories*, 2 vols. (Cambridge: Cambridge University Press, 1986), I, 295–8.

[15] See William G. Searle, *The History of the Queens' College*, 2 vols., Cambridge Antiquarian Society, octavo publications 9, 13 (Cambridge: Deighton, Bell and Co, 1867–71), II, 297–302, at p. 300, with further references to a Latin summary account.

IV

Bodley 647 came to its present repository in 1603 or 1604 from an unknown source.[16] It seems immediately to have attracted the attention of Thomas James, Bodley's librarian, who edited and published item 13 as the second text in his *Two short treatises against the order of begging friars*.[17] This book formed a companion (the letters dedicatory of both are dated the same day, 10 February 1608, from the Bodleian) to *An Apologie for Iohn Wickliffe shewing his conformitie with the now Church of England* (STC 14445; Oxford, 1608).

James presents *Two short treatises* to the public as a modern analogy to Wycliffe's medieval situation. Particularly following the Jesuit scares of the 1590s – and the horrific martyrdoms of English Catholic missionaries like Campion and Southwell – James is engaged in the wars of religion produced by the Counter-Reformation. The Jesuit enemy seeks the corruption of England specifically, and the Protestant cause more generally. In this polarised and paranoia-inducing situation, James fashions himself as an apostolic inheritor of Lollard belief. Intensely conscious of his position as librarian in Sir Thomas Bodley's foundation at Oxford, he seeks to wrap himself in the mantle of Lollard associations with the university. The full title of James's *Two short treatises* parades Wycliffe's Oxford connections, down to his college affiliations. Moreover, with what he took to be an elegant modesty, James – like scribe 2 adding 'apostolic' texts to Bodley 647 – affiliates himself with early local Lollard efforts: 'Wickliffe hath not as yet wanted a *Iames* to follow and embrase his doctrine' (*Two short treatises* [¶ 4ᵛ]). This allusion to the early adherent William James, whom, as his sidenote shows, Thomas knew from his manuscript reading, here of Thomas Netter's *Doctrinale*, places the writer firmly in the line of Lollard succession.[18]

---

[16] See Hunt, *Summary Catalogue*, I, 92 (no. 525). Fol. i has the superseded Bodleian shelfmark 'Arch. B183', and fol. iᵛ, a table of contents, s. xviiᵉˣ.

[17] The title continues: *compiled by that famous doctour of the church and Preacher of Gods word John Wickliffe* (STC 25589; Oxford, 1608), 19–62. Pages 1–17 of the volume reproduce 'The Complaint to the King and Parliament' (Lewis *et al., Index of Printed Middle English Prose*, 542), explicitly here from Corpus 296. As frequently in describing early modern prints, *Index of Printed Middle English Prose* errs in implying that the volume is in two separable parts; it was produced fully in quarto, and 'The Complaint' ends on the first leaf of gathering 'C', to be succeeded by the second text on 'C2'.

[18] On the earlier James, see Hudson, *Premature Reformation*, pp. 88–90.

Succession is indeed central to James's arguments. Early identifying him as 'this stout Champion, reuerend Doctor, & worthie preacher of God's word' (*Apologie* 1), James associates Wycliffe's persecution with that endured by Paul in Acts 25–6 – and with Paul's exoneration by Agrippa. But this apostolic role continues into the present, for Wycliffe is 'a resolued, true, Cath[o]like, English Protestant'; alternatively, 'an indifferent, sober, discreet, learned and iudicious Protestant' (*Apologie* 25, 40; in the first citation, the printer Barnes mis-set 'Catho | tholike' across a line-boundary). On two occasions (*Apologie* 48, 50), James describes the *doctor evangelicus* as self-consciously engaged in 'reformation'. He stands as proof of an ancient English creed, more consonant with Scripture than is Catholic 'noueltrie', one who expressed 'his detestation of al Popish or humane traditions, such as are contrarie to the word of God' (*Apologie* 15). James's argument, accompanied by lengthy marginal references aligning Wycliffe's opinions with the specifics of The Thirty-Nine Articles, implicitly indicates the Church of England's status as a national Church that has persisted in a model Wycliffe established long before: the Church 'doth teach no new Doctrin . . . but the very same doctrine, which was many hundred yeares ago retained and maintained her in England' (*Apologie* 72).[19]

Thus, in James's fervid history, Jesuit apostles/missionaries seek to invade, corrupt and overturn a long local apostolic history. But Wycliffe had already spotted this 'Romish' danger and addressed it. Just as James thinks Wycliffe's opinions generally may be aligned (or wrenched into conformity?) with Elizabethan ecclesiology, so Wycliffe's perception of papist threats directly addresses contemporary issues. In presenting the anti-mendicant tracts of *Two short treatises*, James heralds them as essentially prophetic enunciations, applicable in their argument to new situations: 'in regard of your lordships [James addresses his brother-in-law, James I's Lord Chief Justice] utter detestation of all Iesuitical Friars, and Friarlike Iesuits, for what is spoken of the one, *mutato nomine* may well be vnderstood of the other . . . they are so like in hypocrisie,

---

[19] One might adduce here the discussion at *Apologie*, p. 14, where James ascribes to Wycliffe both the English biblical translation and the Lollard commentary on the Psalter (interpolated into Richard Rolle's original) and judges the latter as inherently in conformity with modern Anglican liturgical usage. A sidenote, including a description of the binding, indicates that James knew the Psalter from what is now Oxford, Bodleian Library, Bodley 877, which he identifies (as *Summary Catalogue*, I, 96 [no. 684] does not) as a donation of Nicholas Bond, President of Magdalen College, 1590–1607/8.

blasphemie, treacheries, treasons, lyings, and damnable *Equiuocations* . . .' James proposes 'to vse *Wickliffs* words' in what he claims as a truly reformative spirit, '*to saue there persons & destroy their errors*'.[20] Thus, the two tracts, gathered from manuscript, provide a comprehensive demolition of yet another papistical 'newe secte'.

But, as is clear from the final movement of *An Apologie*, James's real interests are a great deal more practical than simply pope-baiting. Both the printed anti-mendicant tracts and the theological alignment of Wycliffe's views with contemporary Anglican practice provide only a framework for another Lollard-inspired operation, for James of greater importance. The inspiration for this is another vernacular text James will have known well, because one long in print, the 'general prologue' to the Wycliffite biblical translation.[21] James believes that he faces a situation analogous to that of the fourteenth-century translators, who found their Vulgates littered with corruptions. Similarly, modern Roman editions of the Fathers require a purging and, just as the Lollard biblical scholars had done, the construction of a pure text. But while the authors of Wycliffite scripture understood that their possible source Bibles merely reflected the predictable ravages of time, the multiplication of error inherent in a persistent copying tradition, the paranoic James saw in modern patristic print-editions deliberate acts of corruption.

For James, Roman prints go hand in hand with another papal innovation, the 'Index purgatorium librorum'. Just as the Jesuit censors of provocative books seek to suppress and hide divine truth, so their editions, under the guise of 'correction of [scribal] error', include further silent corrections, the suppression of 'doctrinal error', opinions currently uncomfortable. James is certain that the Fathers no longer appear pristine in many continental printings; they have been altered to accord with new Counter-Reformation, 'Jesuitical' orthodoxies, and thus present only 'Syrenical enchantments, Circean sorceries and Diabolical charmes' (*Apologie* 73–4). To counteract this censorious malignity, James assembled, as had presumably been done in Oxford in the 1380s or 1390s, a staff devoted to textual purification and repromulgation.

---

[20] All three citations come from *Two short sigs* [℗ 3v–℗ 4]; the italicised portion of the last actually quotes the Wycliffite tract James edited; cf. *Select Works* III, 369/24–7.

[21] See STC 25587.5, 25588, published by John Gowgh in 1540 and Robert Crowley in 1550, in the latter sigs R i^{rv} and R iii.

In all this activity, James took very seriously those tasks and duties appropriate to Bodley's librarian, the commitment to the promulgation of proper scholarship. As *An Apologie* shows on every page, James had assiduously scrutinised numerous manuscripts in his care.[22] He planned to put additional Bodleian (and other) books to further use – to make ancient English copies of patristic texts reveal the insidious errors deliberately propagated in modern Catholic editions. Like the Wyclif-fite translators, James and his staff collected numerous copies (many never returned to their owners, probably by forgetfulness and accident, as the project ran aground). They collated these against Italian printed texts, seeking to reveal deliberately intercalated 'papistical doctrinal error', and to expunge it to restore a true ancient text. Just as in the fourteenth century, Oxford became again an apostolic centre, again one of historical, textual, and doctrinal purity.[23]

V

As I indicated at the opening, Bodley 647 returned to prominence as the result of Walter Shirley's investigation of Wycliffe's writings in the mid-nineteenth century. Shirley mined the volume assiduously and care-fully; his catalogue included all but one of the texts here, the brief item 4.[24] Yet, within this carefulness, Shirley never realised the circularity of his procedures. In his researches, he relied upon Bale as an authority, or as Arnold puts it, a source providing 'external evidence of authorship' (*Select Works* III, 366). It occurred to neither researcher, as it did with some other manuscripts, that Bale's information had been derived from perusal of this very volume.[25] In his introduction, Shirley was dismissive about the English texts, seeing them as examples of a presumptively 'dumbed-down' form of 'popular' promulgation. Yet the book, as it has existed since shortly after inception, will rebuff such views, since signifi-cant portions (fols. 65–8, 79–85) presuppose a capacity to engage with

---

[22] Compare Hudson's comments, 'The Survival of Wyclif's Works in England and Bohemia', *Studies in the Transmission*, XVI, 26–8.
[23] On this project, see N. R. Ker, 'Thomas James's Collation of Gregory, Cyprian, and Ambrose', *Bodleian Library Record* 4, i (1952), 16–30 (a list of relevant manuscripts, many unreturned to their sources, at 23–30). Note also James's *The Jesuits Downefall* (STC 14459; Oxford, 1612).
[24] See Arnold's comment, *Select Works*, I, iii.
[25] See Shirley 40–8 passim for various indications of Bale as 'authority' for an ascription, but notice also the comments on Trinity 244 (48, no. 60).

Latin. And more than that: materials such as those in item 12 (a, e, k) presuppose not only Latin literacy but research ability, both access to original texts (here most usually Gratian), and the capacity to use the reference systems that open these volumes to readers.[26]

At this point, I want to decentre that (by now, conventional) perception of Bodley 647 as vernacular Lollardy. I do so by working in from materials always taken as peripheral, the Latin notes, not all of them part of the book's original plan, and none of them actually an integral text. On the one hand, one tends to view such materials as rather like a shopping-list, scrappy 'memoranda', reminders to oneself. Their effect, so this argument would run, is centrifugal, randomising, and these are adventitious additions, rather than ones focusing upon a reading.[27] Yet to this view, one might respond that the theological notes are additions made to this specific volume. At some level, like the added English texts here, they have been inspired by this book, and they respond, with authoritative materials, to what were considered, by some readers at least, themes relevant to the ensemble.

Moreover, book-production like this probably ruffles our sensitivities. We are accustomed to read whole texts and to feel that some integrity attaches to full exposure to complex authorial argument. But one might offer a somewhat counterintuitive riposte to that view, as well. Extraction and excerption form a strongly motivated variety of textual communication. After all, in an excerpt, someone is choosing this bit and not that one and is highlighting for consumption something discrete and readily assimilable. It may be that in such peripheral moments as these one can best discover those impulses driving production of an individual volume.

Certainly, the fairly constant recourse to Gratian's *Decretum* in these additions implies a set of reading procedures that do not privilege whole texts, but important scraps. The Latin, like Wycliffe's own theological materials, authoritatively underwrites opinions expressed, perhaps more availably, in the vernacular. Gratian indeed functions, not simply as a source of various odd bits, but a model for so proceeding. Like Bodley

[26] The penultimate English text of Bodley 647 both implies the need of 'pore prestis' teaching in both languages (*Select Works* III, 391) and heralds the vernacular Bible rather neutrally, as an aid to public 'learnedness' (p. 393).
[27] In these terms, and in the light of my discussion in the next paragraph but one, notice the passing expression of antipathy to canon law in Bodley 647, item 1 (*Select Works* III, 153).

647 itself, it can be construed as forming a model teaching anthology.[28] Its selective procedures, in the foundational volume of canon law, render doubly authoritative statements already authoritative through their attachment to named patristic writers.

Here I should think two extensive discussions in scribe 2's item 12 central. On the one hand, his notes include a treble reference to a single chapter of Gregory's *Cura pastoralis* (item 12 [a], [g]); on the other, he copies, from Gratian's quotation, a very extensive discussion by Jerome (item 12 [f]). Both selections focus upon the proper exercise of the clerical duty of teaching and preaching. Of course, many of the more tendentious selections copied in the Bodley manuscript, especially those drawing attention to the pseudo-prophets of the last days and to the Antichrist, examine the abuse of this function. There is certainly quite immediate carryover of these issues across linguistic boundaries; for example, one of Jerome's discussions (item 12 [a]) is expanded in the latest addition to the volume, the fragmentary and unpublished English item 7, itself a further gathering of authoritative quotation.

I am, of course, arguing that Bodley 647 forms a fairly carefully focused 'thematic miscellany', devoted to discussion of proper priesthood.[29] Here the lengthy citation from Jerome is particularly important (and richly resonant with James's defence of English orthodoxy). In this excerpt, Jerome argues that the duties of priests must not be compromised by the presence of a bishop, for if a priest fails to teach in this context, he has essentially forfeited his office. His point is taken

[28] Of course, as Hudson points out to me, scholarly excerption constitutes one common form of Wycliffite textual production, for example in the *Rosarium/Floretum* and 'the glossed gospels'. For the former, see Hudson, *Lollards*, 13–42, as well as Christina von Nolcken, ed., *The Middle English Translation of the Rosarium Theologie: A Selection*, Middle English Texts 10 (Heidelberg: Karl Winter, 1979); Hudson suggests to me that many of the Latin excerpts here may have been derived from this source. For 'the glossed gospels', see the index entry in Hudson, *Premature Reformation*, p. 545. Both tools, in line with the arguments of this paragraph, are parasitic on (and often, appropriating from) pre-existing academic Latin models, the *Rosarium* on texts like Thomas of Ireland's *Manipulus florum* or Nicholas of Byard's *Distinctiones*; 'the glossed gospels' on Aquinas's *Catena aurea*.

[29] Armando Petrucci, ed. and tr. Charles M. Radding, 'From the Unitary Book to the Miscellany', in *Writers and Readers in Medieval Italy: Studies in the History of Written Culture* (New Haven: Yale University Press, 1995), pp. 1–18, usefully argues that miscellaneity is a distinctively medieval form of book-production. For an exemplary set of analyses, see Philippa Hardman, ed., *Medieval and Early Modern Miscellanies and Anthologies*, Yearbook of English Studies 23 (2003).

up by the author of Bodley 647's longest (and first and keynote) text, the tract on the seven deadly sins. Apostolic Christianity, this writer avers, knew no bishops, only priests; Wycliffism returns to that pristine status of spiritually labouring democracy. As the author of 'The Seven Deadly Sins' reiterates, the Church (and society at large) should represent a single communal body. Ranks and distinctions are alien to such a conception, and it is they (and the special interests they institute) that have produced the world's sins.[30]

As a discussion of the seven sins, this English text is a bit unusual. Since its abiding concern is the harmonious social body, it has been conceived as an analysis *ad status*. While the author, somewhat illogically, accepts that differentiation inherent in the conception of the social 'three estates', he analyses sin as motivated by the divisive and self-seeking activities of knights, clerks, and labourers. Ultimately, social and spiritual harmony depend upon each group adopting a perspective broader than some form of class self-interest. This particular formulation enables the author, not simply to castigate abuses of the laity, great and small, but to devote 'equal time' to clerical malfeasance. (This decision, of course, allows ample space for the excoriation of both lax clerical practice, as well as such divisive behaviour as that indulged by those old enemies, the 'newe sectis' of friars – another focus of 'bad priest' discussion throughout the manuscript.)

A very small citation will clarify the point – and the ethos of Bodley 647. Envy afflicts the clergy, the author claims, because the various clerical orders compete for perquisites, and, in the process, ignore their most basic shared duty, to teach: 'And so [th]e fend has cast a boon, and made [th]ese houndes to feght, and by a bal of talow lettis hom to berke' (*Select Works* Vol. 3/III).

The charge fluctuates between pungent proverbialism and scriptural learnedness. On the one hand, clerics compete for the same 'perks' and, intent on discomfiting their rivals, seek some tangible reward, even a dry bone, to the exclusion of other duties. The metaphor itself plays off a widely recorded pseudo-Aesopian anecdote (recall the jealous Arcite's piously self-serving citation of an analogue at Chaucer, *Knight's Tale*,

---

[30] See *Select Works* III, 130–1. No one, I think, has noticed that this tract, in part, provides another example of Wycliffite appropriation of a pre-existing orthodox text. But chapters 2–6 have been derived from the second half of 'Pride wrath envy', P. S. Jolliffe, *A Check-List of Middle English Prose Writings of Spiritual Guidance* (Toronto: Pontifical Institute of Medieval Studies, 1974), I.19 (for the full tract, see F.21).

1177–82). But ultimately, in this account, there is not even a bone there to struggle over, but worthless worldly offal, refuse of a sort that gums up every dog's mouth, not just to its own discomfiture, but to that of untaught lay people. Yet the anecdote comes to rest in a quite different mode, learned biblicism, an allusion to the great locus of clerical rebuke, 'canes muti, non valentes latrare' (Isaiah 56: 10).[31]

In the last analysis, the Bodley manuscript enacts a succession of rhetorical moves of this sort. At its most typical moments, it replicates the sardonic passion of this comment. As Thomas James (and one of the book's annotators, who elaborated Wycliffe's name here) saw pretty well, Wycliffite rhetoric is that of inversion and parody. Its greatest triumph comes from reversing argumentative terms, from displaying what conventional clerical language calls 'heresy' as the purest apostolic 'orthodoxy'. This small moment in 'The Seven Deadly Sins' makes the case succinctly. The author here takes a typically mendicant form, the *exemplum*, elsewhere in the book excoriated as an improper instructional mode, and makes of it a learned and instructive allusion to the biblical text that should 'ground' all Christian behaviour.[32]

Conclusions

One might draw a variety of conclusions from this account of the descent of Bodley 647. First of all, only with difficulty may one ascribe to the production of the volume any pristine 'intention'. Even in the hands of its original pair of scribes, the developing quires and booklets that form the received manuscript were subject to various shifts of emphasis – and a consequent oscillation between broadening and particularising the 'argument' this collection might be construed as presenting.

Here one might point especially to the effect produced by scribe 2's various activities. On the one hand, as I implicitly argued in my allusions to this book in 1990, his central-text mendicant materials offer a quite specifically professionalised model of 'the bad clerical teacher'/ pseudo-prophet. The vocation of those abused in these texts paradoxically broadens the general scope of analysis in Bodley 647; in general

---

[31] See *Piers Plowman* C, 9.256–80 (ed. George Russell and George Kane [London: Athlone, 1977]) for an analogous evocation of the trope.
[32] For attacks on mendicant efforts to entertain diffusely, rather than concentrate on the educational biblical text, see, for example, *Select Works* III, 143 ('The Seven Deadly Sins' discussion of sloth) and p. 376.

(although item 2 is an exception), scribe 1's texts address themselves to problems associated with parochial, rather than regular, clergy.

On the other hand, scribe 2's additions on previously blank leaves, 'testimonials of the founders', offer resolutely specific materials, statements attached to named and revered predecessors. These, only by indirection, exemplify the general interests of the volume. They stand, like the unglossed Franciscan rule scribe 2 also provided, as samples that attain their full meaning only within an 'already instructed' environment, an 'extracodicological' set of historical particulars. One is to understand Francis's rule (of course, another founder's document) within a contemporary context, in which it describes no living Franciscan.

Conversely, yet analogously, Wycliffe, Hereford *et al.* are emphatically 'true priests' and are recognisable as such in the contemporary context by their concise, and catechetically useful, statements about the sacrament. By implication, other opinions within the volume, to be associated with these or comparable figures, their followers, achieve rhetorical purchase as equally basic sectarian catechesis precisely through such association.

Second, if 'single intention' cannot be predicated of Bodley 647's origins, the volume's use fractures matters yet further. As I have already indicated in various ways, I do not find any of the book's early readers, down to Thomas James, unresponsive to what was before them. It might not be amiss, although it surely runs against the grain of that fixedness implied by Lollard *scriptura sola*, to invoke an idea like 'continuous revelation' to describe the way in which the volume has been resituated by its readers, usually within a continuing, yet discontinuous, anti-Catholic context.

The final conclusion, and the aegis of this volume, is that this manuscript (and by extension, all manuscripts) never exists devoid of a context. One cannot here read Francis's rule as blandly 'informative', a historical document. The text only works as a stimulus to outrage, an implicit commentary upon different circumambient mendicant activities, *c.* 1380–1410 (and beyond). The book always gestures outside itself, at some material conditions, upon which it implicitly encourages intervention.

Obviously, Bodley 647 instructs. But all those who contributed to its production were aware of one thing about the procedure. They were constructing a portable library constructed from much more extensive materials, a further library not directly in evidence here. One goal of the manuscript's instruction is to stimulate readers to seek further materials, ones of greater sophistication and perhaps broader usefulness. Perhaps surprisingly, these materials are not vernacular ones; they include, but are not limited to, Gratian and Grosseteste. In spite of its status as the archetypal vernacular Lollard collection, Bodley 647 persistently alludes to the greater riches provided in the richly polylingual culture of late medieval England.

Appendix: Some further descriptive detail of Bodley 647

Vellum. Fols. iii + 107 + ii (an accurate medieval foliation for fols. 1–80). Overall 193 x 137mm.

Booklet 1 = fols. 1–36
1. Fols. 1–36ᵛ: the Wycliffite tract on the seven deadly sins (IPMEP [Index of Middle English Prose] 596, Shirley's English text 44), ed. Arnold 3: 119–67. The text also appears in Cambridge MA, Harvard University Library, Eng. 738; Dublin, Trinity College 245; Oxford, Bodleian, Bodley 938 and Douce 273. See the published description of Bodley 938, 'The Origins and Production of Westminster School MS. 3', *Studies in Bibliography* 41 (1988), 197–218, at 208–9; Eng. th.e.181, Douce 274 and Douce 273, in that order, originally formed a single volume; see Hudson, 'The *Lay Folks' Catechism*: A Postscript', *Viator* 19 (1988), 307–9.
Collation 1–3⁸ 4¹². No signatures in the manuscript, but regular centred catchwords on the last versos of quires.

Booklet 2 = fols. 37–69
2. Fols. 37–57: 'De blasphemia contra fratres' (IPMEP 401, Shirley 52), ed. Arnold 3:402–29.
3. Fols. 57ᵛ–62ᵛ: *Vita sacerdotum* (IPMEP 692, Shirley 53), ed. Arnold 3:233–41.
4. Fols. 62ᵛ–63ᵛ: *Lincolniensis* (IPMEP 436), ed. Arnold 3:230–2. This and the following items probably added on blank leaves at the end of the booklet's final quire.
5. Fols. 63ᵛ-64ᵛ: *Iohannes Wycliff* <long erasure>, the second confession on the eucharist (IPMEP 802, Shirley 54), also in the two manuscripts of Knighton's *Chronicle*, ed. Arnold 3:502–3; and Hudson, *Selections* 17–18 (a reference to this manuscript at 141).
6. Fols. 65-8: Latin theological notes, added in anglicana on blank leaves, inc. '*Ancelmus* Quia enim viles uestes et nigras fert vt se talem reputet peccatorum . . .'. There are only ten written lines on fol. 68. Given the rather uneven fading of the greyish ink, these

selections may have been added piecemeal, perhaps by the first owner.

(a) Fol. 65^{rv}: the incipit above, a misascription and not from any text in the *Patrologia Latina* (hereafter *PL*).

(b) Fol. 65^v: Jerome, epistle 51, ed. *PL* 22:517.

(c) Fols. 65^v-66: 'Lincolniensis, dicto 135', unpublished, but apparently from a sermon to monks; see S. Harrison Thomson, *The Writings of Robert Grosseteste* . . . (Cambridge, 1940), 179, 231. Hudson generously points out to me that item 4 begins with the same passage in both Latin and English, and that this is the bit of Grosseteste (a worthy English apostolic precursor) most frequently cited in both Wycliffe and his followers.

(d) Fol. 66^{rv}: 'Nota quod Antecristus iiij^{or}. cornibus armabitur scilicet callida persuasione miraculorum operacione . . .', including citation of the gloss on Apoc. 13:13 and of Gregory, perhaps paraphrase of *Moralia* 28.19 (*PL* 76:475).

(e) Fols. 66^v-67: Chrysostom, 'omelia xl. in *Imperfectum*', probably a citation from Gratian, *Decretum* D.40, c.12 ('Non est uere sacerdos omnis, qui nominatur sacerdos'), ed. E. Friedberg et al., *Corpus Juris Canonici*, 2 vols (Leipzig, 1869–71), 1:147–8.

(f) Fols. 67–8: 'Crisostomus in *Inperfectum*, omelia 27 Quando enim vides scripturas prophetarum et euangelii et apostolorum traditas esse', paraphrase probably inspired by Chrysostom's discussion of 'tradita' (Matt. 11:27) in homily 28 (*Patrologia Graeca* 56:777–8), turning into a lengthy analysis of 'similacra'.[33]

7. Fols. 68^v-69: a still unpublished Lollard text, elsewhere only at Cambridge, Trinity College, MS O.1.29, fols. 73–74^v, where it is called 'Documentum Roberti Grosehede'; see further Hudson, *Premature Reformation* 342 n142.[34] Added on leaves originally blank (and only nineteen lines on the added fol. 69, the entire verso still blank.

Collation 5^{16} 6^8 7^{8+1} (+9, the stub showing before fol. 61).

Booklet 3 = fols. 70–85

8. Fol. 70: Nicholas Hereford and Philip Repingdon's joint profession of eucharistic faith, 19 June 1382, ed. Margaret Aston, 'Wyclif

---

[33] The top line of fol. 68 has an interlinear Latinised English/Anglo-French gloss, 'babwynus' to explain 'chimera', in the same hand as the text.

[34] An edition has now appeared; see *Journal of the Early Book Society* 13 (2010), 265–74.

and the Vernacular', *Studies in Church History* subsidia 5 (1987), 281–330, at 328–9 (cf. the discussion at 297–300). This item and the next probably added, on a blank covering leaf, by scribe 2, in different, packed format: writing area 145 x 100, in 35 long lines (the last five on the verso blank).

9. Fol. 70^v: John Aston's similar profession, of the same date, ed. Aston 329–30.

10. Fols. 71–78^v: St Francis's rule and testament, in English, with a concluding commentary on modern efforts to ignore the rule (IPMEP 698 + 522, Shirley 13 + 14), also in Cambridge, Corpus Christi College, MS 296; and Dublin, Trinity College, MS 244, ed. Matthew 40–51.

11. Fols. 79–83: the Latin originals of the preceding texts, this item probably planned for, but the next certainly not and the quire supplemented to hold it, with rather second-rate vellum (fols. 80, 82, and 84 all lack the foot of the leaf, the first decidedly so).

12. Fols. 83–5: More Latin theological notes. There are eight blank lines at the foot of fol. 85, and the verso is also blank.

(a) Fol. 83^{rv}: Gregory, *Cura pastoralis* 2.4, ed. *PL* 77:30–1. These abbreviated selections are followed by references to Jerome, *Decretum* C.1, q.2, c.6 ('Qui sumptibus propriis sustentari possunt, ab ecclesia stipendia non accipiant', ed. 1:409) and Gregory, *Decretum* D.43, c.1 ('De discretione predicationis, et silentii', another extensive citation of the passage at the head of this section, ed. 1:153–5), and then citations of Luke 24:47 (paraphrased) and Mark 16:15, etc.

(b) Fol. 83^v: Augustine, cited from *Decretum* C.1, q.1, c.94 ('Eque seruandum est uerbum Christi et corpus Christi'), ed. 1:391–2.

(c) Fol. 83^v: Cyprian, cited from *Decretum* D.8, c.9 ('Dei veritatem, non hominem consuetudinem sequi oportet'), ed. 1:15–16.

(d) Fols. 83^v-84: an early sixth-century synod, cited from *Decretum* D.10, c.2 ('Nichil quod euangelicis regulis obuiet, imperatori agere licet'), ed. 1:20–1.

(e) Fol. 84: a reference, citation of the incipit only, to Chrysostom at *Decretum* C.11, q.3, c.86 ('Veritatem prodit non solum qui pro ueritate mendacium loquitur, sed etiam qui ueritatem non libere predicat'), ed. 1:167.

(f) Fol. 84^{rv}: Jerome, cited from *Decretum* D.95, c.6 ('Coram episcopis presbiteris docere licet'), ed. 1:333–4, much the longest of these selections.

(g) Fol. 84^v: Gregory, portions of *Cura Pastoralis* 2.4 again, ed. *PL* 77:30.

(h) Fol. 84^v: Augustine, sermon 'de scripturis' 111.3–4 paraphrased (on

Luke 10:2), ed. *PL* 38:607–8, including added discussion of efforts
to silence the apostles in Acts 4–5.

(i) Fol. 84ᵛ: Gregory, *Homiliae in evangelia* 1.18.3–5 paraphrased, ed.
PL 76:1152–3; then becoming a denunciation of 'superba edificia',
with citation of Isa. 5:8, Jer. 22:14, Amos 6:8, Matt. 8:20, and Heb.
13:14.

(j) Fols. 84ᵛ-85: Jerome, epistle 108, ed. *PL* 22:892, succeeded by further
citations, Hab. 2:11 with analysis, Matt. 24:2 (paraphrased), Amos
3:15.

(k) Fol. 85: materials ascribed to Bernard, not in *PL* and likely paraphrase, inc. 'Specialiter autem deberent cohibere claustrales a
superbis edificiis', with a concluding reference to further materials
in 'Parisiensis', i.e. Guillaume Peyrault OP (Peraldus). Hudson
identifies the reference as to *Summa de vitiis*, De superbia, ch. 22.

Collation 8⁸ 9⁶⁺² (+5, fol. 82, its stub preceding fol. 80; +7, fol. 84, its
stub preceding fol. 79).

Booklet 4 = fols. 86–107

13. Fols. 86–106ᵛ: 'Fifty heresies and errors of the friars' (IPMEP 187,
Shirley 15), also in Corpus 296 and Trinity 244, following item 10,
ed. Arnold 3:367–401.

14. Fol. 107ʳᵛ: Wycliffe, 'Letter to Urban VI' (IPMEP 324, Shirley 55),
also in Oxford, New College, MS 95, ed. Arnold 3:504–6, added
by scribe 2 on an originally blank leaf. For a full description of the
other copy, see Hudson, *English Wycliffite Sermons I* (Oxford, 1983),
75–6. In the fifteenth century, this book was at one time reasonably
proximate to areas where Bodley 647 might have circulated, since
an inscription indicates that it was given to dom. John Plumtree
of Dalby (i.e., one of the three villages of that name near Melton
Mowbray, Leics.) by Henry Suanton.

Collation 10⁶ 11–12⁸.

The Idea of the Heart in Byzantium and the History of the Book[1]

ROBERT ROMANCHUK

While historians of the book and of reading in the Middle Ages have pored over the evidence offered up by Christian Latinity – and, betting on cultural continuity, have not been afraid to reach back to Antiquity and forward to the Renaissance to clarify or contextualise their own readings – they have been chary of the abundant materials to be found in Byzantium.[2] Greek, in its Christian idiom, is 'not read' in the pages of specialist studies like Mary Carruthers's *The Book of Memory* and popular surveys such as Alberto Manguel's *A History of Reading*.[3] This 'not read' is not easy to justify: the earliest writings of Byzantium represent the shared patristic and monastic heritage of East and West, while in later texts the 'readerly' gestures and habits of earlier eras are replayed and rearticulated. Here, the celebrated conservatism of the Byzantines might be an advantage. In fact, the history of the book in the Christian East (when this history is 'read')[4] challenges certain

[1] This essay first grew out of conversations with Carol Poster and (especially) with Peter Stallybrass, whose numerous presentations and interventions at the History of Material Texts seminar at the University of Pennsylvania and the 2002–3 Penn Humanities Forum seminar on 'The Book' provided its initial stimulus. William R. Veder read an early draft of this paper and provided me with many useful suggestions and further examples, and Roman Koropeckyj and Lisa R. Wakamiya corrected a number of its stylistic infelicities. Two anonymous reviewers of a later draft likewise suggested substantive and stylistic improvements, and Orietta Da Rold and Elaine Treharne helped it reach its present form. My sincere thanks to the above-mentioned scholars; any mistakes are of course my own.
[2] Here I use 'Byzantium' to stand for the Eastern Christian Roman Empire together with its Eastern European 'Commonwealth'.
[3] M. J. Carruthers, *The Book of Memory: A Study of Memory in Medieval Culture* (Cambridge: Cambridge University Press, 1990); A. Manguel, *A History of Reading* (New York: Viking, 1996).
[4] Two fine descriptive surveys are A. P. Kazhdan, *Kniga i pisatel' v Vizantii* (Moscow: Nauka, 1973) and H. Hunger, *Schreiben und Lesen in Byzanz: Die byzantinische Buchkultur* (Munich: C. H. Beck, 1989); see also the essays in *Byzantine Books and Bookmen. A Dumbarton Oaks Colloquium* (Washington: Dumbarton Oaks, 1971), and B. Mondrain, ed., *Lire et écrire à Byzance* (Paris:

comfortable and well-established disciplinary formulations, necessi-
tating their revision or even rejection. For the purposes of this essay,
Byzantium's role will not be to supplement the (technological) history
of the book that has emerged in the West; rather, by restoring a group
of metaphors usually considered technological to their ethical ground,
an 'Eastern approach' will displace them from the field of inquiry of the
history of material texts and of mnemotechnique. Their estrangement
will, nonetheless, enrich the history of reading, and along the way, as
we will see, Byzantium will provide a new perspective on a *locus clas-
sicus* of this discipline in the West: Augustine's famous encounter with
the silence of his teacher Ambrose, in the face of his book.

As my title suggests, I wish to interrogate the *heart* as master trope
for the book in the European Middle Ages. Tracing a genealogy forward
from Paul's metaphor of the 'fleshy tablets of the heart' in 2 Corinthians 3: 3, Western historians of the book – most notably Eric Jager –
have glossed the heart as a surface for writing, a figure for the memory,
and ultimately a model of the self.[5] To be sure, the heart functions as
a materially book-like metaphor in East and West; doubtless, it acts
as a figure for memory across the whole Christian *oikoumene*. Yet in
Byzantium, the heart is more usually attached to the Scriptural word
by means of metaphors that are not *materially* book-like. It figures an
ethical subject before and after a 'subject who remembers'.[6] And the

---

Association des amis du Centre d'histoire et civilisation de Byzance, 2006).
For Kievan Rus', see S. Franklin, *Writing, Society and Culture in Early Rus, c.
950-1300* (Cambridge: Cambridge University Press, 2002); for a single monas-
tery in Muscovy, see R. Romanchuk, *Byzantine Hermeneutics and Pedagogy in the
Russian North: Monks and Masters at the Kirillo-Belozerskii Monastery, 1397–1501*
(Toronto: University of Toronto Press, 2007). Note as well S. Franklin, 'Book-
learning and Bookmen in Kievan Rus': A Survey of an Idea', *Harvard Ukrainian
Studies* 12–13 (1988–9), 830–48 and G. Lenhoff, 'The "Stepennaja kniga" and
the Idea of the Book in Medieval Russia', in M. Okuka and U. Schweier, eds.,
Germano-slavistische Beiträge. Festschrift für Peter Rehder zum 65. Geburtstag
(Munich: O. Sagner, 2004), pp. 449–58, for particular moments in Kievan Rus'
and Muscovy. Much work remains to be done before truly interdisciplinary
studies in the history of the book and of reading can appear in Byzantine (and
Early Slavic) studies.
[5] See E. Jager, *The Book of the Heart* (Chicago: University of Chicago Press,
2000).
[6] 'So instead of the word "self" or even "individual", we might better speak
of a "subject-who-remembers", and in remembering also feels and thinks and
judges. In other words, we should think of the apprehending and commenting
individual subject ("self") also in rhetorical terms', Carruthers, *The Book of
Memory*, p. 182. As will be seen, I would propose inverting this formula: in

Eastern Christian concept of the heart as the ethical support for the word – not necessarily a material support for the text – echoes across the Western European Middle Ages as well. Western historians of the book have rarely distinguished the various figures of the heart in their own sources, which include *pedagogical* metaphors of response to the word – the *earth*, and the *ears* and *eyes*, of the heart; and *eschatological* metaphors of judgement – the *tablets* of the heart. Spiritual formation is the main force of all these tropes; anything they have to say about technology, material or mnemotechnical, is incidental. An inquiry into the book-like heart in Byzantium will not only provide the 'tropology' of the reading act with a measure of historical precision that has long been wanting; insofar as it attenuates the technologistic lens through which the history of the medieval book has thus far been 'read', the discipline stands to gain in breadth of vision.

Let us, then, open a representative Eastern Christian book: the Old Slavic *Izmaragd* (or *Emerald*), a collection of sermons offering the reader instruction in moral exegesis, the branch of knowledge Seneca called 'preceptive'.[7] In its origin a tenth-century Bulgarian miscellany[8] compiled mostly of translated Greek texts, it was read in several versions (in a very great number of copies) by the East Slavs from the fourteenth century onward.[9] The *Izmaragd*, like other such miscellanies, begins

'feeling' (through the senses of the heart), thinking and judging, the reading subject also remembers.

[7] Seneca gives *praeceptivam* as a translation of *paraeneticem* in his *Ep.* 95. See Lucius Anaeus Seneca, *Moral Epistles*, ed. R. M. Gummere, 3 vols. (Cambridge, MA: Harvard University Press, 1917–25), vol. 3: pp. 58–9.

[8] This is the thesis of William R. Veder. See, for example, W. R. Veder, 'How to Write an Original Old Russian Text', in J. J. van Baak, ed., *Signs of Friendship to Honour A. G. F. van Holk, Slavist, Linguist, Semiotician* (Amsterdam: Rodopi, 1984); W. R. Veder, 'Three Old Slavic Discourses on Reading', in M. Colucci, G. Dell'Agata and H. Goldblatt, eds., *Studia slavica mediaevalia et humanistica Riccardo Picchio dictata*, 2 vols. (Rome: Edizioni Dell'Ateneo, 1986), vol. 2: 717–30, p. 721; W. R. Veder, 'Über erbauliche Kompilationen, die altrussischen Literati zugeschrieben werden', *Studia Slavica et Baltica* 8 (1987), 241–4; W. R. Veder and A. A. Turilov, eds., *The Edificatory Prose of Kievan Rus'* (Cambridge, MA: Harvard Ukrainian Research Institute, 1994): 3 n (but note Veder's caution at xxxv n. 68).

[9] For redactions and copies (85 attested), see B. M. Pudalov, 'Sbornik "Izmaragd" v russkoi pis'mennosti XIV–XVIII vv', *Metodicheskie rekomendatsii po opisaniiu slaviano-russkikh rukopisnykh knig*, 3.2 (1990), 382–405; for the chapters of the two main versions, and one view of the history of the text, see B. M. Pudalov, 'Literaturnaia istoria 1–i ("Drevneishei") redaktsii *Izmaragda*', *Drevniaia Rus'* 2 (1990), 76–95; B. M. Pudalov, 'K literaturnoi istorii sbornika

with a chain of sermons concerning the reading of Scripture.[10] The
first of these, a 'Discourse on how to listen and give heed to lecture',
attributed to John Chrysostom, is largely adapted from the fifth-century
pseudepigraph *De patientia* (itself attributed alternately to Chrysostom
and Ephrem the Syrian),[11] in particular the section called the 'Proposal
of penance, and exhortation to meditate on the divine Scriptures' in
Migne's edition.[12] The 'Discourse' in its entirety is as follows:

> John Chrysostom said: 'When thou sittest (down) to the reading of
> God's words, *first pray to Him that He open the eyes of thy heart, so*

"Izmaragd": formirovanie 2-i ("Osnovnoi") redaktsii', *Trudy otdela drevnerusskoi
literatury* 55 (2004), 330–42. Pudalov's studies largely supersede V. A. Iakovlev, *K literaturnoi istorii drevne-russkikh sbornikov: opyt issledovaniia 'Izmaragda'*
(Odessa: Tipografiia Sht. Voisk Odesskogo voennogo Okruga, 1893), 42–50.

[10] For English translations of excerpts from these sermons, see G. P. Fedotov,
*The Russian Religious Mind II. The Middle Ages: The Thirteenth to the Fifteenth
Centuries* (Belmont, MA: Nordland, 1966), pp. 41–9; for excerpts in Slavic, see
Iakovlev, *K literaturnoi istorii drevne-russkikh sbornikov*, pp. 42–50. The *Izmaragd*
has only been published in one eccentric version, which lacks many of these
sermons: *Izmaragd, izhe vo s(via)tykh o(t)tsa nashego Ioanna Zlatoustago i prochikh
s(via)tykh: bezplatnoe prilozhenie k zhurnalu 'Zlatostrui'*, 2 vols. (Moscow: Mosko-
vskaia staroobriadcheskaia knigopechatnia, 1911–12).

[11] The *De patientia* is published in Greek under Chrysostom's name by Migne
in PG 63, col. 937–42 (CPG 4693). It is published under Ephrem the Syrian's
name in *Sancti Ephraem Syri Opera omnia. Tom. III (Gr. I)*, ed. J. Assemani
(Rome: Typographia Vaticana, 1746), pp. 93–104 (CPG 4007) and in a dual
Slavic and Greek text in G. Bojkovsky and R. Aitzetmüller, eds., *Paraenesis. Die
altbulgarische Übersetzung von Werken Ephraims des Syrers*, 5 vols. (Freiburg im
Breisgau: U. W. Weiher, 1984–90), vol. IV, 232–81. An apophthegm (N670)
derived from the *De patientia*, assigned to Chrysostom's name (and opening the
short Slavic 'Discourse', printed below), concludes the *Alphabetical-Anonymous
Collection* of the *Apophthegmata patrum* (CPG 5561), compiled by c.500. See J.
Guy, *Recherches sur la tradition grecque des Apophthegmata patrum*, 2nd edition
(Brussels: Société des Bollandistes, 1984), pp. 74, 87; D. Burton-Christie, *The
Word in the Desert: Scripture and the Quest for Holiness in Early Christian Monasti-
cism* (New York: Oxford University Press, 1993), pp. 85–8.

[12] The section described as 'Hypothesis exomologēseôs, kai pros tên tôn theiôn
graphôn meletên protropê' is on col. 939–41 of PG 63. Outside the *De patientia*,
it is also found compiled into the *De panoplia* of Ephrem (CPG 4020): see *Sancti
Ephraem Syri Opera*, ed. Assemani, pp. 219–34. The reader's prayer from the
'Proposal of Penance' (present in a modified form in the 'Discourse') has several
verbal parallels to the prayer recited at the Liturgy of St John Chrysostom
prior to the reading of the Epistle (in some contexts, the Gospel). See J. Goar,
Euchologion sive rituale graecorum (Venice: Typ. Bartholomaei Javarina, 1730),
p. 74.

that thou mayest not only read what is written, but do (it) as well; lest
we read to our harm the lives and words of the saints'. When thou
art reading, *read diligently with all thy heart, and read the words with
much diligence*; and do not endeavor only to turn the leaves – if need
be, do not be negligent, but read the words even twice, so that thou
mayest understand their force. When thou shalt sit down to read
or to listen to someone else reading, pray to God with these words:
'*Lord Jesus Christ, open the ears and eyes of my heart to hear Thy word
and to understand it and to do Thy will*, Lord, for I am a stranger in
the earth; hide not Thy commandments from me, but open mine
eyes and I shall understand wondrous things out of Thy law (Psalm
118 [119]: 19, 18); reveal to me the hidden and secret things of Thy
wisdom (Psalm 50 [51]: 6). In Thee I trust, God, that thou illumine
my intellect and reason with the light of Thy intellect not only to
read what is written, but also to do (it); lest I read to my harm the
lives and words of the saints, (but) to the renewal (and) the illumination and to the sanctification and to the salvation of my soul, and
to the achievement of eternal life; for Thou art a light of them that
lie in darkness (Rom. 2: 19) and from Thee is every good gift and
every perfect gift (Jas. 1: 17). To Thee do we offer praise and glory, to
the Father and to the Son and to the Holy Ghost, now and forever
and to the ages of ages. Amen'.[13]

This text and its source (the *De patientia*) are authoritative statements
on reading, popular across the whole Byzantine world.[14]

[13] Critical edition of the Slavic 'Discourse' in Veder, 'Three Old Slavic
Discourses on Reading', p. 724; English translation in W. R. Veder, ed, *The
Scaliger Paterikon, Early Slavic Texts on Microfiche*, 2 vols. (Leiden: Inter Documentation Company, 1976–8), vol. I: fol. 1v–2v. Here and below I have italicised passages of interest; in a few places I have also brought the translations
closer to the originals to maintain the continuity of certain metaphorical and
theological expressions. The sources of the 'Discourse' include the apophthegm
just mentioned (N670) and the section of the *De patientia* entitled 'Proposal of
Penance': see Veder, 'Three Old Slavic Discourses on Reading', p. 718; as well
as the seventh pre-communion prayer, attributed to John Chrysostom in Old
Believer prayer-books (the sixth, attributed to Basil the Great, in canonical
prayer-books): see R. Romanchuk, 'Lectio divina: monasheskoe chtenie na
vostoke i na zapade', in E. G. Vodolazkin, ed., *Monastyrskaia kul'tura: vostok i
zapad* (St. Petersburg: Al'manakh 'Kanun', 1999), pp. 36–43, at p. 41.
[14] Aside from the various Greek and Slavic versions, the *De patientia* was translated into Georgian in the tenth century: I. Abuladze, ed., *Mamat'a scavlani X
da XI s.-t'a xelnacerebis mixedvit' (Poucheniia Ottsov po rukopisiam X i XI vekov)*
(Tbilisi: Izd. AN GSSR, 1955), pp. 12–24.

The 'Basic' redaction of the *Izmaragd* continues with the following 'Foreword to all the instructions and parables in these books, for the confirmation of the faithful':

> If one shall read, let him read first this parable, which the Savior said of us in the Gospel.
>
> A sower went forth to sow: And when he sowed, some seeds fell by the way side, and the fowls came and devoured them up: Some fell upon stony places, where they had not much earth: and forthwith they sprung up, and withered away. And some fell among thorns: But other fell into good earth, and brought forth fruit (Matt. 13: 3–8). If one, O brother, shall hear the holy words, and enter the heavenly kingdom by true learning, *then first soften the earth of thy heart, and thou shalt receive the fruit of the saving grain.* It is said: if we only hear the word of God and do not do it, we will accomplish nothing, and cannot be saved. [. . .]
>
> HEAR THE MEANING OF THIS PARABLE.
>
> The sower is Christ, and the seed is the teaching of Divine Scripture; and the seed that falls upon stone is [as Scripture] among the Jews; and that by the wayside, is [as Scripture] among the heretics; and that among thorns, is that done by Christians, but doing the Devil's deeds, and following only the will of the flesh, in drunkenness and so forth. And that into good earth, is [as Scripture] among the meek and humble, *who with all their heart trust in God,* not only with faith, but also with good deeds endeavoring to receive eternal life in Christ Jesus our Lord.[15]

The 'Discourse' and the 'Foreword' are 'preceptive' writings. George Fedotov compared them to the introductions of catechetics, and Ivan Porfir'ev noted that they prescribe a regimen for the reading of books.[16] The reader is exhorted to 'read diligently with all thy heart', and to accept Scripture's teaching as do the meek and humble, 'who with all their heart trust in God'. Two particular metaphors of the heart as a locus of Scripture are present here: the senses (the ears and eyes) of the heart, and the earth of the heart. Both tropes have been linked with the 'book of the heart' and with mnemotechnique in the Western history of the book. Yet we will be disappointed if we expect a memory

---

[15] Text printed in *Izmaragd*, I, fol. 1v.
[16] See Fedotov, *The Russian Religious Mind II*, p. 41; I. I. Porfir'ev, 'O chtenii knig (o pochitanii knizhnom) v drevnie vremena Rossii', *Pravoslavnyi sobesednik* 2 (1858), 173–98, 443–61, at p. 178.

treatise, for *memoria* has been mostly forgotten here. Mnemotechnique may perhaps be detected behind (or better, *after*) the exhortation to 'read the words even twice, so that thou mayest understand their force' in the 'Discourse' – the lesson is repeated insistently enough for the words to become embodied on the lips and in the ears of the reader, and ultimately in his or her heart, as it were – but here the 'force' of the words aims at a place that is not memorial or material. What is its aim? To answer this question, I will examine each of the Byzantine metaphors of the book-like heart in turn.

Earth of the heart

The earth of the heart, as the compiler of the *Izmaragd* recognised, has its origin in the parable of the sower. The seed is the word of God, which the reader endeavours to hear, understand and put into practice:

> When any one heareth the word of the kingdom and understandeth it not [. . .] this is he which received seed by the way side. But he that received the seed into stony places, the same is he that heareth the word [. . .] Yet hath he not root in himself [. . .] He also that received seed among the thorns is he that heareth the word; and the care of this world [. . .] choke[s] the word [. . .] But he that received seed into the good ground is he that heareth the word, and understandeth it; which also beareth fruit, and bringeth forth [*poiei*, 'doeth'], some an hundredfold, some sixty, some thirty. (Matthew 13: 19–23)

This three-part approach to the word (it is heard, understood and enacted), adumbrated and articulated in the parable of the sower, reappears in the hermeneutics of Gadamer and Jauss as the 'Pietist' triad of understanding, interpretation and application.[17] The word is understood by a subject as a *kerygma*, a proclamation that demands an

---

[17] On the hermeneutic triad, see H. Gadamer, *Truth and Method*, trans. J. Winsheimer and D. G. Marshall, 2nd, revised edition (New York: Continuum, 1998), pp. 307–11; H. R. Jauss, *Toward an Aesthetic of Reception* (Minneapolis: University of Minnesota Press, 1982), pp. 139–48; P. Ricoeur, *A Ricoeur Reader: Reflection and Imagination*, ed. M. J. Valdes (Toronto: University of Toronto Press, 1991), pp. 407–11. Gadamer attributed this triad to the pietist J. J. Rambach, but this has been shown to be a lapse on Gadamer's part: see L. Kisbali, 'In Pursuit of a Phantom Quotation: Gadamer and Pietist Hermeneutics', *Budapest Review of Books* 8.2 (1998), 50–6.

ethical response. It is heard as a 'preaching', reflectively interpreted, and realised in the subject's practice. In this way the Scriptural word maintains the primitive Christian ideal of direct communion with God. The 'occasionalising' force of this word is not properly rhetorical: as Gadamer remarks, such a word has the power to 'call men to repentance even though the sermon is a bad one'.[18] The word is retained in the heart,[19] effecting not a store of common places, but a conversion. It is effectively 'remembered' by means of its ethical fruits.

The image of the earth of the heart, if it proceeds from the parable of the sower, is not, to the best of my knowledge, articulated in Scripture. It is found in the fourth-century corpus of writings known as the *Fifty Spiritual Homilies*, probably originating among the Messalians[20] but accepted by the Orthodox Church and assigned to Macarius of Egypt. It is a sufficiently characteristic image to provide the name of Columba Stewart's study of this corpus, *Working the Earth of the Heart*.[21] In his Homily 26, for instance, Pseudo-Macarius invokes the earth of the heart in a bucolic metaphor for a joint operation of grace and labour that seems to exclude the Scriptural word altogether:

> In the material world of things around us, the farmer works the earth. So also in the spiritual world there are two elements to be considered. It is necessary for man to work the earth of his heart by a free deliberation and hard work. For God looks to man's hard work and toil and labor. But if the heavenly clouds from above do not appear and the showers of grace, the farmer for all his labor avails nothing.[22]

Grace is planted in the heart directly by God; Pseudo-Macarius's image suggests no bookish mediation. Indeed the Word is consistently defined as incarnate in the *Homilies*: 'The Word of God is God'; 'The individual person progresses, once he has received the life of the Holy Spirit and

[18] Gadamer, *Truth and Method*, p. 330.
[19] On the heart as the *sedes sapientiae* in the Bible, see Jager, *The Book of the Heart*, pp. 9–12.
[20] The Messalians were Syrian monastic proponents of 'pure prayer', holding the sacraments to be useless. They were condemned at the Third Ecumenical Council in 431, but the writings later attributed to Macarius continued to circulate. For an overview of the Messalian controversy and the problem of the Pseudo-Macarian corpus, see Pseudo-Macarius, *The Fifty Spiritual Homilies and the Great Letter*, ed. G. A. Maloney (New York: Paulist Press, 1992), pp. 1–33.
[21] C. Stewart, *'Working the Earth of the Heart': The Messalian Controversy in History, Texts, and Language to AD 431* (Oxford: Clarendon Press, 1991).
[22] Pseudo-Macarius, *Homilies*, p. 167

has eaten the Lamb and has been anointed by his blood and has eaten the true Bread, the living Word' (Homilies 46, 47).[23] This concept of grace that circumvents the kerygmatic Scriptural word is representative of a bookless strain in the spirituality of the desert fathers, as Douglas Burton-Christie has shown.[24] However, a metropolitan (and bookish) Byzantine tendency – originating in a 'Roman' capital in Asia Minor or at the Bulgarian court in Preslav, where the *Izmaragd* was compiled – rearticulated the link of the earth of the heart with the Gospel parable of the sower of the Scriptural word. Should the reader lazily forget his bookish vocation and be tempted to seek grace in 'pure prayer', the foreword of the *Izmaragd* would remind him: 'The sower is Christ, and the seed is the teaching of Divine Scripture'.

The sower of the word – whether encountered in Scripture or in the person of a teacher of flesh and blood through whom Scripture speaks – plants the word in the heart of a reader-student through pedagogy. Many pedagogical traditions of late antiquity – the value placed on the *viva vox* of a teacher, the division of study into phases of *moralia* and *mystica*, and the provision of introductory material before the study of writings – were preserved in Christian *paideia*, and are evoked from Origen to the great Byzantine saints, John Climacus and John Damascene.[25] The pedagogical aptness of the metaphor of the earth of the heart is seen in a text (preserving more Macarian imagery: the farmer's toil, the showers of God) copied in the *Izmaragd* (c. 24 of the 'Archaic' redaction) and the tenth-century Bulgarian *Miscellany* of John the Sinner:

> My child, I would say to you even more that is to your salvation. *But the words of God are prolific, and if you will loosen the earth of your heart and receive the small seed of teaching, you will very greatly multiply within yourself the grain of salvation. If you truly aspire to all my small words*

---

[23] Pseudo-Macarius, *Homilies*, pp. 230, 236.

[24] See D. Burton-Christie, *The Word in the Desert: Scripture and the Quest for Holiness in Early Christian Monasticism* (New York: Oxford University Press, 1993), pp. 54–62.

[25] For studies of these and other late antique pedagogical traditions, see I. Hadot, *Arts libéraux et philosophie dans la pensée antique*, 2nd, revised and augmented edition (Paris: Vrin, 2005); J. Mansfeld, *Prolegomena: Questions to be settled before the study of an author, or a text* (Leiden: E. J. Brill, 1994). For their appropriation by Christianity, see A. Louth, *The Origins of the Christian Mystical Tradition: From Plato to Denys* (Oxford: Oxford University Press, 1981); P. Hadot, *Exercices spirituels et philosophie antique*, revised and augmented edition (Paris: Albin Michel, 2002), pp. 19–98.

of teaching and live your days accordingly, then the field of your heart will be watered by God who desires that all men be saved (cf. 1 Timothy 2: 4). And the fruit of salvation will so multiply within you that you will not be able to accommodate the abundance in the home of your soul, but will distribute it to the others who long for their own salvation.[26]

In John's *Miscellany*, this follows immediately upon a recompilation of Pseudo-Chrysostom's 'Discourse'. The earth of the heart is here bound to the senses of the heart, in a structural echo of the 'Basic' version of the *Izmaragd*.

Augustine knew the earth of the heart as a pedagogical metaphor, although his version (in *Confessions* II.3.5) connotes the absence of a teacher:

> Still, this same father troubled himself not at all as to how I was progressing toward thee nor how chaste I was, just so long as I was skillful in speaking – no matter how barren I was to thy tillage, O God, who art the one true and good Lord of my heart, which is thy field ['qui es unus verus et bonus dominus agri tui, cordis mei'].[27]

The trope was known as well to the Orthodox saints (or at least, to their hagiographers). At the end of the fourteenth century, according to Pachomius the Logothete, the Russian monastic Saint Cyril of Beloozero laboured in the bakery of the Moscow Simonov monastery, developing his abundant gift of tears. His teacher was Sergius of Radonezh, the great Muscovite cenobitic reformer and hesychast. Whenever Sergius would come to Simonov, says Pachomius, he would head straightaway to the bakery to converse with Cyril. Pachomius's description of their 'discussions on the good of the soul' binds the Macarian metaphor of the showers of God to a lachrymose image from the Psalms: 'So to say, the two made a spiritual furrow: the one (i.e. Sergius) sowed the seeds of good deeds, the other (i.e. Cyril) watered with tears: "They that sow in tears shall reap in joy" (Psalm 125 [126]: 5)'.[28] This is a

---

[26] English text cited from Veder and Turilov, eds., *The Edificatory Prose of Kievan Rus'*, p. 8; for the text's place in the *Izmaragd*, see Pudalov, 'Literaturnaia istoria 1–i', p. 84. The Greek original of the instruction is untraced.

[27] English translation: Augustine, *Confessions and Enchiridion*, ed. A. C. Outler (Philadelphia: The Westminster Press, 1955), p. 52; see text and commentary in Augustine, *Confessions*, ed. J. J. O'Donnell, 3 vols. (Oxford: Clarendon Press, 1992), I, 17 and II, 119.

[28] Pachomius's *Life* of Cyril of Beloozero, line 440. V. Iablonskii, *Pakhomii Serb*

description of Sergius's spiritual pedagogy, and almost certainly figures a bookish Scriptural exegesis of the moral or 'tropological' kind favoured by monastics. These discussions, Pachomius writes, would continue for an hour or more until the abbot and the brethren arrived in the bakery, amazed that Sergius wished to tarry so long with Cyril.

In summary, the metaphor of the earth of the heart as a vessel for Scripture grew out of the parable of the sower. In its earliest form, articulated in the bookless and quasi-Messalian desert milieu, the image describes a subject seeking grace directly from God, unmediated by Scripture. Later, in a metropolitan context, the metaphor is explicitly bound to the parable of the sower and comes to imply a *reading subject*. Figuring the place where this subject holds the word, the earth of the heart becomes a book-like image in Byzantium. Yet it is not a material-technological metaphor for a writing surface, even if it may be joined to such imagery (see below). It suggests no mnemotechnique; the earth of the heart is softened, not to aid memory storage, but so that word may grow and the subject bear the fruits of repentance. It is thus natural that this earth should be softened by tears, the visible signs of compunction.[29] Insofar as the earth of the heart requires a sower of the word, the trope makes the reader a student discoursing with a teacher. This pedagogy may at times be literally bookless – certainly, books were not permitted in the Simonov bakery – but it is still rooted in the book.

Ears and eyes of the heart

The *Izmaragd*'s opening sermon instructs the reader to pray that Christ 'open the ears and eyes of my heart to hear Thy word and to understand

i ego agiograficheskie pisaniia. Biograficheskii i bibliograficheskii-literaturnyi ocherk (St. Petersburg: Sinodal'naia tipografiia, 1908), p. x; G. M. Prokhorov, E. G. Vodolazkin and E. E. Shevchenko, eds., *Prepodobnye Kirill, Ferapont i Martinian Belozerskie*, 2nd edition (St Petersburg: Glagol, 1994), p. 66. See also Romanchuk, *Byzantine Hermeneutics*, pp. 88–9. The metaphor of the furrow is traced from Isidore of Seville to Peter the Venerable by Ivan Illich, who takes it to mean an amanuensis (ploughman) taking his master's (the sower's) dictation; see I. Illich, *In the Vineyard of the Text* (Chicago: University of Chicago Press, 1993), p. 89. Illich seems to have overlooked the ethical aspect of the trope.
[29] In Greek, *penthos* or *katanyxis*, in Slavic *plach* or *umilenie*. For an overview of the concept, see I. Hausherr, *Penthos: The Doctrine of Compunction in the Christian East*, trans. A. Hufstader (Kalamazoo, MI: Cistercian Publications, 1982).

it and to do Thy will'. The ears and eyes of the heart are here connected
with the triad of hearing, understanding and enacting the word previously encountered in the parable of the sower, and were thus linked, in
the Byzantine mind, to the kerygmatic word and its ethical application.
Historians of the book, however, have glossed the senses of the heart
(as widespread in the Latin tradition as in its Byzantine counterpart)
rather differently – as a memory trope.[30] The eye of the heart serves
to figure the 'seeing' of memorial *phantasmata*, visual images to aid the
memory, in Carruthers's *The Book of Memory*: this image frames Carruthers's preliminary discussion of 'the material, and therefore spatial,
nature of memory images, [which] also helps to account for why the
ancients persistently thought of memoria as a kind of eye-dependent
reading, a visual process'.[31] As the spoken word 'is turned into visual
form so frequently and persistently', there is – it goes without saying –
no place for aural tropes. Carruthers states categorically: 'There simply
is no classical or Hebrew or medieval tradition regarding an "ear of the
mind" equivalent to that of the "eye of the mind".'[32] Of course, such a
claim is untenable; as Curtius pointed out, Augustine knew of the ears
of the heart, and they open Benedict's *Rule*.[33]

The eyes of the heart, according to Bauer, are attested in the
Hermetic Corpus.[34] Their Scriptural usage, whether dependent upon
an earlier tradition or not, is probably related to Christ's sixth beatitude from the Sermon on the Mount: 'Blessed are the pure in heart: for
they shall see God' (Matthew 5: 8). These eyes are found only once in
canonical Scripture, in a bookless and revelatory context (as proceeds
from the beatitude), at Ephesians 1: 17–18:

> That the God of our Lord Jesus Christ, the Father of glory, may give
> unto you the spirit of wisdom and revelation in the knowledge of

---

[30] Although Carruthers, in *The Book of Memory*, p. 46, links memory in the
Middle Ages with the 'praxis of liturgical and devotional prayer', this praxis is
discussed almost exclusively in its mnemotechnical aspects.
[31] Carruthers, *The Book of Memory*, pp. 16–17, 27, introduces *phantasmata* by
citing Jerome on the eyes of the heart.
[32] Ibid., p. 27.
[33] See E. R. Curtius, *European Literature and the Latin Middle Ages*, trans. W.
R. Trask (Princeton: Princeton University Press, 1953), pp. 136–7. Paulinus of
Nola also knew the 'eyes and ears of the mind'.
[34] W. Bauer, *A Greek-English Lexicon of the New Testament and Other Early
Christian Literature*, 2nd edition (Chicago: University of Chicago Press, 1979)
p. 599, s.v. *ophthalmos* 2.

him: *The eyes of your heart being enlightened*; that ye may know what is the hope of his calling, and what the riches of the glory of his inheritance in the saints.

The eyes of the heart are 'opened' (as in the reader's prayer) to light and revelation several times in the Apostolic Fathers, for example in 1 Clement 36: 2:

> Through him [i.e., Christ] we fix our gaze on the heights of heaven, through him we see the reflection of his faultless and lofty countenance, *through him the eyes of our hearts were opened*, through him our foolish and darkened understanding blossoms towards the light, through him the Master willed that we should taste the immortal knowledge [. . .].[35]

Thus far we are not, it seems, dealing with much more than textual reminiscence.[36] The late-antique-*cum*-medieval tradition that assigned particular roles to the eyes and ears of the heart goes back to Origen's doctrine of the spiritual senses, which has been discussed in a classic article by Karl Rahner.[37] Origen (especially in his *Contra Celsum*) claimed that the perfected Christian perceives, and receives, divine grace through five spiritual senses that correspond to the five bodily senses. Out of the (mistranslated) 'divine sense' of Proverbs 2: 5 and the senses of the 'perfect' in Hebrews 5: 14, Origen delineated five separate spiritual faculties, assigned alternately to the soul, spirit or intellect (*nous*). In the *Contra Celsum* he speaks of

> a sight which can see things superior to corporeal beings, the cherubim or seraphim being obvious instances, and a hearing which can receive impressions of sounds that have no objective existence in

[35] K. Lake, ed. *The Apostolic Fathers*, 2 vols. (Cambridge, MA: Harvard University Press, 1912–13), I, 71.
[36] The 'eye of the soul' is, of course, found in Plato, Aristotle and Plotinus, and was known to Celsus. See for example Plato, *Republic* 533d.
[37] K. Rahner, *Theological Investigations. Volume XVI. Experience of the Spirit: Source of Theology*, trans. D. Morland (New York: Crossroad, 1983), pp. 81–103. For a similar doctrine in Plotinus and a possible source for both Origen and Plotinus, see J. Dillon, 'Aisthêsis noêtê: A Doctrine of Spiritual Senses in Origen and in Plotinus', in A. Caquot, ed., *Hellenica et Judaica: Hommage à Valentin Nikiprowetsky* (Liuven: Peeters, 1986), pp. 443–55.

the air, and a taste which feeds on living bread that has come down from heaven and gives life to the world (John 6: 33)[38]

– and so forth, all the way to the touch of 1 John 1: 1.

Origen maintains a Platonic-Plotinian noetic ('intellectual') locus for the spiritual senses; they are not connected with the heart in the *Contra Celsum*.[39] It was Pseudo-Macarius who reoriented Origenist doctrine upon the heart, most probably under the influence of the Scriptural passages discussed above. Pseudo-Macarius makes frequent reference to the senses, in particular the eyes, of the heart.[40] He treats the image of the eyes of the heart much like the earth of the heart – even invoking the heart's eyes in tandem with his rustic metaphor in Homily 14:

> For the farmer sows seeds in the hope of fruit and he undergoes toils on account of what he hopes to receive. [. . .] So also in the Kingdom of Heaven – *in the hope of having the eyes of his heart illumined*, a person gives himself up to seek the kingdom, putting aside all worldly pursuits, intent on prayers and supplications.[41]

It is striking that the eyes of the heart do not perceive the Scriptural word in Pseudo-Macarius. The senses of the heart – like its earth – receive direct revelation from God. They are opened in the perfected Christian, who does not require Scripture. Rather, as the eye of the heart is identified in the Pseudo-Macarian writings with the *nous* – which is held to be the organ of divine perception, *theoria* (as was Plotinus's eye of the intellect or Origen's spiritual eye) – prayers and supplications, as well as a perfected life, open it to the vision of God.[42] Pseudo-Macarius does not, to the best of my knowledge, refer explicitly to the ears of the heart, although he often speaks in one breath of the 'eyes and ears' that are 'deeper', 'inner' or 'new' (e.g. in Homilies 28,

---

[38] Origen, *Contra Celsum*, ed. H. Chadwick, revised edition (Cambridge: Cambridge University Press, 1980), I.48, p. 44.

[39] *De principiis* I.1.9, however, refers to the 'faculties of the heart'. See Rahner, *Theological Investigations*, p. 85 n. 20.

[40] Pseudo-Macarius speaks of five spiritual senses (for example in Homily 4: see Pseudo-Macarius, *Homilies*, p. 53), but is especially interested in the eye of the heart. See Rahner, *Theological Investigations*, pp. 101–2.

[41] Pseudo-Macarius, *Homilies*, p. 105.

[42] Homily 15; see Pseudo-Macarius, *Homilies*, p. 116. See also Louth, *The Origins of the Christian Mystical Tradition*, chapters 3 and 4.

33, 44).[43] The fact that Chrysostom and Ephrem – to both of whom
the *De patientia* is ascribed – as well as Pseudo-Macarius, were Syrian,
could suggest that the image of the 'ears of the heart' originated in Syria,
although Stewart does not remark on this in his thorough study of the
Syriac origins of Macarian vocabulary.[44]

As was the case with the earth of the heart, it was in a metropolitan
Byzantine context (as reflected in the *De patientia* and the *Izmaragd*)
that the senses of the heart were turned explicitly toward the Scriptural
word: 'When you wish to sit and read, or again, to listen to another
reading, beg first of God, saying: "Lord Jesus Christ, open the ears and
eyes of my heart for me to hear Thy word, and to understand it, and to
do Thy will, Lord".'[45] Pseudo-Chrysostom, invoking the heart's senses,
prescribes the same response to the word implied by the Byzantine
image of the earth of the heart: hearing the *kerygma* and conversion, in
a broadly pedagogical context. It is in such a form that the eyes and ears
of the heart migrated to the West, for the Latin use of these metaphors
is typically connected to the book, rather than (as in Pseudo-Macarius)
with a grace that lies beyond it. And, just as in Byzantium, in Latinity
the ears and eyes of the heart are opened to the *ethical* effect of the
Scriptural word, before and after they encounter any *phantasmata* of
mnemotechnique. Augustine's use of the metaphors is unexceptional:
'Behold, *the ears of my heart* are before thee, O Lord; *open them* and "say
to my soul, I am your salvation" (Psalm 34 [35]: 3)', *Confessions* I.5.5;
'Those who *remember the words less closely* but penetrate to the heart of

---

[43] See Pseudo-Macarius, *Homilies*, pp. 185, 202, 223. The coupling of eyes and
ears is found in Matthew 13: 15 (based on Isaiah 6: 10) and 1 Corinthians 2: 9
(based on Isaiah 64: 4).
[44] For Stewart's discussion of the *aisthêsis noera* in Pseudo-Macarius see Stewart,
'*Working the Earth of the Heart*', pp. 124–31. The 'ears of the heart' are distinct
from the Mariological trope of 'conception through hearing' employed by the
fifth-century Proclus of Constantinople, and discussed in Constas's fine study:
see N. Constas, *Proclus of Constantinople and the Cult of the Virgin in Late Antiquity. Homilies 1–5, Texts and Translations* (Leiden: Brill, 2003), pp. 273–313.
Constas (pp. 308–9) assimilates the *voces paginarum* to the notion of spiritual
midwifery, an image I have not encountered in the instructions I have studied.
[45] Ephrem (in his 'Homily on Our Lord', XXXII.3) uses typology to gloss the
'interior eyes': 'Even though the eyes of Moses were physical, like those of Paul,
his interior eyes were Christian. For "Moses wrote concerning me . . ."' (Acts
9: 4). Ephrem cites Ephesians 1: 18 in this passage. See Saint Ephrem, *Selected
Prose Works*, ed. K. McVey, E. G. Mathews Jr and J. P. Amar (Washington:
Catholic University of America Press, 1994), p. 308. This use of the figure
seems eccentric, however, and in any case does not refer explicitly to reading.

Scripture *with the eyes of their own heart* are much to be preferred', *De doctrina christiana* IV.5.[46] It is worth noting that in the last instance, as in Gadamer's example, the *kerygma* has its effect despite the failure of (rhetorical) *memoria*.

This excursus into Origenist and Macarian theology makes the meaning of the ears and eyes of the heart in the context of reading Scripture sufficiently clear. Origen states in his *Commentary on the Song of Songs* that 'Christ [. . .] is called the true light, therefore, so that the soul's eyes may have something to lighten them. He is the Word, so that her ears may have something to hear [. . .]'.[47] In the *Contra Celsum*, he claims that the spiritual ear 'can receive impressions of sounds that have no objective existence in the air'. Opened to Scripture, the ears of the heart perceive the *kerygma* within the silent pages – they 'hear' the word, in Pseudo-Chrysostom's tripartite scheme – in a way that the bodily ears do not.[48] This 'hearing' precedes interpretation *per se*, corresponding to Gadamer's *understanding*. The eyes of the heart, if we may take Origen's definition of the spiritual eye, open to 'see things superior to corporeal beings'. Contemplation, the vision of God, is the elect way of 'doing God's will', putting the Scriptural word into practice. This was the achievement of the above-mentioned Cyril of Beloozero, whose reading culminated in a mystical vision.[49] The beginner's task is to meditate upon the word 'with the intent to do it', as Jean Leclercq has written,[50] and hence to become perfected in the virtues; when Augustine uses the image of the eyes of the heart in *De doctrina*, he seems to have such a result in mind. In both instances, spiritual vision corresponds to Gadamer's *application*; various applications of the word accompany the surmounting of 'steps' in the pedagogical programmes

---

[46] Passages cited from Augustine, ed. Outler, p. 34.; St Augustine, *On Christian Teaching*, ed. R. P. H. Green (Oxford: Oxford University Press, 1997), p. 105.

[47] *In Cant.* II.9. See Origen, *The Song of Songs: Commentary and Homilies*, ed. R. P. Lawson (New York: The Newman Press, 1956), p. 162.

[48] The ears of the heart may also be the ears that hear the spiritual father's silent words: see John Climacus's interpretation of John the Theban's apophthegm in John Climacus, *The Ladder of Divine Ascent*, ed. C. Luibheid and N. Russell (Manwah, NJ: Paulist Press, 1982), p. 114.

[49] Pachomius's *Life* of Cyril of Beloozero, lines 630–50: Iablonskii, *Pakhomii Serb*, p. xiv, Prokhorov, Vodolazkin and Shevchenko, eds., *Prepodobnye Kirill*, p. 72. See also Romanchuk, *Byzantine Hermeneutics*, pp. 92–4.

[50] J. Leclercq, *The Love of Learning and the Desire for God: A Study of Monastic Culture*, trans. C. Misrahi, 3rd edition (New York: Fordham University Press, 1982), p. 16.

articulated by authorities such as Origen and John Climacus. Any mnemotechnique must, out of necessity, operate in the space *between* these two openings.

Whether reading alone or listening, the reader implores Christ to first open the ears of the heart, and then the corresponding eyes. This offers a useful perspective on Frithjof Schuon's conceptualisation of the doctrine of the spiritual senses:

> This evident correspondence between sight and the intellect is due to the static and total character of the former: sight [. . .] simultaneously realizes by far the widest possibilities in the domain of sensible knowledge, whereas the other senses react only to influences linked to vital sensibility; except, however, for hearing which reflects intellection not in its static and simultaneous, but in its dynamic and successive mode, and which plays what could be termed a 'lunar' role in relation to sight [. . .].[51]

For the Byzantines, spiritual hearing played no such 'lunar' role, at least not during the reading of Scripture; the eyes of the heart could be opened to 'doing' the word only if the ears of the heart 'heard' it first as an ethical preaching. Indeed, the typical (i.e. monkish) Byzantine reader's first approach to the book – his 'hearing' of its message – might be described as 'static and simultaneous'. Fedotov has noted that in the *Izmaragd*'s instructions '[a]ll religious literature is "sacred" and "divine", and tradition is included in the Scriptures and participates in the charisma of divine inspiration'.[52] By the same token, the application linked to the eyes of the heart – the *praxis* of interpretation – may be quite dynamic in such a reader, as recent studies (for the West, John Dagenais's *The Ethics of Reading in Manuscript Culture*)[53] have shown. If Schuon's treatment of the ears and eyes of the heart as 'lunar' and 'solar' figures is infelicitous, Carruthers's subsuming the eyes of the heart into a general transformation of the heard into the visual, for the ends of mnemotechnique, is also unjustified. Reading 'by heart' is the activity of a medieval subject in an ethical-pedagogical context. If we were to call him a 'subject who remembers', he would likely agree that he is remembering, in his life and *through his internalisation of Scripture*, the

---

[51] F. Schuon, *The Eye of the Heart* (Bloomington, IN: World Wisdom Books, 1997), p. 3.
[52] Fedotov, *The Russian Religious Mind II*, p.41.
[53] J. Dagenais, *The Ethics of Reading in Manuscript Culture: Glossing the Libro de buen amor* (Princeton: Princeton University Press, 1994).

world to come. This mindfulness, the 'memory of God' (*mnêmê theou*) of the Pseudo-Macarian homilies,[54] becomes for the Byzantine reader a hermeneutical *act*.

Tablets of the heart

That the earth of the heart and the senses of the heart – bookless, 'desert' images of unmediated receptivity to grace – accommodated themselves readily to the Scriptural word in a metropolitan milieu is not surprising, for mainstream Byzantine culture valued the book and its 'conversants' highly. By the time of the *Izmaragd's* compilation these images had become stereotyped expressions of *how to read* – they are no longer aligned with 'orality' or 'pure prayer'. Yet it may come as a surprise that the instructions on reading found at the head of the *Izmaragd* and elsewhere are disinclined to use Paul's well-known metaphor of Christ writing grace on the 'fleshy tablets of the heart' (2 Corinthians 3: 3) – the starting point of the Western discussion of the book-like heart.[55] Indeed, the few instances of 'writing in the heart' in these sermons do not make explicit reference to 2 Corinthians 3: 3. To be sure, Paul's tablets of the heart were well known to the Byzantines. Jager offers several examples in the first chapter of *The Book of the Heart*. Here are two more. First, Pseudo-Macarius's Homily 15:

> It is like this in Christianity for anyone who tastes the grace of God. For it says: 'Taste and see that the Lord is good' (Psalm 33 [34]: 8). Such a taste is this power of the Spirit working to effect full certainty in faith which operates in the heart. For as many as are sons of light and in the service of the New Covenant through the Holy Spirit have nothing to learn from men. For they are taught by God. His

---

[54] For the 'memory of God' see Homily 43.3, 19.2, Pseudo-Macarius, *Homilies*, pp. 220, 146); see also, Louth, *The Origins of the Christian Mystical Tradition*, pp. 126–7 and Hausherr, *Penthos*, p. 46. Of course, memory *ad verbum* was linked to the heart as well in Byzantium. The *De patientia* invokes memory as 'writing in the heart' (see PG 63, col. 940; Bojkovsky and Aitzetmüller, eds., *Paraenesis*, IV, 262–4); Climacus's step 4 does likewise: see John Climacus, ed. Luibheid and Russell, p. 93. Yet the authorities do not prescribe any memorial reading or writing practices; at the same time, they maintain a sharp *ethical* focus on the memory of 'good deeds'. Cf. Pseudo-Chrysostom's exegesis of Psalm 118 (119): 'See, brother, that remembering the words of God, man makes his way straight.'
[55] It occupies most of chapter 1 of Jager, *The Book of the Heart*.

very grace writes in their hearts the laws of the Spirit. They should not put all their trusting hope solely in the Scriptures written in ink. For divine grace writes on the 'tables of the heart' (2 Cor. 3: 3) the laws of the Spirit and the heavenly mysteries. For the heart directs and governs all the other organs of the body. And when grace pastures the heart, it rules over all the members and the thoughts. For there, in the heart, the intellect [nous] abides as well as all the thoughts of the soul and all its hopes.[56]

Next, step 1 ('On renunciation of life') of John Climacus's *Ladder of Divine Ascent*:

Let us make a treatise, with their knowledge (i.e., that of the true servants of God: cf. Luke 17:10) as the implement of writing, a pen dipped in their subdued yet glorious humility, applied to the smooth white parchments [chartais] of their hearts [kardiais], or rather resting on the tablets of the spirit (cf. 2 Corinthians 3: 3). Let us write on it divine words, or rather seeds (cf. Matthew 13; not present in all manuscripts), and let us begin like this.[57]

The Byzantines perceived a similitude between the 'good earth' of the heart that receives the seed and the 'fleshy tablets of the heart' on which grace is written, even if (as we can see) the connections are awkward and the linking seems rather mechanical.[58]

Yet the reason the metaphors have been 'mixed' in the above examples from Pseudo-Macarius and John Climacus, while Paul's tablets of the heart do not appear in the *Izmaragd*'s sermons, is not far to seek. The main goal of the first chapters of the *Izmaragd* is to teach readers the ethics of reading and interpretation, the *force* of the word. Hence the images of the earth, and the ears and eyes, of the heart predominate. Pseudo-Macarius and John Climacus have a pedagogical goal as well (the latter does especially), but they endeavour to teach perfection in the virtues and the contemplative achievement of grace *with an eye to the last things* – hence their use of the Pauline metaphor from 2 Corinthians. The tablets of the heart, which become transformed into the book of the heart and conflated with the book of life (Revelation 20: 12), were associated early on in East and West with the Last Judgement,

---

[56] Pseudo-Macarius, *Homilies*, pp. 115–16.
[57] John Climacus, ed. Luibheid and Russell, pp. 73–4.
[58] The linking of the softened 'heart of stone' (Ezekiel 11: 18–21) with Paul's tablets of the heart in the West seems to have been made on the same basis.

and the metaphor usually retains this eschatological meaning.[59] Jager's examples illustrate this well: 'But these books of our soul or tablets of our heart shall be opened before the throne' (Origen, *Commentarii in epistolam ad Romanos* 9: 41); 'The book of your conscience shall be opened; the book of your heart shall be opened; our guilt shall be read aloud' (Ambrose, *Explanatio Psalmorum* XII 1: 52); 'Each person carries in his heart a written record, as it were, whereby his conscience accuses or defends him' (Richard of St Victor, *De judiciaria*).[60] These figures are effective for the teacher of compunction, but less so for the Byzantine instructor of reading and exegesis. The latter preferred the tropes of the earth of the heart and the senses of the heart in his instructions. Paradoxically, then, the trope that has inspired historians of the book – the tablets of the heart – articulates the history of the book and its pedagogy of reading rather poorly, at least in Byzantium; while those that have been ignored, or subsumed into the Pauline metaphor – the earth, and the ears and eyes, of the heart – are more closely bound to this history. They are heard insistently in the prayers of Byzantine schoolboys, depictions of saintly readers and introductions to books like the *Izmaragd*.[61]

---

[59] See P. Adnès, 'Jugement', in A. Rayez, A. Derville and A. Solignac, eds., *Dictionnaire de spiritualité, ascétique et mystique doctrine et histoire* (Paris: Beauchense, 1974). One Byzantine authority whose use of the trope is not eschatological is Gregory Nazianzenus: for example, his *Orations* I.6, XL.45, and XLIII.67: see P. Schaff and H. Wace, eds., *Cyril of Jerusalem, Gregory Nazianzen*. Vol. 7, A *Select Library of the Nicene and Post-Nicene Fathers of the Christian Church, Second Series* (New York: Christian Literature Publishing Co., 1894), pp. 204, 376, 418, where the tables of the heart are invoked in a pedagogical context.

[60] See Jager, *The Book of the Heart*, pp. 21, 24, 49.

[61] The schoolboys' prayers (remarkably close to Pseudo-Chrysostom's, and perhaps deriving from his version) are collected in P. Koukoulès, *Vie et civilization byzantines*, tome I, fasc. I (Athens: Institut Français d'Athenes, 1948), pp. 71–3. Pseudo-Chrysostom's prayer is adapted in Nestor's *Life* of Boris and Gleb: see P. Hollingsworth, ed., *The Hagiography of Kievan Rus'* (Cambridge, MA: Harvard Ukrainian Research Institute, 1992), pp. 7–8, and in Feodosii's *Life* of Aleksandr Oshevenskii, to characterise the saint's study of Scripture; the senses of the heart are invoked in the latter (unpublished) *Life*: see I. Iakhontov, *Zhitiia sviatykh Severnorusskikh podvizhnikov Pomorskogo kraia kak istoricheskii istochnik* (Kazan: Tipografiia Imp. Universiteta, 1881), p. 95. Apart from the *Izmaragd*, the *Scaliger Patericon* open with Pseudo-Chrysostom's 'Discourse'; see Veder, *The Scaliger Paterikon*, I, fol. 1v–2v; J. Popovski, ed., *The Pandects of Antiochus: Slavic Text in Transcription, Polata Knigopisnaja* 23–24 (1989), p. 1.

Augustine's book of the heart

The utility of distinguishing pedagogical tropes of the book-like heart from their eschatological counterparts is not limited to Byzantine studies, as the examples I have cited from Latin texts illustrate. Likewise, the ethical force of all these metaphors is felt strongly in their Western usage. Indeed, a 'Byzantine' approach to these tropes may help to contextualise a moment in the history of the book that has been frequently glossed:[62] this is Augustine's description, in *Confessions* VI.3.3, of Ambrose's reading. Historians of the book will likely be familiar with Carruthers's interpretation of the passage: 'Ambrose withdraws over a book into silence, *meditatio*, even though others are present; Augustine contrasts it specifically here with the activity of *lectio*, delivered in a loud voice to a listener who freely asks questions.'[63] Carruthers's reading, which here privileges the pedagogical relationship over technological matters, is exemplary. Aleksandr Gavrilov, in his article 'Techniques of Silent Reading in Antiquity', has shown that Augustine's depiction of his master's silent reading is not paradoxographical in genre; he is not depicting an extraordinary phenomenon *as such*.[64] And Carruthers pins down the reason for Augustine's surprise – 'that Ambrose never read in the *other* way, though others were present'. Gavrilov is more explicit:

> The story becomes more coherent, and fits both the narrower and broader contexts, if we accept that what puzzles Augustine is not Ambrose's method of reading in and of itself, but his resorting to that method *in the presence of his parishioners*. Why doesn't he read a book *with* them (aloud, naturally) so that they can discuss it together?[65]

Why not, indeed? Augustine's spiritual formation, after all, is the theme of the *Confessions* as a whole, and Ambrose's role as Augustine's teacher offers the key to the passage. Yet, having identified the ethical-pedagogical crux of the passage, Carruthers falls back upon an interpretation of its heart imagery as exclusively mnemotechnical.

---

[62] Rather than reproducing the entire passage, I will excerpt O'Donnell's text and Outler's translation in the paragraphs below.

[63] Carruthers, *The Book of Memory*, p. 171.

[64] See A. K. Gavrilov, 'Techniques of Silent Reading in Classical Antiquity', *Classical Quarterly* 47 (1997), 56–73, p. 63.

[65] Carruthers, *The Book of Memory*, p. 171 and Gavrilov, 'Techniques of Silent Reading', p. 63 (his italics).

Ambrose's 'hidden mouth' which is in his heart (memory) 'rumi-
nates' the texts of Scripture. Such reading was nourishment for his
mind [. . .]. When he read for this purpose, his eyes were led over
the page as his recollection ('heart') 'pored over [*rimabatur*]' the
meaning. The verb *rimor* is related to the noun *rima*, meaning 'crack,
fissure', and was used originally in an agricultural context to mean
'turn up' or 'tear open' the ground. [. . .] All of this indicates that
meditative reading, 'legere tacite', was a slow, thorough process in
keeping with its memorative function, one in which each word was
examined thoroughly ('broken into pieces') as one stored a piece of
text away together with its heuristic associations.[66]

I would, rather, place the initial insights of Carruthers (and those of
Gavrilov) against the ethical-pedagogical tropes of the heart as used
in Byzantium and, as we have seen, in the medieval West. It is the
relationship of Ambrose and Augustine, spiritual father and son, that
frames Augustine's discomfort at Ambrose's silence, and the appearance
(as well as the failure, or 'breaking')[67] of metaphors of the book-like
heart.

Augustine begins by describing Ambrose's grace; he employs an
image joining the metaphors of the earth of the heart (its fruits) and
the heart's senses:

> But what hope he cherished, what struggles he had against the temp-
> tations that beset his high station, what solace in adversity, and what
> savory joys thy bread possessed for the hidden mouth of his heart
> when feeding on it ['et occultum os eius, quod erat in corde eius,
> quam sapida gaudia de pane tuo ruminaret'], I could neither conjec-
> ture nor experience.[68]

The passage comes immediately after the recollection of Ambrose's celi-
bacy, another factor that Augustine did not comprehend at the time.
Writing a decade and a half after the events he described, Augustine
now understands that his master's asceticism, together with his reading
and study, had perfected him and allowed the seed of the word to grow
into the 'saving grain'. Ambrose ruminated this grain with the mouth

---

[66] Carruthers, *The Book of Memory*, p. 172.

[67] I borrow the notion of a 'broken metaphor' from Illich, *In the Vineyard of the
Text*, p. 2.

[68] English translation: Augustine, ed. Outler, pp. 115–16; text and commentary on the entire passage in Augustine, ed. O'Donnell, vol. I, 59, and vol. II,
339–46.

of his heart (Origen: 'taste in order to savour the living bread'). It is his teacher's parsimony with this bread that troubles Augustine, causing the metaphors of the earth, and senses, of the heart to 'break' – to cease functioning as tropes for pedagogy:

> Now, as he read, his eyes glanced over the pages and his heart searched out [or: 'turned over'] the sense, but his voice and tongue were silent ['oculi ducebantur per paginas et cor intellectum rima-batur, vox autem et lingua quiescebant']. Often when we came to his room – for no one was forbidden to enter, nor was it his custom that the arrival of visitors should be announced to him – we would see him thus reading to himself.[69]

The saint would till the earth of his own heart, as his heart's mouth ruminated God's word – 'but his voice and tongue were silent'. The ears of the student's heart were not opened. Augustine could practically be describing Ambrose's reading – unfavourably – against the strictures of Pseudo-Chrysostom:

> *When thou art reading, read diligently with all thy heart, and read the words with much diligence; and do not endeavor only to turn the leaves – if need be, do not be negligent, but read the words even twice, so that thou mayest understand their force.* When thou shalt sit down to read *or to listen to someone else reading,* pray to God with these words:[70] '*Lord Jesus Christ, open the ears and eyes of my heart to hear Thy word and to understand it and to do Thy will, Lord,* for I am a stranger in the earth; *hide not Thy commandments from me,* but open mine eyes and I shall understand wondrous things out of Thy law (Psalm 118 [119]: 19, 18); *reveal to me the hidden and secret things of Thy wisdom* (Psalm 50 [51]: 6).

To understand the force of the word is to hear it, understand it and 'do God's will'. For the student, understanding begins when a teacher plants the Scriptural seed in the earth of his heart – through conversation. Augustine depicts Ambrose as a perfect Christian, his own master:

---

[69] English translation: Augustine, ed. Outler, p. 116; text in O'Donnell, ed., I, 60.

[70] It is perhaps worth noting that at this point the Georgian text incorpo-rates a reminiscence of Psalm 50 (51): 15: 'Lord Jesus Christ, *open my mouth* and the eyes of my intellect'. See Abuladze, ed., *Mamat'a scavlani X da XI s.-t'a xelnacerebis mixedvit'*, p. 21. I wish to thank Anna Melua, formerly of the Russian National Library's Manuscript Division, for help with the Old Geor-gian version.

'Whatever his motive was in so doing, it was doubtless, in such a man, a good one'. But precisely how Ambrose was 'doing God's will' remained elusive to the student. Augustine 'could not request of him what I wanted as I wanted it'.[71] Gavrilov refers to Augustine's schoolboy resentment, and perhaps this is not far from the truth.[72]

The Byzantine tropes of the book-like heart open perspectives onto the book and its reading far broader than the Pauline metaphor of the tablets of the heart, and deeper than a technological treatment allows. Here are the voice, flavour and vision of the Word and the bookish colloquy with the spiritual father; here too is the moment of application, the ethical place beyond the book, where the reader grapples with the word 'in a realm beyond language' (Dagenais).[73] I hope to be forgiven if I end this essay on a somewhat speculative note. Just as the most book-like Byzantine metaphors of the heart bear the least material resemblance to the book, it seems that the book *itself* in Byzantium – at least, from an iconographic perspective – is not a book at all; it is not a material object made of parchment, leather, boards and nails. The book itself, like the codex that Christ Pantocrator holds, clasped shut, in the dome fresco of the Byzantine church, is a figure for the reader's corrected heart, bearing the seeds that the teacher has sown.[74]

[71] Augustine, ed. Outler, p. 116.
[72] See Gavrilov, 'Techniques of Silent Reading', pp. 63–4.
[73] Dagenais, *The Ethics of Reading*, p. 5.
[74] See the writer Nicholas Mesarites's description of the Christ Pantocrator in the dome of Constantinople's Church of the Holy Apostles: 'His eyes, to those who have achieved a clean understanding, are gentle and friendly and instill the joy of contrition in the souls of the pure in heart . . . to those, however, who are condemned by their own judgment, (the eyes) are scornful and hostile and boding of ill'. Cited from H. Maguire, 'The Cycle of Images in the Church', in L. Safran, ed., *Heaven on Earth: Art and the Church in Byzantium* (University Park, PA: Pennsylvania State University Press, 1998), p. 137. Maguire (p. 138) goes on to characterise Christ as judge and the church as a courtroom on the basis of the second part of this ecphrasis, but it seems to me that the first part conforms rather well to the pedagogical metaphors of the heart discussed in my paper.

Red as a Textual Element during the Transition from Manuscript to Print

MARGARET M. SMITH

Introduction

THERE IS AN IRONY about the use of red as an element of textual articulation. Its role over the several centuries before the invention of printing was to be visible, and thereby to distinguish what was rendered in red from other parts of the text. But to many modern scholars of the printed book, red is an invisible element, written off as insignificant because it is assumed to be merely decorative. Manuscript specialists, including the palaeographers Christopher de Hamel and J. P. Gumbert, are well aware of the value of red in medieval books, but incunabulists and those studying early printed books have, on the whole, ignored it, or worse, categorised it as part of the early printers' attempts to imitate manuscripts.[1] This paper aims to demonstrate the articulatory value of red as it was used in incunables, and so to make the case for a better understanding of the use of colour in books during the transition from manuscript to print, as it had been used in their manuscript predecessors.

The reasons behind the neglect of red may lie in our ambiguous attitude to the term *decoration* in relation to books. On the one hand we find that manuscript specialists equate decoration with what I am calling textual articulation, which is the system within a book that signals to the reader the structure of the text and the relationships of

---

[1] See my refutation of this point in 'The Design Relationship between the Manuscript and the Incunable', in Robin Myers and Michael Harris, eds., *A Millennium of the Book: Production, Design and Illustration in Manuscript and Print 900–1900* (Winchester and New Castle: St Paul's Bibliographies and Oak Knoll, 1994), pp. 23–43; for the appreciation of red by some palaeographers, see Christopher De Hamel, *A History of Illuminated Manuscripts*, 2nd edition (London: Phaidon, 1994), p. 98; *Medieval Craftsmen: Scribes and Illuminators* (London: British Library, 1992), p. 33; *The British Library Guide to Manuscript Illumination: History and Techniques* (London: British Library, 2001), especially pp. 16–17; De Hamel, *The Book: A History of the Bible* (London: Phaidon, 2001), pp. 103–4; and J. P. Gumbert, '"Typography" in the Manuscript Book', *Journal of the Printing Historical Society* 22 (1995), 5–28.

parts of a text to each other. It sets up a hierarchy, which uses relationships of size and elaborateness of treatment (in terms of the number of colours and the use of gold and historiation); the hierarchy is applied to the books, chapters and subsections of chapters so that, for example, ten-line initials indicate books, and three-line initials chapters, etc. On the other hand, we find scholars of later books apparently partaking of the modernist distaste for decoration as a mere 'knick-knack on the mantel piece'.[2] For them decoration is adventitious, and to be avoided. The use of red in books has been caught up in this ambiguous attitude because of its own development over time. The very important role of red in the textual articulation of incunables more or less disappeared when, some time in the early sixteenth century, the texts of books became monochrome and fully functional in black and white. Red was retained for a few categories of books, in particular liturgical books and some legal books. And it was always available for luxury books. But apart from these uses, the red that remained was indeed used decoratively in the dismissable sense, often isolated on the title-page where it might be used for alternate lines, or to pick out a few words. This later role for red may be largely responsible for the scholarly assumption that red was, *and had always been*, basically decorative. Once placed in that category, it became invisible and scholars have become colour-blind. Or they are inclined to search for symbolic meaning where there may be none.

How to get red into books

In manuscripts the red was added by a scribe, most often by the same scribe who wrote the main text. In printed books there were two methods available: by a scribe/rubricator, or by printing. Printing the red was attempted even for the earliest complete book, the Gutenberg Bible. However, research has shown that only a few copies of this edition have a few pages with their printed red chapter headings.[3] All

---

[2]   E. H. Gombrich, *The Sense of Order: A Study in the Psychology of Decorative Art*, 2nd edition (Oxford: Phaidon, 1984), p. x; in a milder form this has been expressed by F. R. Goff as 'title pages [being] *brightened up with accents of red*' (my emphasis), in 'Rubrication in American Books of the Eighteenth Century', *Proceedings of the American Antiquarian Society* 79 (1969), 29–43, at p. 30.

[3]   Frederick R. Goff, 'Printing in Red in the Gutenberg Bible (B42)', *Gutenberg Jahrbuch* 56 (1981), 130–5.

the others were added by hand, by a rubricator. These two methods would continue throughout the incunable period, but not at all equally. Hand rubrication became the more common, for the simple reason that the printers found two-colour printing to be too expensive for most books.[4] The printers gradually replaced the red by various means. The different uses of red (to be discussed in detail below) were each substituted differently. The fact that red printing was attempted so early, combined with the struggles that the printers had with replacing it, can be taken as evidence that they fully understood its importance. It could not simply be eliminated, but had to be dealt with. Ultimately, though, it was indeed eliminated and how this was accomplished can be determined by analytical study of books from the transitional period of the late fifteenth century.

The norm in the incunable period was that books would be rubricated, even those that might seem to the modern eye not to need it. Some scholars have identified relatively early editions, which apparently do not need the work of a rubricator, and yet there are copies of these same editions, which have, nevertheless, been rubricated. Having said that, there are also a great many copies of most incunable editions that never received their intended rubrication. Even the Gutenberg Bible exists in some unrubricated copies. From my own research I estimate that perhaps just under half of all extant copies received their handwork, and that in the course of the late fifteenth century an increasingly smaller proportion of copies were rubricated.

Hand rubrication: a case study of this widespread practice

To demonstrate the nature of rubrication, including what was rubricated, and why, a case study of copies of one particular printed edition is useful. I am unaware of other publications offering the level of analysis to be provided here. It brings out the essentially functional nature of the elements that have been added in red, and allows me to make some general comments about rubrication, drawn on many years of observations. The finding below that rubrication has been applied somewhat differently in each case-study copy has many implications, which form the basis of my concluding remarks.

---

[4] Margaret M. Smith and Alan May 'Early Two-Colour Printing', *Bulletin* of the Printing Historical Society 44 (Winter 1997), 1–4.

The case-study edition, Johannes Nider's *De morali lepra* printed in Cologne by Ulrich Zel in 1470[5] was selected for two principal reasons: first, there are seven rubricated copies[6] readily available to me for close study, and second, it exemplifies the very common practice of printing incunables entirely in a single type of one size, a fact that is of considerable relevance to the use of rubrication for textual articulation.[7]

Johannes Nider (1380–1438), an important German Dominican theologian and reformer[8] active in the Councils of Constance and Basle, taught theology at the University of Vienna. Nine of his works, and a broadside, were published during the incunable period, in over eighty incunable editions, the most frequently printed being his *Preceptorium divinae legis, sive Expositio decalogi*. His most famous work, though, was *Formicarius* (The ant hill) (three incunable editions, and a total of seven editions by 1692), which treats witchcraft in Part V; this part was sometimes partnered with Jakob Sprenger's *Malleus malificarum*, the infamous, slightly later, treatise against witchcraft, for which Nider's writings had been an important source. Nider's early treatise on business ethics, *De contractibus mercatorum* and *Formicarius* were reprinted in the sixteenth and seventeenth centuries.[9]

De morali lepra (On moral leprosy) is a work of moral theology addressed to confessors, consisting of an introduction followed by

---

[5] ISTC in 00188000, dated before 10 October 1470 on the basis of a purchase note in one of the Besançon copies; fifty-six copies were recorded as extant as of 22 May 2009.
[6] Some of the copies were first seen as part of my Leverhulme Fellowship research project in 2001, and I am extremely grateful to the Leverhulme Foundation for the purchase of the photograph of a page from one of the British Library's copies. No attempt has been made to establish the state of rubrication of all the extant copies listed in ISTC, but it has been possible to establish that the copies at Harvard, the Newberry Library, Rostock University Library and Württembergische Landesbibliothek Stuttgart all are rubricated, although exactly how they compare to the seven copies detailed here is not known
[7] Margaret M. Smith, 'The Pre-history of "Small Caps": From All Caps to Smaller Capitals to Small Caps', *Journal of the Printing Historical Society* 22 (1993), 79–106, discusses how many incunables used only one type.
[8] On Nider, see Michael D. Bailey, 'From Sorcery to Witchcraft: Clerical Conceptions of Magic in the Later Middle Ages', *Speculum* 76 (2001), 960–90, and his *Battling Demons: Witchcraft, Heresy and Reform in the Late Middle Ages* (University Park, PA: Pennsylvania State University Press, 2003).
[9] A translation of the *De contractibus: On the Contracts of Merchants*, transl. Charles H. Reeves, ed. Ronald B. Shuman (Norman: University of Oklahoma Press, 1966). This work is of an entirely different nature from most of Nider's others.

eighteen numbered chapters. In common with *Formicarius* and *Preceptorium divinae legis*, it deals with magic and witchcraft among other
sins, and has been called Nider's most misogynous work. Eight separate
editions of this text were printed between 1470 and 1500, and three
further incunable printings are found in French editions combined
with his *Manuale confessorum*. The case-study edition, the first separate edition of *De morali lepra*, was printer by Ulrich Zel in 1470. Zel,
Cologne's earliest printer, began his work by 1466. By 1470 he had
printed over eighty editions. Altogether, the *ISTC* records 196 incunable editions printed by Zel.

The design of Zel's 1470 De morali lepra

The edition is a quarto of 104 leaves, quired in 8s (i.e. each quire has
eight leaves = sixteen pages), without a title-page, headlines, foliation,
signatures or illustrations of any kind. The text is laid out in twenty-
seven long lines, the text-area measuring 146 by 89 mm.

Its one type is used throughout, a fere-humanistica measuring 106
mm/20 lines,[10] for incipit and explicit, body text and headings to the
chapters. The introduction and eighteen chapters are signalled in two
ways. The text of each new chapter begins with a space for an enlarged
initial, which is to be added by hand. The initial for the introduction
is four lines deep, the other chapter initials are three lines, with a few
only two lines when space does not allow three. The heading to each
chapter announces the subject and then gives its number; in Fig. 1
the heading to Chapter three concerning avarice reads 'de Auaricia[m]
Capitulum.3.' Within chapters there are further subdivisions, some
more or less equivalent to paragraphs, but others, apparently arguments broken down into numbered points, each point introduced by
an ordinal number *primo*, *secundo*, etc. The page shown in Figs. 1 and 2

[10] *Catalogue of Books Printed in the XVth Century Now in the British Museum,
Part I* (London: British Museum, 1908), I, 178 describes the type: '96 [mm for
20 lines] text type, recast after 1467 on a body measuring 99, leaded later to
106–11. At first the h is round, then, between 1467 and 1469, a tailed h was
introduced and mixed with the former; in 1472 T from type 115 begins to be
mixed with that of this type.' In the BMC description of the copy the type is
represented as 96 (108); my own measurement of 106 mm for 20 lines is within
the two per cent variation suggested by Philip Gaskell in *A New Introduction to
Bibliography* (Oxford: Clarendon Press, 1972) as normal due to paper expansion
and contraction.

has no fewer than four sets of such numbered points, occurring in lines 1–3 (only the end of a sequence, *tercio* and *quarto*), 5–9 (1, 2 and 3), 16–19 (1, 2, and 3), 23–6 (1, 2 and *ultimo*). Two other characteristics of this text need to be mentioned. First there are frequent references to authorities in the running text, especially the three particularly important ones mentioned in the introduction, St Thomas Aquinas, Alexander de Hales and Jean Gerson (referred to as 'Cancellarius'), but also others Augustine, Gregorius, Ambrosius and other patristic writers. Second, there are quite highly abbreviated additional references, i.e. in Fig. 1, lines 25–6 'de hoc vide § 8' ('about this see section 8'). These are mostly internal cross-references to the eighteen numbered chapters and the subdivisions (paragraphs or sections) within chapters. Each of the subdivisions in the sequence is preceded by a space, but the subdivisions are not numbered in print. These spaces are considerably larger than normal word spaces. In Fig. 1, see the space before 'Aua[r]icia potest . . .' in the sixth line from the foot, which has received a hand paragraph mark (to be discussed below).

There is no contents table as such, but a brief chapter-by-chapter descriptive list forms the final part of the introduction. Most of these chapter descriptions in the introduction are given their own paragraph, beginning with the chapter number. Within the rest of the text, chapter headings have been handled variously by their 'designer'. A very few of the headings are centred on their own line, as in Fig. 1, but most of them are tucked into the final line of the preceding chapter; in some cases they are started in the final line, and then turned over at the right margin to finish flush right, occupying the end of the first line of the following chapter. Such variation, or lack of consistent treatment, is common in incunables.[11] The headings themselves, printed in the one type used in the book, are only distinguished from body text by their proximity to the enlarged initials, and, in a few cases, by the centring just described. They are, and were, prime candidates for hand rubrication to further distinguish them, as will be seen below.

The incipit and the explicit to the entire work (again printed in the book's only type) are each separated from the text by one line-space, with all the lines of each indented, so they are set apart from the body text by means of spacing, i.e. the line-spaces and the indentions.

---

[11] See my 'Space-Saving Techniques in Early Printed Books', *Printing Historical Society Journal* n.s. 6 (2003), 19–39, for other examples of the tucking in of headings.

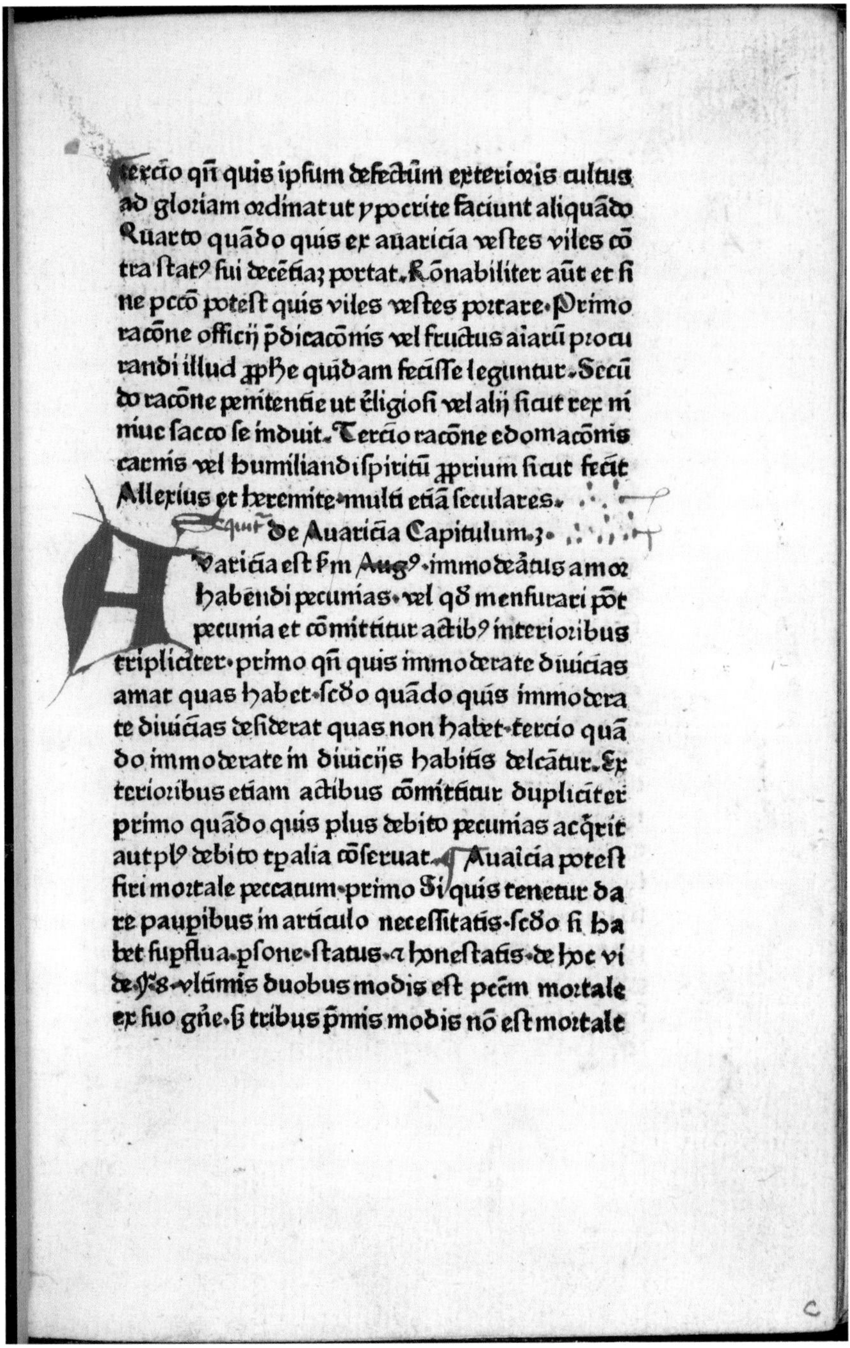

tercio qñ quis ipſum defectum exterioris cultus
ad gloriam ordinat ut ypocrite faciunt aliquãdo
Quarto quãdo quis ex auaricia veſtes viles cõ
tra ſtat? ſui decétiaʒ portat. Rõnabiliter aũt et ſi
ne pcõ poteſt quis viles veſtes portare. Primo
racõne officij pdicacõnis vel fructus aiarũ procu
randi illud ꝓphe quidam feciſſe leguntur. Secũ
do racõne penitentie ut eligioſi vel alij ſicut rex ṁ
niue ſacco ſe induit. Tercio racõne edomacõnis
carnis vel humiliandi ſpiritũ ꝓprium ſicut fecit
Allexius et heremite multi etiã ſeculares.

De Auaricia Capitulum 3.
Auaricia eſt ſm Aug? immoderatus amor
habendi pecunias vel qd menſurari pot
pecunia et cõmittitur actib? interioribus
tripliciter. primo qñ quis immoderate diuicias
amat quas habet. ſcdo quãdo quis immodera
te diuicias deſiderat quas non habet. tercio quã
do immoderate in diuicijs habitis delcãtur. Ex
terioribus etiam actibus cõmittitur dupliciter
primo quãdo quis plus debito pecunias acꝗrit
aut plꝰ debito tpalia cõſeruat. Auaicia poteſt
firi mortale peccatum. primo Si quis tenetur da
re paupibus in articulo neceſſitatis. ſcdo ſi ha
bet ſupflua. pſone. ſtatus. ɇ honeſtatis. de hoc vi
de ſ?8 vltimis duobus modis eſt pctm mortale
ex ſuo gñe. ſ tribus pmis modis nõ eſt mortale

Figure 1: Johannes Nider, *De morali lepra* (Cologne: Zel, 1470), copy 6 of the study.
©British Library Board, IA.2826, fol. [17] recto.

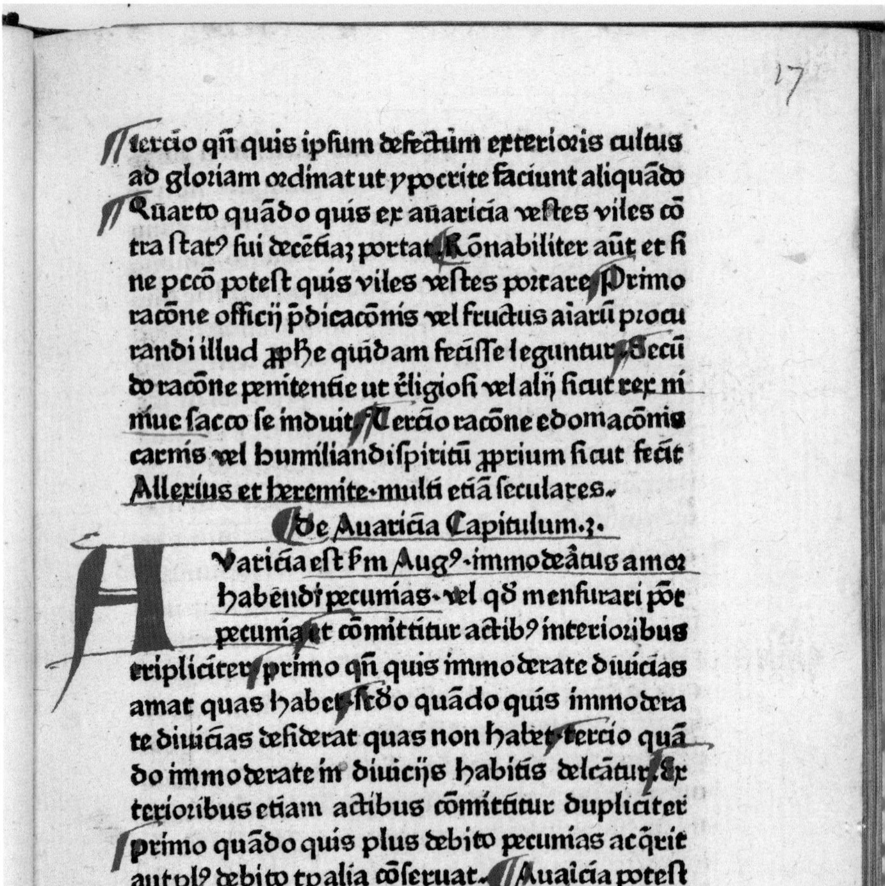

Tercio qñ quis ipfum defectum exterioris cultus
ad gloriam ordinat ut ypocrite faciunt aliquãdo
Quarto quãdo quis ex auaricia veftes viles cõ
tra ftat? sui decẽtia? portat Ronabiliter aũt et fi
ne pccõ poteft quis viles veftes portare Primo
racõne officij pdicacõnis vel fructus aiarũ procu
randi illud xpħe quĩdam feũffe leguntur Secũ
do racõne penitentie ut ẽligiofi vel alij ficut rex mi
nue facco se induit Tercio racõne edomacõnis
carnis vel humiliandi fpiritũ xprium ficut fẽcit
Allexius et heremite multi etĩa feculares.

De Auaricia Capitulum .z.

Auaricia eft ƒm Aug? immoderatus amor
habendi pecunias vel qd menfurari põt
pecunia et cõmittitur actib? interioribus
tripliciter primo qñ quis immoderate diuicias
amat quas habet ftdo quãdo quis immodera
te diuicias defiderat quas non habet tercio quã
do immoderate in diuicijs habitis delcãtur Ex
terioribus etiam actibus cõmittitur dupliciter
primo quãdo quis plus debito pecunias acqrit
aut pl? debito tpalia cõferuat. Auaicia poteft
firi mortale peccatum primo Si quis tenetur da
re paupibus in articulo neceffitatis ftdo fi ha
bet fupflua pfone ftatus et honeftatis et hoc vi
de f? s vltimis duobus modis eft pccm mortale
ex fuo gñe ƒ tribus pmis modis nõ eft mortale

Figure 2: Johannes Nider, *De morali lepra* (Cologne: Zel, 1470), copy 7 of the study.
Reproduced by kind permission of the Syndics of Cambridge University Library,
Inc.5.A.4.1 (269), fol. [17] recto.

Analysis of the rubrication in the seven copies

Table 1 provides details about the principal uses of rubrication (enlarged initials, paragraph marks, initial-strokes and underlining) in the copies, together with comments on the differences observed. These four elements are the most common types of rubrication, and other types are discussed where they occur.[12] In case the term *initial-stroke* is not self explanatory, it consists of one stroke of red ink through a capital letter; usually vertical, although it sometimes follows a letter's contour. Copies 1 to 4 have somewhat simpler rubrication programmes than the other three, and will be discussed first. Reproductions have been provided only for copies 6 and 7.

The simple rubrication programmes, copies 1 to 4
Copies 1 and 2 use no initial-strokes at all, and differ from all five other copies in this. The incipit, the explicit, chapter headings and subdivisions are marked by means of paragraph marks. In copy 1 the incipit, explicit and chapter headings are also underlined, and compared to copy 2 the only difference is that copy 2 does not have its chapter headings underlined. So, what these two copies mark is the same, but how they are marked, in the case of the chapter headings, differs slightly. Copy 3 uses the same programme as copy 2, but adds sporadic initial-strokes. A difference is that its enlarged initials and paragraph marks are alternately red and blue. So copy 3 marks a different feature compared to 1 and 2 (initial-strokes), and differs from all six other copies in the use of some blue. Copy 4 also uses initial-strokes; its paragraph marks are not used for the incipit or the explicit, but are reserved for the chapter headings and subdivisions, while its underlining adds two new uses, for the names of authorities and for internal cross-references (both sporadically applied). Copy 4 therefore differs from the other three in this group both in how it marks the incipit and the explicit, and in what it marks (adding authorities and cross-references).

---

[12] See my 'Patterns of Incomplete Rubrication in Incunables and What They Suggest About Working Methods', in L. L. Brownrigg, ed., *Medieval Book Production: Assessing the Evidence* (Los Altos Hills: Anderson-Lovelace, 1990), pp. 133–46, for further verification of these as the most common.

Table 1. Analysis of the rubrication of the seven copies

Copy number, shelfmark, bibliographical reference	enlarged initials	paragraph marks	initial-strokes	under-lines	other comment
1. British Library c.11.a.12(1)[1] BMC, I, 185	X	X	O	X	

No initial-strokes; paragraph marks only at incipit, explicit, chapter headings and subdivisions; underlines only at incipit, explicit and chapter headings; compare to 2 below

2. University of Cologne, GB IV 3400; complete facsimile online at http://www.inkunabeln.ub.uni-koeln.de, linked from ISTC	X	X	O	X	

No initial-strokes; paragraph marks only at incipit, explicit, chapter headings and subdivisions; underlining at incipit and explicit, but not chapter headings; lack of underlining at chapter headings is the only difference from 1 above

3. Cambridge Inc.5.A.4.1 (3842) Oates 332[2]	X	X	X	X	Red and blue

Initial strokes irregular with some pages completely missed; paragraph marks only at chapter headings and subdivisions, not incipit or explicit; underlining at incipit, explicit and some chapter headings. Red and blue alternation of enlarged initials and paragraph marks, but altogether rather careless in execution

4. Cambridge Inc.5.A.4.1 (270) Oates 331	X	X	X	X	

Initial strokes; paragraph marks only at chapter headings and subdivisions, not incipit or explicit; underlining at incipit, explicit, chapter headings, names of authorities (sporadically) and some cross-references. Underlining of authorities and cross-references differentiates copy 4 from 1–3

5. Bodleian Auct.Q.sup.1.4 Coates N 085[3]	X	X	X	X	Variant paragraph marks

Underlining used for incipit, explicit, chapter headings, and also for cross references, names of authorities, keywords and occasional key sentences, the last two unique to this copy. Two differently shaped paragraph marks; a rounded one combined with an underline reserved for chapter headings; an angular one to mark subdivisions, and this sometimes alternating with a large red dot, or a bold vertical stroke (heavier than initial-strokes), so there are four shapes used here where the other six copies make do with one

[1]   The British Library online catalogue wrongly attributes this copy to Conrad Winters [1480]; this information has been superseded by the information in both BMC, and ISTC. It was possible to study c.11.a.12(1) alongside verified copies both of Winter's 1480 edition, and of Zel's edition, and thus to see for myself that c.11.a.12(1) is correctly identified as Zel's, proving ISTC to be correct.

[2]   J. C. T. Oates, A Catalogue of the Fifteenth-Century Printed Books in the University Library Cambridge (Cambridge: Cambridge University Library, 1954).

[3]   Alan Coates, Kristian Jensen, Cristina Dondi, Bettina Wagner and Helen Dixon, with the assistance of Carolinne White and Elizabeth Mathew, A Catalogue of Books Printed in the Fifteenth Century Now in the Bodleian Library, 6 vols. (Oxford, 2005); online pdf at http://www.bodley.ox.ac.uk/csb/bod-inc.

6. British Library IA.2826   X   X   X   X   Several
BMC, I, 185; see Fig. 1   unusual uses
  Underlining reserved to mark the chapter list at end of the introduction;
  authorities highlighted by horizontal red line (a variant of underlining?);
  chapter headings distinguished by line-filling pattern of dots and the addition of
  word 'Sequitur' before chapter headings; red dots on all the full stops; only copy
  of the seven to mark chapter transitions in this manner, or to mark full stops.
  Paragraph marks at subdivisions

7. Cambridge Inc.5.A.4.1 (269)   X   X   X   X
Oates 330; see Fig. 2
  Underlining used at incipit, explicit, chapter headings, names of authorities,
  cross-references, and occasional key words or sentences. Paragraph marks at
  headings and subdivisions, but also squeezed into word spaces before lists of
  numbered points and elsewhere. Initial-strokes often placed on uncapitalised
  words. Altogether the most extensively and eccentrically executed work in the
  copies

The more complex rubrication programmes, copies 5 to 7

Copy 5, almost uniquely among the seven, underlines new elements –
key words and key sentences.[13] It also uses two differently shaped paragraph marks, reserving the rounded shape for chapter headings. The
rounded mark is combined with one stroke to form an underline. Its
second paragraph mark is angular and is used at subdivisions, where it
alternates with a large red dot, and a bold vertical stroke (which is not
to be confused with this copy's much lighter initial strokes). It could
be argued therefore that this copy uses four different marks where the
other case-study copies make do with a single one. The angular paragraph mark and its variants, the red dot and the vertical, seem to be
applied randomly rather than significantly.

Copy 6 (Fig. 1) reserves underlining for marking the chapter titles
listed at the end of the introduction, but otherwise does not use underlining at all. However, it does highlight the names of authorities by a
red line running horizontally through the name, which could be considered to be a variant form of underlining.[14] Uniquely among the seven,
this copy has small red dots on top of its full stops, line-fillers at the
ends of chapters, and the addition of the word 'Sequitur' before the
chapter headings. The marking of full stops and the use of line-fillers
and rubricated words to mark chapter transitions mean that copy 6's
methods differ considerably from the other copies.

---

[13] A few of each also turn up on copy 7.
[14] This form of highlighting was sometimes used in manuscripts.

Copy 7 (Fig. 2) underlines all the elements already mentioned for underlining – incipit, explicit, chapter headings, names of authorities, internal cross-references, and a few key words and sentences. It goes overboard on the use of paragraph marks, not only at the subdivisions, but also marking the many lists of numbered points found in the running text, which are signalled by the words *primo, secundo, tercio* (Fig. 2 lines 5, 7 and 9, among others on the page) often squeezing these marks into normal word spaces. There are initial-strokes not only on all the capitals, but also on a number of uncapitalised words; as with the extra paragraph marks, these unusually liberal initial-strokes seem to be excessive. There is so much red on the pages of this copy that it is easy to suspect that any attempt to help the reader pick out the various elements has been compromised by over-enthusiasm and lack of discipline, and that textual articulation has suffered.

General observations

The single most important observation is that the work on every one of the seven copies is different from every other one, even among the four with simpler rubrication. They differ either in what features they mark, or in how the features are marked, or both. In some cases the differences are relatively small, in others they are more significant. Had the copies been rubricated more or less identically, I think we would be entitled to assume that there was a high level of quality control in the work. The control might have been exercised by being undertaken in a single workshop, such as the printer's, or there might have been some strong, shared understanding of what was to be marked. The differences suggest less control rather than more, although not the complete absence of shared understandings by the rubricators. The differences found in these copies basically fortify our current general understanding that most rubrication, like binding, was undertaken after the copies left the printer's workshop, often at the point of retail sale. They also suggest that individual rubricators had somewhat personal understandings of their responsibilities, which leads to the point that rubrication as an activity is more complex and less obvious than might be assumed. To describe a copy as 'rubricated' does not provide very complete information.

There are a number of ways to group the observed differences in rubrication. First, there are the rubrications that were planned for by the printer, in that he provided spaces for them, as compared to the rubrications that were added on top of printed elements and for which the printer had not necessarily planned. Second, there are the named rubrications and how they were used variably, as compared to the different features that were rubricated. Third, there are the consistently observed rubrications, compared to those that were only sometimes added. Fourth, there are the different colours used.

To begin with the least complicated issue, colour, only one of the copies uses anything but red: copy 3 has alternating red and blue enlarged initials and paragraph marks. Such red and blue alternation was quite common in incunables, as it had been in fifteenth-century manuscripts. If only one colour was used, it would be red; if two, usually red and blue, although occasionally red and green. The purpose of the alternation was apparently decorative, with no particular significance attached to the different colours. Underlines were almost always red. Red initial strokes were sometimes replaced by yellow wash, but the strokes were never blue. I have always assumed that the use of red and blue alternation was merely a step up in luxury from all red.

Rubrications planned by the printer

For the enlarged initials used at the first word of each new chapter, the printer has left square spaces, usually three lines deep. A space is quite obviously a call for a letter, because what follows is a word lacking its first letter. In the case study edition these spaces do not have the small printed guide letters, which are often found in later incunables. In general, if copies are minimally rubricated, it will be the initials that have been provided; all of the case-study copies have their initials. There is another rubrication which also has a space provided by the printer, and that is the paragraph mark. This space is not so obvious, because it is just somewhat larger than a normal word space. Nor is the space's purpose so obvious; it has often been misunderstood by modern observers, who take it to be there for purposes of justification, or use it to prove that the printer had low standards. All seven copies use paragraph marks in these spaces, and elsewhere I have discussed the space more fully.[15] Altogether the very most consistently found rubrications

[15] See my '"Le Blanc aldin" and the Paragraph Mark', in William J. Jones, William A. Kelly and Frank Shaw, eds.,'*Vir ingenio mirandus*': *Studies Presented to John L. Flood* (Göppingen: Kümmerle, 2003), 2 vols., II, 537–57. The term 'blanc aldin' was somewhat inappropriately coined for such spaces in later

in the case study are those that were planned for by the printer, the enlarged initials and the paragraph marks at subdivisions. The other principal rubrications (underlines and initial-strokes) are not in spaces provided by the printer, and it is probably no coincidence that these have been found to be much more variable in application. They are placed under words (underlining, roughly placed on the baseline), on top of parts of letters (initial-strokes, a red stroke usually vertical on part of a printed capital; or highlighting running horizontally through a word), or in spaces created by a new heading (line-fillers; introductory words), or in spaces between words (other paragraph marks).[16] Apparently, with no signals from the printer that something is required, these rubrications had to be applied according to the rubricator's own standards, which must account for some of the variations observed.

Rubrications named, compared to features rubricated

I have said above that there are four kinds of rubrication found most often: initials, initial-strokes, paragraph marks and underlines. In the case of paragraph marks and underlines, simply naming them is really not very informative. These two rubrications are not tied to specific uses, but are general marks, the specific role of which must be contextually interpreted by the reader. This is perhaps the more surprising for the paragraph mark, which is not reserved to mark the equivalent of the modern paragraph, but is also used to mark headings (here the incipit and explicit as well as the chapter headings), numbered lists, and in some cases even words in the wrong place, as when a final word is placed at the right margin.[17] Similarly underlining marks a number of features: headings (here including incipit and explicit), names of authorities, cross-references, the beginnings of numbered lists. The paragraph mark and the underline are thus quite close in function, and

editions by the eminent book historian Henri Jean Martin, *La naissance du livre moderne (XIVᵉ–XVIIᵉ siècles); mise en page et mise en texte du livre français* (Paris: Éditions de Cercle de la Librairie, 2000), pp. 301–2.

[16] Rubrications can also appear in the margins, for example leaf numbering, chapter numbers, brackets, or shoulder notes, although none of these are found in the case study copies.

[17] Smith, 'Le Blanc aldin'. The role of the medieval paragraph mark might usefully be compared to the computer screen's paragraph mark, which occurs at every hard return; in medieval usage it would be placed before its text segment (paragraph or heading, etc.), rather than following it as on the screen.

often used together, so that a heading will have both a paragraph mark, and an underline. Such double marking of features is not uncommon, although equally common are examples in which one copy marks a feature by an underline, while in another copy the same feature is marked by a paragraph mark.

Conclusions

Studying the nature of rubrication requires direct observation. Most catalogues of incunable collections are of little help. Older catalogues are often completely silent on rubrication in the copies, concentrating only on the printed portions of copies. Many of the more recent ones will provide the barest of information, so that one can only separate the rubricated copies from the unrubricated, without even knowing whether the rubricated copies are worked throughout, or have as little as only their very first page done (not an infrequently encountered circum-stance). The very best will indicate which rubrications are present, and it is from these that I have formed the list of the most common ones. But what is actually marked, and what is also there beyond the easily named rubrications, must be determined by examination. Each rubricated copy represents the meeting of a pristine copy and at least one rubricator, who has added his red elements according to what the printer has called for, plus his understanding of what else the text needs. The case study copies sometimes have rubricated indications of which authorities had been drawn upon, and where the internal cross-references occur, but often they only show the reader where the chapter and subdivision transitions occur. Altogether these copies use red as a textual element quite differently. The rubrication of copy 7 with what appears to be too many uses of paragraph marks, underlines and even initial-strokes may very well confuse the reader. Its rubricator may have subverted the very purpose of rubrication to help in textual articulation.

We cannot know what the printers thought about the variations in the rubrication of the books they printed, or about the fact that their books were increasingly likely never to receive any rubrication. It is possible that they were unconcerned. However, we do know that even-tually the printers took back to themselves all the decisions about what to mark and how to mark it, turning the book from a multi-colour to a monochrome object, complete when it left the printer's shop, apart from its binding. To accomplish this, they did away with red, substituting a change of type style or size for the change of colour, or accepting a large black initial, or a large black paragraph mark as the functional equivalent of red ones. And they began to exploit space internal to the text in a more systematic manner. We can suspect that variations like those demonstrated in these seven copies of a single edition contributed to the beginnings of the demise of red as an important textual element. More importantly, analysis of the role(s) of rubrication in these early printed books restores red to its proper place as a textual element.

Problematising Textual Authority in the York Register

LIBERTY STANAVAGE

Recent work on medieval textuality has disrupted the popular notion that books in the Middle Ages were universally treated with reverence as almost magical objects, although the notion remains disturbingly persistent.[1] The past two decades have seen an increasing interest in destabilised texts, in reified meanings and in marginalia and glosses as a component of the text, rather than a defacement. Critics such as Peter Diehl, Siân Echard, Ralph Hanna and Carol Braun Pasternack have suggested variant editorial practices that recognise the complexity of texts, rather than reducing them to a single 'correct' edition.[2] Other critics have argued the need for considering extra-codicological materials as part of the text; for instance, Andrew Taylor's argument about the need to consider sound as part of the text for the *Song of Roland*.[3]

---

[1] Much of this destabilisation has come in the wake of New Philology (heralded by the 1990 *Speculum* special issue by the same title edited by Stephen Nichols). Work by Bernard Cerquiglini (*In Praise of the Variant: A Critical History of Philology* (Baltimore: Johns Hopkins Press, 1999)) on variance and Paul Zumthor (*Towards a Medieval Poetics* (Minneapolis: University of Minnesota Press, 1992)) on *mouvance* initiated (or facilitated, according to some older scholars) a wave of interest moving away from the fixed text to the variant, and recognising that many medieval attitudes to the text were themselves also varied and complex. These intersected with and drew from non-medieval discussions of New Philology like Jerome McGann's *A Critique of Modern Textual Criticism* (Charlottesville: University Press of Virginia, 1983).
[2] Representative works include: P. Diehl, 'An Inquisitor in Manuscript and in Print: The *Tractatus super materiale hereticorum* of Zanchino Ugolini', in Siân Echard and Stephen Partridge, eds., *The Book Unbound: Editing and Reading Medieval Manuscripts and Texts* (Toronto: University of Toronto Press, 2004), pp. 58–77.; S. Echard, *Printing the Middle Ages* (Philadelphia, PA: University of Pennsylvania Press, 2008); Ralph Hanna, *Pursuing History: Middle English Manuscripts and their Texts* (Stanford, CA; Stanford University Press, 1996) and C. B. Pasternack, *The Textuality of Old English Poetry*, Cambridge Studies in Anglo-Saxon England (Cambridge: Cambridge University Press, 1992).
[3] Andrew Taylor, 'Editing Sung Objects: The Challenge of Digby', in Echard and Partridge, eds., *The Book Unbound*, pp. 78–104

Indeed, many texts seem to indicate, self-reflexively, a pragmatic or flexible sensibility in their role in medieval culture. The physical book shows that the medieval sense of the codex was far from static, through the meta-text provided by marginalia, the emendation or alteration of the text, and the willingness to adapt, alter, and excerpt in transcription. These dynamic elements reveal the medieval use of the codex as a technology of information, rather than identical to the information it contains. Despite its visual similarity to the printed codex, a manuscript functions differently; the two are, in fact, fundamentally different technologies of information, working towards different purposes.

The dramatic

Critics of medieval drama have not been absent from these New Philological movements; in fact particularly relevant to this study is work that opened the medieval drama up to being more than a purely literary text. I am particularly indebted to scholars who have worked to clarify the material conditions of playing the Corpus Christi cycles: scholars such as David Bevington, Alexandra F. Johnston, David Mills or Pamela King, whose work has done so much to clarify the social contexts of the plays.[4]

Nevertheless, despite these changes, ideas of the primacy of the written word over performance have endured. The dramatic manuscript has often rested in a liminal position between these fields of study, examined for clues to the performance, but rarely subjected to the same questions about its internal logic as other types of books; in other words, dramatic texts are examined for what they can tell us about the performance, but are often assumed to be dead 'fixed' texts, snapshots of a particular moment of performance, representing a (possibly abortive) attempt to close down performance variants. Some scholars[5] cite the

---

[4] For representative works, see A. F. Johnston, 'The York Cycle and the Chester Cycle: What do the records tell us?', in A. F. Johnston, ed., *Editing Early English Drama: Special Problems and New Directions* (New York: AMS Press, 1983), pp. 121–39; P. King, *The York Mystery Cycle and the Worship of the City* (Cambridge: D. S. Brewer, 2006); and D. Mills, *Recycling the Cycle: The City of Chester and its Whitsun Plays* (Toronto: Univeristy of Toronto Press, 1998).
[5] In *Signifying God*, Sarah Beckwith argues that the York plays' 'confinement to a civic manuscript . . . is undoubtedly part of an attempt at control and censorship over extemporizing and unpredictable performance': S. Beckwith, *Signifying God: Social Relation and Symbolic Act in the New York Corpus Christi*

very creation of the codicological playtext to signify the rejection of any further performance innovation.

Thus, revived performances of the medieval cycle plays that try to render them more understandable to a modern audience are often derided for deviating from the medieval language or practice 'preserved' in dramatic records. Perhaps resulting from a reverence for the past or a simple desire to identify some form of 'authentic' drama, critical handling of the drama has largely ignored the question of the manuscript's controlling logic. Concerned with the text of the plays, discussions and editions of the York Corpus Christi cycle largely omit the meta-textual apparatus. When the marginalia or textual irregularities are included, they nevertheless tend either to be considered separately from the 'real' text or, similarly problematic, to be incorporated with no acknowledgment of their different chronological or marginal origins.[6] The plays are presented as fixed texts for interpretation, disregarding the emendations, additions or blatant rejections contained in the codex's marginalia, which prioritise the current performance, rather than the codicological record.[7]

In this paper I discuss the York Register of the Corpus Christi Cycle (London, British Library, Additional 35290) in order to examine criti-

Plays (Chicago: University of Chicago Press, 2003), p. 4. On the contrary, in his essay 'Chester's Mystery Cycle and the "Mystery" of the Past', David Mills suggests that 'the creation of a play-book may well signal the end of a cycle as a living art-form, *Transactions of the Historic Society of Lancashire and Cheshire*, 137 (1988), 1–23, at p. 4.

6   Carol Symes discusses the danger of incorporating later additions undifferentiated into a fixed play text in her discussion of the medieval French *Le garçon et l'aveugle*, noting that: 'certain modern editorial practices, many of which have already been abandoned by scholars working with non-dramatic texts, still pose a fundamental threat to our understanding of how plays were variously transmitted and reconceived during this period' (p. 116). While Symes is arguing against overweighting these marginalia as part of the text, the point remains that any attempt to produce a fixed play text from these transhistorical manuscripts is problematised by the fact of their multilayered history; see Carol Symes, 'The Boy and the Blind Man: A Medieval Play Script and Its Editors', in *The Book Unbound*, pp. 105–27.

7   The difference between this approach and the reworking of textual criticism and editorial practice argued for by scholars is striking. Ralph Hanna's discussion of conflicts between print and manuscript highlights the very different nature of the codices' logic, stating that with regard to audience relations, the medieval manuscript 'hovers between oral and written, inasmuch as its consumption may be supervised by authorial reading and/or conversational commentary': Hanna, *Pursuing History*, pp. 67–8.

cally some of these assumptions about the authority (textual, political and social) of the manuscript, both in its original context and for contemporary scholars and audiences. The manuscript of the Register functions simultaneously as visual text, performance record and civic document, and reflects in its form and structure the conflicting demands of these roles. Rather than attempting and failing to fix the text, the register instead seems to have had from its beginnings a more complex and unsettled relationship to its own authority. This is a text that questions its own textual authority, a civic document that lacks permanence, and a performance record that defers its authority to later performance.

Much of the research done on the York Register of the Corpus Christi plays is concerned with scribal and authorial identity, with the struggle between the guilds and civic authority signalled by the creation of the register, or with issues of power and authority in the language of the plays. In considering these issues discretely, we impair our ability to understand the ways in which the physical manuscript itself reveals a conflicted sense of its own function, as a technology, as an object and as a symbol, relevant not only to these individual questions, but also to broader issues of textual roles and manuscript authority.[8]

This essay considers the material manuscript of the York Register, and what its physical layout reveals about its own textual sensibilities. I discuss the ways that the different functions of the text manifest themselves in the codex and how the complex and unsettled identity of the manuscript reveals broader social conflicts in late medieval York, as well as conflicts between different textual identities. In other words, I am examining how the physical text articulates social and ideological conflicts over textual authority and, in fact, the very nature of textuality.

---

[8] Jerome McGann discusses 'editing as a theoretical pursuit' in the chapter of the same name in his *Radiant Textualities*, arguing for the practice of 'un-editing', of attempting to produce a documentary replica of the original material, as helping to clarify questions of documentary identity. He suggests that texts like Michael Warren's 'The Parallel King Lear' function as 'an investigation into the character and status of documents and their relationships (intra – as well as extratextual)' (p. 77). McGann promotes digital media as allowing us to surpass the limitations of print reproduction. According to McGann 'using books to study books constrains the analysis to the same conceptual level as the materials to be studied' (p. 82): Jerome McGann, *Radiant Textuality: Literature after the World Wide Web* (New York: Palgrave Macmillan, 2001).

The York Corpus Christi Plays and Register

While the feast of Corpus Christi was established in 1264 by Pope Urban IV, it was not adopted in England until the second decade of the fourteenth century. In York, the celebration first took the form of a procession and feast day, but when this was expanded to include the pageants is unclear.[9] The York Register was compiled some time between 1463 and 1477, at the behest of the York city council, and provides our only surviving copy of the pageants other than one surviving guild copy, the Scriveners' 'Incredulity of Thomas'. Four scribes contributed to the text of the register, two in the initial compilation of the manuscript, and two with additions and glosses in the sixteenth century. One of these sixteenth-century scribes, John Clerke (1510–80), whom we shall return to later, copied pageants 4 and 18, and an interpolation in 7 as well as providing the majority of the later marginal glosses.[10]

In addition to the plays that were added whole, the manuscript contains a large number of added or expanded stage directions, speakers' names and marginal glosses, which make this text interesting from a broad range of perspectives. I will discuss the multiple identities of the manuscript individually, and return to the issues presented by these marginalia.

The visual text

When I discuss the role of the manuscript as a visual text, I am referring to those aspects of it that are specifically geared for a visual experience. This includes illuminations, structured layout and other elements geared to produce a 'bookish-looking' text. It is in these ways that the manuscript reflects the sense (well developed by the fifteenth century) of texts as geared for a silent, solitary reader rather than intended to be read aloud.

The existence of the York Register as a visual text may seem self-evident. After all, the text shows a definite awareness of a reader in

---

[9]   Dating generally places the plays in the 1360s, although a record of the plays as an already established practice appears in 1378. The *Ordo paginarum*, listing the order and guild assignments of plays, was created later, in 1415.
[10] R. Beadle and Peter Meredith, eds., *The York Play: A Facsimile of British Library MS Additional 35290, together with a Facsimile of the Ordo Paginarum Section of the A/Y Memorandum Book* (Ilkley: Moxon Press, 1983), pp. xix–xxi.

its inclusion of decorations, such as the marginal faces at fol. 6v and fol. 224, that appear to have no bearing on the content.[11] The pages commonly begin with initial capitals, betraying again a concern with the appearance of the page itself, as the capitals are linked to the layout, not to significant moments in the content of the text.

The overall layout of the text is oriented towards a reader, and seems formally and visually oriented. Much of the layout and format is more elaborate than simple necessity would warrant. As Beadle and Meredith note, the scripts used in the project are formal, making copying and rubrication more expensive, and are clearly geared toward the creation of a dignified, uniform manuscript. That the manuscript is specifically planned for homogeneity in appearance seems clear in that the only surviving probable exemplar, the Sykes manuscript of the Scriveners' play, shows considerable differences in layout from the Register.

However, this visual homogeneity breaks down at a number of points. The varying poetic structure of the plays repeatedly causes the text to overrun the frames (as at fol. 35). Rough initial capitals appear at points in the text, and the initial capitals are blocked out, but not completed, for several of the pageants. Decorations and illustrations are irregularly applied throughout the codex. Another disruption to this homogeneous appearance occurs with the rhyme brackets. Beadle and Meredith argue that early in the manuscript, rubrication, including these rhyme brackets, seems to have allowed the scribe to check for error,[12] but these brackets get increasingly less accurate in their reflection of the rhyme scheme, and by fol. 123 the brackets do not reflect the scheme at all. They appear only intermittently after the verso of this page.

So what should we make of these irregular rhyme brackets? Is the scribe trying to follow some convention about what play texts should look like? After all, a number of other cycle play manuscripts,[13] as well as some poetic manuscripts[14] show rhyme brackets, so their inclusion might be an attempt to help this text look more like other formal manuscripts, following a particular visual trope. However, the gradual breakdown of this system undermines the manuscript's coherence of

---

[11] All references use Beadle and Meredith's facsimile numbering for foliation.
[12] Beadle and Meredith, *The York Play*, p. xxiii.
[13] Among these are the Brome Abraham and Isaac and the N-Town plays.
[14] Including the Digby Wisdom poem and some poems in London, British Library, Harley 2253.

appearance,[15] and, ultimately, denies the importance of its visual presentation.[16]

Civic document

The creation of the Register for the city of York suggests an attempt to establish a firm civic identity, both through the city's assertion of its right to incorporate the guilds' records into its own, as well as through the attempt to collect the plays into a unified cycle, identified with the city (rather than existing solely as individual guild-identified pageants). As a significant celebration, the Corpus Christi festivities could serve as both a source of and as a destabilising force in the establishment of a unified civic identity.[17] The creation of the register as a civic document plays a role in this struggle by attempting to position the civic government as the authoritative agency for the cycle as a whole.

---

[15] In addition to disruptions that occur in the initial creation of the manuscript, the neatly homogenous layout is disrupted by John Clerke when he re-does the ruled frames for pageants four and eight. Also, the omission of some illuminated capitals where guide letters indicate spaces problematises thinking about the literary nature of the text. The manuscript obviously continued to be updated and to involve expenditures by the city on the clerks who kept the register and entered missing pageants, but these later scribes failed to add the capitals. With late additions, as well as entire plays scribed *and rubricated* later, we cannot simply ascribe this to a lack of funds for the ink or the craftsmen.

[16] We can compare this text with the Towneley Manuscript of the Corpus Christi plays. Briefly, while the preparation of the York page by the scribe, with the fairly even ruling and design of the pages, shows a visual intent and hand, the Towneley is a visually orientated text; more attention and space is given to the visual in the Towneley manuscript, with large lavishly illuminated capitals that often occur mid-page, and the extended rubrication and regularity of the text. Notably, the margins of the Towneley copy are considerably narrower than those of the York, although the membrane is of better quality. This suggests that the wider margins in the York do not simply function as a show of extravagance, but may rather suggest an anticipated need to provide wide margins for future glosses and additions.

[17] Alan Justice argues that the celebration itself, despite its religious nature, did not find its genesis with the church in the city, but was a civic project from its beginnings. With authority for the pageants shared between the city and the guilds, without the moderation of ecclesiastic authorities, the plays naturally provided a venue in which the power struggles between the guilds and city could play out. See, A. D. Justice, 'The English Corpus Christi Play in its Social Setting', unpublished PhD dissertation, University of California Santa Barbara (1977), p. 13.

However, the text functions oddly as a civic record. Most of the York civic records tend to be chronological, not recursive: static, dormant chronicles, not living documents like the register. Other registers in York, like the A/Y record book,[18] were subject to some emendation or change, but served, in their corrected form, as an authoritative information source. The *Ordo paginarum* from the A/Y record book would be copied out each year and sent to the guilds to remind them of the proper order of the plays. The Register, in contrast, is unique in that it was not only subject to change from decisions of the council, but continually open to change as the plays themselves changed.

The very creation of the task of 'keeping' the register highlights the role of the Register as a living text. From 1501 on, the common clerk of the city was allocated a space at the first of the twelve performance stations for the pageants, although no specific indication as to why is given until 1538, when a reference appears to the clerk being there 'keeping the register'.[19] The register was 'kept', for the period of most of these emendations, by the city clerk's representative, John Clerke (1510–80). He might correct a speaker (as at fol. 125v, where Cayphus is added as a speaker and then corrected to Pilatus), add a stage direction, or emend one, or note that the pageant contained entirely different material from what was recorded (as the note on fol. 79v, which says that 'This matter of the gyrdlers agreyth not with the coucher in no point it begynnyth Lysten lordes unto my Lawe'). The nature of many of the marginal comments in the manuscript suggests an oral source, and the performances appear to have provided this material.[20]

---

[18] The A/Y Record Book is a contemporaneous fourteenth- and fifteenth-century register from the city of York which includes an assortment of entries related to the city. The section of the volume most clearly related to the city's Mystery Cycle is the *Ordo paginarum*, reproduced by Beadle and Meredith in their facsimile of the play register, listing the order of the plays, and which guilds were responsible for the performance of each pageant. A note at the head of the section directs that the information should be copied out and sent to the guilds early in Lent (Beadle and Meredith, p. liii). The *Ordo paginarum* thus served as an authoritative source from which the city could draw to assert its authority. This contrasts markedly with the repeated emendations of the play register itself (British Library, Additional 35290), which seem to track changes instead of asserting a set order.

[19] Beadle and Meredith, *The York Play*, p. xxii.

[20] As Beadle and Meredith, *The York Play*, p. xxii, note, 'The brevity and piecemeal nature of most of the snippets of text which have been recorded look very much like snatches of speech caught by the Common clerk or his deputy and entered on the spot into the Register'.

The idea of a civic document that needs continual management is very different from the concept of the civic record embodied in the chronicles of the council or the authoritative order of the *Ordo paginarum*. The manuscript of the Register is heavily thumbed, and obviously an actively used record; this is not a text that was made for an archive, but one that was used as a constantly mutable document of changing civic reality in its reflection of the changing pageant experience.

The textual layout of the pageants also emphasises the role of the manuscript as civic record. The plays are labelled with the name of the guild that performed them, not with the subject matter or title of the pageant. This is not intended for a reader to be able to navigate easily through the biblical history, or to see the scope and subjects of the cycle. Instead, dividing the plays up by craft headings connects the pageants explicitly to the agents who perform them, and this manuscript explicitly to its purpose as civic record. The later additions of guild names (like the addition of the hatmakers to the capmakers' pageant on fol. 111), and the notation of pageants that have become joined, serves to illustrate the importance of this function of the manuscript. The record here is not just of the cycle, but of the role that each guild plays in this civic project. This practice affirms the power of the York civic government, showing the guilds' contributions towards the York cycle, a unified civic project. It also, however, shows the authority of the guilds, in the city's interest in maintaining the identity of the guild associated with each pageant.

By adding the names of additional guilds, the scribes demonstrate the city's concern with not just the matter of the pageants (for which the shorthand of the initial guild could have been sufficient), but with the mechanisms and agents of production. In addition, the updating of the Osteleres guild name with 'alias Inholders' (in the header to fol. 257) shows the importance of clarity here in exactly who is contributing what. If the concern of the record keepers were simply with the ownership of the pageants, instead of with the immediate contributions of the guilds as civic subjects, this updating would be unnecessary, as this does not show a change of agent, but simply of current name.

What makes this manuscript particularly interesting as a civic record is its lack of fixity or permanent authority. Instead of the Register taking precedence over the records of the plays kept by the guilds or choosing to reflect a particular moment in the history of the city, the manuscript undermines its own role as a fixed record by continually transforming in response to changes in the pageants.

Performance record

While the York register has a number of specifically visual features and elements, and also serves a number of important functions as a civic record, the most compelling aspect of the manuscript is its function as performance record. Instead of the manuscript acting as the authoritative text for the plays, authority is vested in the acted pageant. Rather than the civic record of the plays assuming dominance over future performance, the literary text is corrected and emended from the acted plays.

Strikingly, the manuscript does not attempt to create a fixed play or even to record the specifics of performance at one moment in time. The two later hands (primarily John Clerke[21]) continue to edit and revise the plays, but also to note the lack of current text. Instead of supplying a script for the performance, these corrections highlight the difference between record and civic experience. The initial stage directions are rubricated and use an ornamental script, while these later additions are in a less formal hand and are often abbreviated. The importance of adding the stage directions and comments seems to have even overwhelmed John Clerke at one point, when he glosses in English at fol. 71v: 'Nota – the harrode passeth & the iij kynges commyth again to make there offerynges'. The original stage directions and the rest of Clerke's additions are in Latin, suggesting that this anomaly might result from the distraction of trying to keep up with the moment. The text was originally created with stage directions copied from the guild pageant, which could arguably reflect the model that the scribe is using. However, the addition of later stage directions, and the expansion of the originals, suggest a concern with not just the text but the performance. The addition of extended stage directions reinforces this concern with the actual event.

It is therefore not just the language of these plays that the city is interested in recording, but the changing state of the pageants.[22] Clerke's note on fol. 94 that 'This matter is newly mayd . . . we have

---

[21] As Beadle and Meredith suggest, *The York Play*, p. xxxiii, it can be hard to determine whether some of the later marginalia are made by John Clerke, due to his extraordinarily long career with the register, and the changes that occur in his hand over time.

[22] The original guild copies do not seem to hold as much authority in themselves, as the main scribe altered the format considerably from the surviving examplar of the Scriveners' play to create a homogeneous manuscript when undertaking the layout and initial copying of the pageant.

no coppy', seems to argue incontestably for these corrections being from the oral source, which seems logically enough to have happened during the 'keeping of the register'. This correction defers authority to the living performance – to the state of the pageant in the street, not at a particular moment but continuously in its evolution. The concern of the city is not to force performance of the existing copy, nor to call in the guild copies for correction, but rather specifically to note that the record no longer accurately reflects the performance. Similarly, the Vintners' pageant (like the Ironmongers') simply notes the opening line of the play, despite a fully blocked out space for it to be recorded, indicating that an exemplar may not have been available to the civic authorities. These corrections do not logically seem to come from the guild copy as they note only a lack, instead of supplying the new material.

The Register thus operates in a liminal space between visual text and civic record, in which neither the record nor the text has authority over the performance they record. Contrary to examples in which the creation of a text or record seems to in some way fix an authoritative copy for future performances, here the text lacks any fixity, being subject to annual emendation and replacement. When the record for a pageant consists primarily of the notation that there is no record, its authority is denied. The Register's authority as literary manuscript and as civic record is thus undermined by its own repeated insistence on the primacy of the changing pageants themselves; not even the details of the performance seem as essential to John Clerke's use of the register as the fact that the book needs continual updating.

Indeed, this conflict between textual purposes did not go unnoticed or uncontested by the keepers of the text. A number of these recorded omissions have been erased, although legible traces remain, without the incorporation of the missing material. The erasures of these 'here lacks' entries (as at fol. 75, where the note that 'This matter is mayd of niwe after anoyther forme' has been struck through) would seem to reflect differing opinions of the function of the text. Here, ideas of the register as literary record and the register as experiential record come into conflict. It seems difficult to believe that all of these erasures merely reflect Clerke's inaccurate perception of the plays' material, and more likely that the incorporation of these notes was uncomfortable for some record keeper. As I have noted, the inclusion of these recorded omissions problematises the authority of the text, and the erasure of these seems to indicate some attempt to restore its authority, perhaps after unsuccessful attempts to obtain the new guild copies (a consistent

problem, if we are to judge by the still-missing Ironmongers' pageant).
Even the dynamic nature of the manuscript seems to have varied for
different users.

Power and authority in Corpus Christi York

The power of the city council over the Corpus Christi festival can be
seen in a few different ways. The mayor and the city council directed
the guilds' efforts with the pageants and penalised them for failing to
deliver on their commitments. As a marginal note at the beginning
of the *Ordo paginarum* informs us,[23] the descriptions of the pageants
were to be copied out annually and delivered to the guilds early in
Lent.[24] The plays were thus not just administratively connected with
this central authority, but visually and symbolically so. The council
not only reminded guilds of their duties and resolved disputes, but also
imposed fines on guilds that failed to meet expected standards. R. B.
Dobson has argued that the acceptance of these fines by the guilds
demonstrates the unchallenged power of the council.[25]

Dobson's claim that the mayor and council's power was 'unchallenged', however, ignores the contestation of this power clear in both
the town records and the York register itself.

The register and the civic records around it, such as the *A/Y Memorandum Book*, simultaneously display the attempted consolidation of
power by the civic authorities and the tensions around this attempted
consolidation. We can see that not all the guilds were willing to submit
their play texts to the central authorities. Not only are plays missing,
despite the repeated attempts of the council to call them in for copying,
but the plays that are recorded frequently change substantially as shown
by John Clerke's marginal notations. Indeed, the very need to 'keep the

---

[23] On fol. 252v.

[24] Beadle and Meredith, *The York Play*, p. liii.

[25] 'The well-documented practice of levying fines (to be paid into the civic
chamber) for a craft's negligence in maintaining its pageant is recorded as early
as 1386/7. In this sphere more than any other perhaps, for such fines can hardly
have been popular, the mystery play cycle at York reflects the exercise of the
civic council's unchallenged political power over the craft fraternities': R. B.
Dobson, 'Craft Guilds and City: The Historical Origins of the York Mystery
Plays Reassessed', in Alan E. Knight, ed., *The Stage as Mirror: Civic Theatre in
Late Medieval Europe* (Cambridge: D. S. Brewer, 1997), pp. 91–106, at p. 104.

register' betrays the resistance of the guilds to turning over their texts for copying.

Another element of the register that suggests the friction between the guilds and the civic authorities around the manuscript is the inaccurate plotting of pageant length in the initial layout of the text. Some pageants are accorded far too much space, suggesting that the scribes did not have all of their exempla available when plotting out the composition of the manuscript. These signs within the manuscript undermine its own attempt at establishing authority. The register thus stands, not as a marker of consolidated power, but as a visual record of the struggle between the guilds and the council.

Conclusion

Looking at the physical manuscript of the York Register makes us aware of the ways in which it demonstrates conflicting ideas of civic and guild authority over the plays, and particularly of how it articulates conflicting ideas of how books work. The physical make-up of the register expresses recursively shifting ideas about the fixity of the text, its importance as a visual record, its role as an evolving performance record and its own authority over its contents.

In approaching these plays as scholars and as editors, we should beware of our inclination to view the manuscript as reflecting single or even multiple fixed moments in the cycle's history, but should rather attempt to begin our examinations of the manuscript, its history and the text with an understanding and awareness of the manuscript's own insistence on its mutability and its continually revisionary sense of its own identity as record, as civic document and as text. For us to treat the text of these plays as fixed, as when we analyse their language using a modern edition, or indeed, even in the creation of modern print editions,[26] denies the manuscript's own insistence on the primacy of the living performance as a textual source. To attempt to make a singular claim about the cycle as a fixed text is to ignore the facts of its physical

---

[26] Modern editions of 'the York play' display a fundamentally erroneous underlying idea that the 'cycle' is a static text that we can make representative selections from. Although often extremely attentive to issues of performance and reconstruction, they nevertheless present a text that has eliminated the sense of its own mutability that exists in the original codex or its facsimile.

history. Modern recreations of these plays thus seem almost predicated on a fallacy in their assumption of a fixed and final text.

This statement should not be taken as an attempt to discredit these recreations or their 'authenticity', but rather as an attempt to destabilise the notion of these plays as unchanging materials.[27] If we are to follow the logic of the manuscript itself, the most 'authentic' of modern productions would be those that do not regard the language of the plays as unchanging or unchangeable, but those that attempt to rework the plays to more immediately appeal and connect to contemporary audiences, as seems to have happened more than once in the medieval performance history of the cycle.

In our current hypertext age, as the idea of the fixed text continues to break down, we can understand, by looking at pre-modern manuscripts, the ways in which contemporary evolving textual sensibilities are not new inventions, but re-explorations, discoveries and evolutions of the sensibilities of an earlier age. While I am hardly the first to gesture to the connections between manuscript and hypertext sensibilities,[28] the York Register is particularly loaded with these as a manuscript in not simply being subject to change, but requiring it; by subjecting its own authority to the continuing performances of the diverse plays, the Register behaves like a hypertext collection of external resources, continuously demanding upkeep to reflect the changing reality of the works that it defers its own authority to. In other words, the authority of the Register seems to come from its mutability and willingness to unfix its authority: not a prescriptive but a descriptive text. Its failures to record the changed plays serve to mark the irrelevance of those sections, marking 'broken links' that require updating before they can rejoin the living register.

---

[27] Many contemporary approaches to the materials are shaped by a sense of the text as an unchanging relic. For example, Sarah Beckwith's discussion of the connection between the abbey ruins in York and the performance of the revived cycle there in *Signifying God*, particularly at pp. 8–16.

[28] Indeed, some have argued for the manuscript as more authentically hypertext than some digital documents, including Joseph Tabbi in discussing a modern authorial manuscript: 'in fact, the visual presentation of diverse materials on a single two dimensional page may well be closer to Theodor Nelson's conception of hypertext than any hypertext fiction composed since the advent of the Internet': J. Tabbi, 'The Processual Page: Materiality and Consciousness in Print and Hypertext', in Peter Stoicheff and Andrew Taylor, eds., *The Future of the Page* (Buffalo, NY: University of Toronto Press, 2004), pp. 201–30, at p. 203.

The insistence of the register on its own impermanence requires us to reconsider our sense of hypertext and new media documents as uniquely open to change, when we have before us a fifteenth-century model of the same textual concept, and to reconsider our denial of this concept in our creation of contemporary print editions of the text. While the creation of digital facsimiles is an expensive and often daunting process, we need to acknowledge that texts like the register, open-ended evolving documents, virtually require an equally mutable medium (one that can contain all of the information in the codex, not simply the text) in order to properly express for a modern reader their own hypertext sensibilities.

Index

Lort, Michael 113
Llywelyn ap Gruffudd 23–24, 30,
    32–35
Lydgate, John 61

Macarius of Egypt (and Pseudo-
    Macarius) 170, 176, 180–81
Macpherson, David 112–13
Magdalene College, Cambridge 103–4,
    112
Manguel, Alberto 163
Manly and Rickert, 64
Mann, Jill 68
manuscripts
  Aberystwyth, National Library of
      Wales
    Peniarth 28   34
    Peniarth 392   65–69
  California, Henry E. Huntington
      Library, EL 26 C 9   59–73
  Cambridge, Corpus Christi College
    419 and 421   5–19
    198   6
    190   9, 16
    296   142
  Cambridge, Trinity College, B.
      14.39   45, 50, 51
  Cambridge, University Library
    Gg. 3. 28   6
    Gg. 4. 21   72
    Ii. 1. 33   47
  Dublin, Trinity College 244   142
  Edinburgh, National Library of
      Scotland, Advocates 19. 2. 1
      44, 51–52, 70
  Exeter Cathedral Library
      3514   21–42
  London, British Library
    Additional 35290   203–15
    Arundel 119   61
    Cotton Vitellius A. xv (Beowulf-
        manuscript) 75–120, 88 fig. 2
    Cotton Cleopatra B. xiii   9, 11,
        14, 17, 18
    Cotton Vitellius D. xvii   6
    Cotton Vitellius D. iii   50, 51
    Cotton Nero A. x (the Gawain-
        Manuscript)   44
    Egerton 1993   51

Harley 53   147
Harley 2253   44, 206
London, Lambeth Palace 327   31
    489   11, 14, 17, 18
Manchester, John Rylands University
    Library, Eng. 63   72
Oxford, Bodleian Library
  Bodley 340 and 342   6
  Bodley 579   15
  Bodley 647   141–61
  Bodley 938   143
  Digby 86   45, 50, 51, 54
  Eng. poet. a. 1   70
  Hatton 113 and 114   6
  Hatton 115   6
  Laud Misc. 108   45, 50
Oxford, St John's Library 17   86
    fig. 1, 88 fig. 3
Paris, Bibliotheque Nationale, lat.
    943   16
Philadelphia, Rosenbach Museum
    and Library, 1084/2   72
Manuscripts of the West Midlands
    AHRC-funded Project 43
manuscript decoration 187–200, 206–7;
    use 18, 156–59; production 33,
    43–58, 187–200
material media 83
Mattelart, Armand 77–78, 89
Matthews, F. D. 141
Matthews, William 99, 102–3, 108, 115
media studies 76
Mendle, Michael 106–7
Mindwheel 132–34, 137
miscellanies 50
mise-en-page (incunabula) 191–92
multilingualism 46–55, 156–58

Naegling 87
nation-building 22
Netter, Thomas 149; Doctrinale 149
Neville, George 112
Newman, Jane 75
Nider, Johannes De morali lepra
    190–96; Formicarius 190–91;
    De contractibus mercatorum 190;
    Preceptorium 190–91
Nielson, James 101, 103
Niles, John 94–5